INSIDE THE
CLASSROOM
(AND OUT)

INSIDE THE CLASSROOM (AND OUT):

HOW WE LEARN THROUGH FOLKLORE

Edited by
Kenneth L. Untiedt

Publications of the Texas
Folklore Society LXI

UNT
PRESS

University of North Texas Press
Denton, Texas

Permissions:
University of North Texas Press
P.O. Box 311336
Denton, TX 76203-1336

The paper used in this book meets the minimum requirements of the
American National Standard for Permanence of Paper for Printed Library
Materials, z39.48.1984. Binding materials have been chosen for durability.

Library of Congress Cataloging-in-Publication Data

Inside the classroom (and out): how we learn through folklore/edited by Kenneth L.
Untiedt.
   p.cm.
Includes bibliographical references and index.
  ISBN-13: 978-1-57441-202-4 (cloth : alk. paper)
  ISBN-10: 1-57441-202-7 (cloth : alk. paper)
  1. Folklore and education—United States. I. Untiedt, Kenneth L., 1966-
  LB1583.8.I57 2005
  371.39—dc22

                              2005017061

Inside the Classroom (and Out): How We Learn Through Folklore is Number LXII in the
Publications of the Texas Folklore Society

Text design by Carol Sawyer/Rose Design

Contents

Preface

Folklore's place in academe was a natural subject for my first Publications of the Texas Folklore Society (PTFS). I love school. This statement would probably surprise many of my junior and senior high school teachers, some of whom recommended that I be asked to *leave* school a time or two, but it's true. I didn't go to college immediately after high school, instead deciding to "discover myself" for a couple of years in the U. S. Air Force, but I couldn't stay away from the classroom for long. Once I found my way back in, I knew I never wanted to leave again. I remember walking across the Texas Tech campus to turn in the final copies of my master's thesis to be bound and suddenly being nearly overwhelmed by a feeling of uncertainty. Or perhaps, it was certainty that I'd no longer have a good reason to return to the campus or any other. Luckily, I made up my mind right then that I would continue on and get my doctorate, no matter how many bad guys I had to deal with in my job at the Lubbock Police Department in the meantime. That choice, I'm sure, led directly to my sitting here and writing this now.

Back to the subject of this book. "Academe" at first sounds rather stuffy, eliciting images of ivory towers and institutions of higher learning. However, the term includes many things—indeed, practically anything—to do with education. As I was reading through potential papers for this book, I found a reference to

Mody Boatright's "Folklore in a Literate Society," which was published in PTFS XXVIII in 1957. I realized that, according to Boatright, one might substitute "educated" for literate. Practically everyone in America gets a high school education, whether they want it (or deserve it) or not. The same goes for college, and folklore can be found in every part of the learning process. As secretary-editor of the Texas Folklore Society, headquartered at Stephen F. Austin State University, I have had the pleasure of once again teaching the introductory folklore course here. Boatright's article is a good way to convince the students that they are interested in folklore, even if they don't know it yet. I'm a back-to-basics kind of guy, so I'm ready to go back to the beginning, to start over by referring to the standards set by Jan Harold Brunvand, Mody Boatright, J. Frank Dobie, and other principal folklorists, but also to use whatever tools necessary to make the study of folklore interesting and useful to everyone possible.

We learn from everything and everyone around us. Much of our learning is formal, but a lot also comes from family, friends, or other people or organizations not necessarily associated with education. Unlike a previous PTFS that examined teaching folklore (*Between the Cracks of History: Essays on Teaching and Illustrating Folklore*, PTFS LV, 1997), this book shows how folklore plays a fundamental role in the learning process in many areas, from lessons learned in the home and day cares to the more traditional academic environments of elementary and high schools, as well as college. School is a major part of our lives; it is where we form lasting relationships, establish ourselves as individuals, and learn the skills and knowledge that gets us through the rest of our lives. This learning process is vital to us, and we share stories, rituals, and beliefs with fellow learners, and these become part of our academic culture at every level. This book covers folklore in education over the past century, with narratives about teachers in small school houses, as well as ghost stories at major universities. There are humorous anecdotes, family sagas, and some rather sophisticated studies of folklore. Some articles include accounts of oral narratives that would otherwise be lost forever. Several examine unique traditions and ceremonies of high school and college life. Some look at ways in which we utilize folkloric methods to learn certain things better, including, as Hamlet says, "Words, words, words"—understanding them and learning how to use them more effectively.

The five sections of this book follow a practical, chronological order of sorts. The first contains articles pertaining to the early years of learning, in more than one sense of the word "early." A couple of them focus on very young children, before and just after they enter kindergarten. One article tells how young boys learn important life lessons in fun ways through traditions taught in the Boy Scouts. Lou Rodenberger recalls her parents' schoolwork from a time when teachers taught with limited resources in one- or two-room school houses. The first two articles in this section provide a foundation for the rest of the book. "Folklore 101" takes a very basic look at what we do: study folklore. Boatright's article is included for a couple of reasons. It completes the basic definition of what we mean by "folklore," and it also shows that folklore is still relevant, no matter how "educated" or sophisticated we become.

The other sections progress through high school and eventually on to college, ending with a section of more erudite articles on various topics, from linguistics to a comprehensive examination of folklore scholarship itself. It is interesting to see how influential even the simplest things can be. Yearbooks capture cultural elements from a cherished time in people's lives. Cheerleading and the rituals associated with it teach young girls dedication, social skills, and the value of hard work. There is no secret about the significance of football in Texas or the myths that often surround legendary programs or coaches. One article looks at how education affects Mexican Americans in unique ways, particularly when they are caught not only between two ethnic groups but also between generations and differing academic beliefs. The section on college life has ghost stories, memories of wise advice given about the

importance of getting an education, and stories about former professors and their antics. These days, we have Internet sites that rate
professors, recording their eccentricities and issuing warnings
about them before students enroll in courses. My, how times have
changed. The last article has been resurrected from the dust of
James Bratcher's files. Written roughly thirty years ago, it has been
updated and concluded to serve as a thorough review of folklore
scholarship from its earliest incarnation.

One entire section of this book is dedicated to Paul Patterson,
one of our most charismatic and recognized members. Three of
the papers on Paul come from a panel dedicated to him at the
1990 meeting in Kingsville. Paul has been many things: a cowboy,
a poet, a storyteller, a mentor, a writer, and a public speaker. But of
the numerous papers written about him, the common theme that I
found in all of them is that he is a *teacher*. A book on folklore and
its place in education would not be complete without this tribute
to Paul Patterson's influence on the many students he has taught
over the years. Together, these sections show how relevant folklore
is to our basic learning practices at all levels. More importantly,
they show that folklore never stops. My son and daughter transferred to a new school this year, and they almost immediately
began telling stories they'd heard about how Miss Nettie Marshall
still haunts the school that bears her name. In one way or another,
folklore affects everywhere and every way we learn.

I won't spend a lot of time discussing how I became the secretary-
editor of the Texas Folklore Society and therefore, responsible for
this publication. Let me just say that it is truly an honor. Ab wrote
in the preface of his first PTFS (back in 1972) about the "um-
bilical" nature of these volumes. He carried on that life-sustaining
tradition for three decades, and I hope to continue his tradition
of excellence in this and future publications. Putting this book
together has certainly been challenging at times, but it has also
been tremendously fun. Through the efforts of several key people
already mentioned elsewhere, we were able to keep the TFS headquartered at Stephen F. Austin State University. I trust that this

relationship will continue to be favorable to all involved. As with any transition, there were minor bumps here and there, but I've settled in now, and I find SFA to be a very productive atmosphere. After living in Lubbock for nineteen years, Nacogdoches is a perfect fit for our family, and we're adjusting to medium-city life. As an organization, we have many great achievements for which we should be proud: we're the third oldest academic organization in the state of Texas, the oldest continuously running state folklore organization in America, and we've produced over sixty volumes of solid academic research while keeping it accessible to the common reader. However, I feel this is just the beginning. What can we do next? I want to increase membership, attract younger members, appeal to people of varied ethnic groups, and explore new ways to collect, preserve, and study folklore and all that is associated with it. I think the possibilities are endless.

I give thanks to many people, including Barbara Carr, Chair of the English Department at SFA, and Robert Herbert, Dean of Liberal Arts. Special thanks go to Heather Gotti, the TFS office secretary. Working on this book has, appropriately for its theme, been a learning experience for both of us—no pun intended. I also want to thank my family. Their enduring patience and understanding has allowed me to fulfill all of my dreams, and now we're able to fulfill our dreams together. Of course, I thank Kenneth W. Davis, who encouraged me to attend my very first TFS meeting just ten years ago. For those who read the newsletters or hear me speak at meetings or other public venues (or even in my classes), my thanks to him may seem somewhat repetitive by now. Well, when I stop benefiting from his wisdom, humor, and friendship, I'll stop thanking him at every opportunity.

Finally, fittingly, I want to dedicate this book to Francis Edward Abernethy, a driving force behind the Texas Folklore Society for thirty-three years—and then some. Don't think he's done yet. I hope he's not. Ab has been, among many things, a remarkable educator. I hear stories from people I meet everywhere I go about how they remember Ab as a musician, a storyteller, a civic leader, an actor, a hunter, a fisherman . . . an adventurer. However, the most heartfelt stories—and the ones people remember most vividly—are about Ab as a teacher. I hear these tales from people in the grocery store, people at the theater, from people who are now teachers themselves, and even from my insurance man. He has also been a great teacher to me and still is every day. Thanks, Ab.

Kenneth L. Untiedt
Stepehn F. Austin State University
Nacogdoches, Texas
May 22, 2005

Passing on words of wisdom at the 2004 meeting in Allen, Texas.

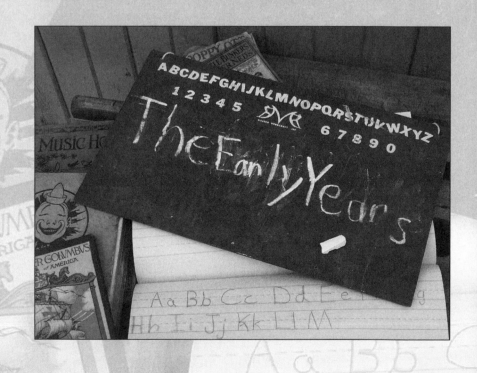

The Early Years

1

Folklore in a Literate Society

by Mody C. Boatright

There will, I predict, be readers, particularly among those who teach English composition to college freshmen and have made the frustrating discovery that Johnny can't read, who will maintain that this essay can have no reference to the United States. Yet, that is the reference intended. For even though Johnny can't read as well as his teacher wishes, and even though Americans read fewer books than the British, the scripts they listen to have been written by somebody. Besides, nearly everybody reads something—if not the Philadelphia *Bulletin*, then the *Readers' Digest*, the *Wall Street Journal*, the Dell Comic books, or the Rexall Almanacs. But even if there is an American who reads nothing at all, he lives in a culture whose most important determinant is the written word.

What happens in America, therefore, has a significant bearing on what happens to folklore in a literate society.

When you read, let us say, Louis Adamic's description of a peasant wedding in Yugoslavia, with its mock fight for possession of the bride, suggestive of a remote antiquity when marriages were made by capture, you say, "How quaint. This is folklore." What do you say when you read about the weddings reported in the society pages of your local newspaper? Here are a couple of examples:

Given in marriage by her father, the bride wore a white crystal waltz length gown with inset eyelet crystalette panels and bouffant skirt. The shoulder length veil of illusion was held by pearlized orange blossoms. . . . Following the ceremony, a reception was held in the fellowship hall of the church. After a trip to Florida, the couple will live in——.

Given in marriage by her father, the bride wore a floor length dress of lace over taffeta designed with a basque bodice, brief

sleeves and a tiered skirt. Her fingertip veil was attached to a cap
of Chantilly lace re-embroidered with pearls and sequins.

[Honor attendants] wore waltz length dresses of seafoam
green chiffon over taffeta and net with matching crown head-
pieces and carried baskets of majestic daisies and English ivy.

Are the American weddings any less folkish because the bride
and her mother had the advice of Emily Post and Neiman-Marcus
rather than, or in addition to, that of the village elders? At least the
veil remains, though its antique function has long been forgotten.

Other questions arise. When a carpenter learns to frame a roof by
serving an apprenticeship and receiving instruction by word of
mouth from a man who has received his in the same way, you may
call his art a folk craft, that is, a tradition that has been handed down
orally. But suppose the carpenter has studied a book on roof fram-
ing? Or—what is often true these days—he has gone to school and
can prove the Euclidean propositions upon which the craft is based?

I have read in collections of folklore descriptions of Czech beer
parties in honor of a christening. But I have never found in what
purported to be a collection of folklore a description of a pub-
lisher's cocktail party in honor of an author's latest book. Yet, each
follows a historically determined pattern; each is a custom of a
group with a common body of tradition. This is not to say that the
traditions are of equal duration, or that they have been transmitted
in exactly the same way.

One effect of literacy is high specialization and another is
nationalism. As a nation gets bigger, its people become increasingly
divided into occupational and other groups. Folklore has been
mainly concerned with certain of these groups, to the exclusion of
others. It began in Europe as a study of "vulgar errors" or "popular antiquities," and even after Thoms proposed the term *folklore*
in 1846, its content, for the most part, continued to be the
social anthropology of European peasants and later of "primitive"
people of other continents. Thus arose the concepts of survival and
arrested development.

Thus arose too the idea that a "folk" must be a primitive group isolated from the contaminating influence of modern civilization. Mary Austin, for example, was able to find only three folk groups in the United States: the Red Indians, the Southern Negroes, and the Southern Mountaineers. These are all isolated geographically or socially or both. But there are other kinds of isolation, and there arc many groups within the mass. An occupation, for example, unites its members, and at the same time partially separates them from the mass. Each occupation has its lore—partly belief, partly custom, partly skills—expressed in anecdotes, sagas, tales, and the like. Each individual in a literate society plays a multiplicity of roles, belonging as he does to more than one group. Take for example the railroad conductor who is also a baseball fan. He has a body of tradition appropriate to each role. He knows how to behave in each role, and he knows the verbal lore of each. He knows the witticisms that pass between conductors and passengers. He can tell you apocryphal tales about Jay Gould and Collis Huntington; he knows about Casey Jones and the slow train through Arkansas. He knows too about Casey at the bat and has at his command all the formulas for heckling the other team and the umpire. Our culture is the richer for this pluralism.

Yet, the mass in the United States may, I think, be properly referred to as a folk. For in spite of divisive influences of specialization, of geography, of race, the American people have more in common than in diversity. Charles Wilson and Walter Reuther are divided by class interest. Wilson believes that what is good for General Motors is good for the United States. Reuther believes that what is good for labor is good for the United States. One believes in the trickle-down theory of prosperity; the other in the seep-up theory of prosperity. But they both believe in prosperity. They speak the same language, have much the same concept of the mission and destiny of America, and neither is a conscious enemy of capitalism. One cannot assert that there is any one belief that every American accepts, but the presence of dissent does not prove the absence of a common body of tradition.

Even in a preliterate society tradition is never wholly static. One consequence of literacy is an acceleration of change. Learning develops not only new techniques but new values as well. As long as the American Negro saw no prospect of sharing in the white man's rising standard of living, his folklore concerned the values available to him. Charms took the place of the medical service he could not afford; superstition took the place of the education that was denied him. He consoled himself with tales covertly satirical of the white man and with the hope of justice when he crossed the River Jordan and was gathered to Abraham's bosom. Once convinced of the possibility of sharing in the good things about him, however, he announces without regret that Uncle Tom is dead— but not Uncle Tom's music, which he will cite with justifiable pride as a major contribution to American culture. This shift in emphasis is illustrative of one change folklore undergoes in a literate society.

Another change involves the crafts. The first effect of the industrial revolution is to drive out the folk crafts. Blankets from New England mills take the place of homemade quilts. Brussels and Axminster carpets appear on floors once covered by hooked rugs and rag carpets. Furniture comes from Grand Rapids rather than from the shop of the local cabinetmaker. In time, however, certain countervailing influences assert themselves. There is a revolt against the monotony of both the mass-produced article and the routine job by which most Americans earn their living; and as the shorter work week, the expansion of the service industries, and the availability of household appliances create leisure, and often boredom, people take up hobbies, and hobbies germinate new industries serving them. Markets are found for textile mill-ends, and the Rose of Sharon and the Wedding Ring begin to appear on beds; department stores display yarn and burlap, and hooked rugs reappear. The makers of power tools put on do-it-yourself campaigns, and men begin turning out coffee tables and four-posters in their basements. Most of the craftsmen will work from patterns furnished by their suppliers or the hobby magazine, but a few will create their own designs.

New crafts appear. Teen-aged boys learn that by doing certain things to their motors they can increase the noise, if not the power, of their jalopies. When this activity spreads over the country, somebody realizes that here is a clientele for a new magazine, and *Hot Rod* appears on the newsstands. Then machine shops begin making the parts and selling kits to non-craftsmen, who, if they can afford to, may have their mechanics install them.

Even so, for the first time since the Stone Age great masses of people have opportunity to give play to the instinct of workmanship, to find relief from the monotony of their jobs, and, in some degree, to express whatever individuality they are endowed with.

As has been suggested by reference to the wedding veil, not all old customs perish. In a culture dedicated as ours is to a continuously rising standard of material well-being, a custom is likely to survive, though with a changed significance, if its observance increases the sales of goods and services. Readers of Keats know that at one time a girl could, by performing certain rites on the Eve of St. Agnes, see a vision of her future husband. The rites are no longer performed. They required no purchasable equipment. Not so with the suitable observance of Christmas, Thanksgiving, Easter—and now Halloween, for of late we bribe the tricksters with store-bought candy. We invent Mother's Day and Father's Day, spacing them carefully so they will not come too close to other already established occasions for spending money.

The pageantry that used to be associated with other occasions—the tournament for example—will be adapted to the publicizing of local products. The Queen of Love and Beauty becomes the Queen of Goats:

FREDERICKSBURG [Texas], July 25 (CTS)—A beautiful queen, as much at home in ranching jeans as in regal robes that denote her reign over the Mohair Realm, will officiate at the 38th annual coronation, show and sale of the Texas Angora Goat Raisers' Association here Aug. 1, 2, and 3.

Her Mohair Majesty, we learn, will have the title of "Angora Queen of the Universe," will be attended by "a score of attractive duchesses," and will receive the homage of the queen of the South Texas Fairs and Fat Stock Shows, the queen of the Gillespie County Fair, and the Farm Bureau queen.

In a literate society, verbal folklore will be disseminated not only by loggers, cotton pickers, oil field workers, and traveling salesmen but also by historians, biographers, fictionists, and journalists, not to say folklorists. Songs, tales, and proverbs will be published and read and some of them put into a wider oral circulation. In this process, narrative lore, in particular, will undergo change. In the 1920s, the journalists discover Paul Bunyan, who by this time is not only a logger but also an oil field worker and begin writing about him for the general magazines. In order to make their material go as far as possible, they invent some tales and rewrite others long in the oral tradition, including many that have no connection with either logging or oil field work. In the meantime, the loggers and oil field workers have become skilled manipulators of machines—power saws, power loaders, tractors, rotary rigs, and the like—and have lost interest in Bunyan. He becomes a national rather than a local or occupational folk character, standing for little more than bigness and strength. As Richard Dorson has observed, the journalists take him from the folk and give him back to a larger folk but with a changed character and significance. And this will be true of any hero who attains more than local fame. Without the aid of writers, he cannot move out of the province in which he has been created. The writers in moving him out must remold him into a type intelligible to the larger audience. Thus bad men become Robin Hoods, cowboys become knights-errant, backwoods politicians become symbols of militant democracy, and lowly animals become symbols of lowly folk. Incidents are reported and transferred from one region to another. The journalists who covered the first oil boom, for example, garnered a considerable sheaf of rags-to-riches stories. Later, journalists reported the same stories from other fields and often in good faith, for the stories appear sometimes to have come from Pennsylvania to Texas first by word of mouth.

This essay will have achieved its purpose if it has raised more questions than it has answered. It has been written on the assumption that the processes which create folklore do not cease when a society becomes literate and that folklore of any culture will reflect the values of that culture. If it has demonstrated anything, it is that the oral and written traditions are not most fruitfully conceived as separate and distinct. Each is continually borrowing from the other as the processes of adaptation and creation continue.

Mody Boatright, secretary-editor from 1943–1963, hard at work.

2

Folklore 101

by Cynthia Savage

What is folklore? And how do we know it when we see it? These are not necessarily easy questions to answer. Sometimes adults even have trouble figuring out what folklore is; they may even disagree on whether something is or is not folklore. This, however, should not discourage any of us from trying to identify, study, understand, and repeat the folklore that we find around us.

As many of us have heard or said, folklore is the study of folk. That sounds so easy, but it may not be as easy as it sounds. So let's take the word apart and see if we can discover what really is the study of folk. Folk, of course, are people. To study them, we need to look at them as members of groups. We generally join with others who think as we do, feel as we do, and believe as we do. In other words, we will create groups with others who reinforce what we think, feel, and believe. So a great way to analyze people is to look at the groups they form.

Let's take a minute to think of the groups to which we might belong. We can categorize ourselves by age: Are you young or old? We can categorize ourselves by place: Are you an American, a Texan, both, or do you identify with being one more than the other? Are you more comfortable in the country or in the city? We can classify ourselves by ethnicity: Did your ancestors come from Ireland, Russia, Africa, or Mexico? We can group ourselves by religious beliefs: Will you follow the teachings of Buddha, Christ, or Muhammad? Will you be baptized, saved, or confirmed? We can classify ourselves by gender: Will you have a bar mitzvah or a bat mitzvah? Will you have a quinceañera? Will you be on the football team? Will you be the bride or the groom?

Once we find to which groups we belong, we can begin to speak, dress, act, and believe as the others in our groups. We can identify them through these distinguishing actions, and they can identify us as one of them. We will sing the same songs, dance the same dances, tell the same stories, laugh at the same jokes, wear the same type clothing, and speak the same slang. We will also agree on what actions of ourselves and others are heroic or weak. We will agree that certain actions or people are good or evil. We will agree on what actions are forbidden. We will accept our beliefs as the truth. We will heal ourselves, both physically and mentally, using the same cures as others in our group. We will see the world around us in the same light.

Once we can see where we belong, we can look around at others and see that they too have their groups. These groups may not be the same as ours. Their songs, dances, stories, manner of speaking, clothing, and beliefs may well be different than ours. Or, you may find that there are elements that are shared. Maybe their song's tune is the same, but the words are different. Maybe they have a fairy tale with the message that you should not enter another's home uninvited and take things without asking. Only the name of the character is not Goldilocks. Sometimes, it's not enough to find the differences but the degrees of difference.

We look to others' ceremonies, rituals, formalities, and customs to discover their beliefs. These beliefs are their knowledge or truth that they have gained over time. In many cases, one generation passes to another this knowledge or these truths that a group believes. It is this knowledge that is passed that is lore. So once you define the group, you can begin to find the knowledge or the beliefs that they share.

How do we let each other know what we believe? How do we express our lore? You are going to see a number of ways today, as each member of this panel shares with you the lore they have studied.[1] We tell nursery rhymes that reveal our idea of good behavior. "Ladybug, ladybug fly away home. Your house is on fire and your children are alone." What mother would not get the message that children should not be left alone? Or, what of Humpty Dumpty who so foolishly sat on a wall high enough to make his fall a great one, one that is so bad that the wounds cannot be healed? We tell tales about the sadness that will overwhelm you and condemn you to a life of walking river banks and wailing if you let a moment of weakness overcome you and you choose a lover over your children, as did La Llorona. We sing songs about our love for our homeland or those who have attributes that we, and our group, find attractive. After all, the Yellow Rose of Texas, whose beauty beats the belles of Tennessee, had eyes as bright as diamonds that sparkle like the dew. We listen to legends about knights who gathered at a round table. From the stories told there, we can decide what characteristics make a hero. And from those same stories, we know of the heartache experienced by those who fall short.

We mix up age-old recipes passed from one generation to the next, for foods that remind us of those who came before and allow us to leave something to those who will come after us. We reach for remedies that we know helped our parents and their parents when they needed healing. And we believe that we too will feel better after we've slathered ourselves with Vick's VaporRub. We pray prayers that our parents learned on their knees—even though we may have to grow in experience before we understand for what we are asking or for what we are thankful.

To find the lore you must find the people. This is such an obvious statement, but it might not be apparent. You will have to follow the people with the lore to the kitchen table, the campfire, the drilling rig, the herb garden, the place of worship . . . wherever the stories are told and the beliefs passed down. And the people and places, the groups and stories change, but the underlying beliefs seldom do.

What changes are occurring now that will be studied by the younger folklorists? For one, people will live longer, and it will be interesting to see how that affects the passing of beliefs. We were once a rural society, but as statistics show, we are becoming an urban society. What will the stories of city folk be and how will they differ from stories based on country knowledge? The lines of ethnicity are blurring more and more. Tiger Woods does not declare one ethnicity, but many. How does this change the lore? Or does it? Gender lines are also blurring. In the war in Iraq, we are seeing women in combat roles. Will this change the traditional war stories? Will this have an effect on who our heroes are?

Not only may the lore evolve, but where will our young folklorists go to gather this information? Instead of the glow of a campfire, will they share their stores in the glow of a computer monitor? Will typing messages in chat rooms and email overtake the oral storytelling circle of the past? Will coffee shops with computers actually replace Dairy Queen? Will people still gather around the microwave in the same way they gathered around the old stove?

It might be exciting and maybe even hard to imagine the wonderful adventure folklore will take these young folklorists on in the future; however, we hope that our knowledge can be passed to

Children participating in special activities at the 2004 meeting in Allen, Texas.

them as they learn. This is why the Texas Folklore Society has such an important place in the lives of those who wish to understand not just folklore but how we view the world as we try to discover the different groups, the patterns they create, and the beliefs that they hold dear.

The founders of the Society, who first met over three quarters of a century ago, enjoyed gathering to share, study, and celebrate the folk and the lore of Texas. Just think of the foresight of the first person who said, "Give me a copy of your paper for the archives." What a treasure! The Society has also shared its knowledge every year through at least one publication. As much as any historical support that the Society can give anyone searching for lore, it may be this opportunity to share and contribute to the vast wealth of knowledge that is most appealing. We look forward to the young folklorists of today sharing with us the groups they see, the patterns and the differences of the groups, and the lore the groups share. The possibilities are theirs to explore.

ENDNOTES

1. This paper was presented as an Introduction to the first regular Children's Session at the 2003 meeting in Kerrville.

3

The Faultless Starch Library

by Ellisene Davis

An unusual collection of thirty-six little booklets called *The Faultless Starch Library* records an interesting era of history in a very different mode. Created in the early 1900s to advertise Faultless Starch, the contents of the library and the story of its creator give an interesting picture of "the folk" at the turn of the century in a unique and interesting manner.

Located in the "west bottoms" of Kansas City, Missouri, near the point where the Kansas River flows into the Missouri River, the Faultless Starch Company still produces starch for Americans. The company lost vital information about their history in two well-remembered floods in June 1903 and July 1951. Although the company still retains three complete sets of the original booklets, the flood destroyed the records of the creators of *The Faultless Starch Library*.[1]

There is one clue to the past that time and the flood did not erase. Although none of the booklets carried his name, the company believes that D. Arthur Brown wrote the text. Who was this man? Certainly a large part of the character of D. Arthur Brown can be seen in the spirit of the light-hearted little booklets. An intense search in Kansas City revealed new answers—a testimony to the immortality of a very special printer.[2]

The Faultless Starch Company distributed starch in early 1900 to many rural homes. A peddler made his rounds with his horse

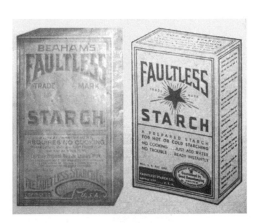

The original Faultless Starch.

and wagon. To each ten cent box of starch, the distributor banded a booklet. Oftentimes, the mercantile store kept a supply of the booklets. On Saturday trips to the general store to get supplies—a two hour trip by wagon—my family collected and stored away in an old trunk a complete set of *The Faultless Starch Library*. Many poor and isolated families made the trips to town no more than once a week. Sometimes, circumstances delayed travel for as long as three weeks. The infrequent trips for supplies made collecting the booklets difficult, and children considered the starch advertisements a very special prize. Distributed first in Texas, the booklets became a text for some parents who used the library to teach their children to read.[3]

Children in the cities as well as in the country collected and traded the booklets as a pastime. In the thirties, the Faultless Starch Company distributed the booklets wrapped in a pad and placed on top of the cartons in the corrugated cases before the workers sealed the boxes. When the retailer opened the case to stock his shelves, he would keep the booklets "under the counter" for the children of his customers or rubber band one booklet to each individual package. Random distribution led to a lively trading market among the kids.[4]

The mystery of the man who created the advertising copy for Faultless Starch nettled my curiosity. I knew the man loved jokes, life, parlor games, the Bible, and children. A query to the Kansas City library revealed a newspaper obituary dated December 20, 1944. "D. Arthur Brown, president of the Charles E. Brown Printing company, died today at St. Petersburg Florida. Mr. Brown, 74 years old, formerly was a Baptist minister and was a leader for many years at the First Baptist Church. He learned the printing trade as a youth in Missouri and worked on newspapers at Kidder, Plattsburg, and Lathrop before attending William Jewell College. There he studied for the ministry, and became pastor of the First Baptist Church at Salt Lake City. . . . As an early member of the Old Advertising Club, Mr. Brown was among the first in Kansas City to emphasize the value of church advertising. For many years he was on the executive committee of the Graphic Arts Association."[5]

The Faultless Starch Company hired D. Arthur Brown to advertise starch. Merchandisers wanted to make the product more appealing. Charles Brown believes his father wrote the booklets as an extra to get the printing. Because D. Arthur Brown understood the mind of "the folk" and possessed an incredible optimism, he began a very successful campaign.[6]

Collecting *The Faultless Starch Library* can be an interesting hobby for the folklorist. The original printing of the books carried the word "Beaham's" above the Faultless trademark. In the thirties, the starch company reprinted the booklets, and reproductions did not have the word Beaham's written above the trademark.[7]

An examination of *The Faultless Starch Library* reveals that D. Arthur Brown felt an appreciation and understanding of how much "Ordinary People" needed laughter and goodness in their lives. Arthur wrote that for *Elisa May* ironin' day is just "the worst, it's worser lots 'n th' day before." Don't sass Elisa on that day. Of course ironin' day is just like play. "Since she buys this Faultless Starch, ironin's as gay as a circus march."[8] Arthur Brown tucked in the pages of *The Tuttles Fourth of July* games and the "Secret of

Several titles from the Faultless Starch Library, including *Elisa May*, *Little Jack*, and *Honey*.

Success" (A Comical Travesty). "'Push,' said the Button; 'Take pains,' said the window; 'Be up to date,' said the calendar; 'Make light of everything,' said the Fire. . . . And naturally, 'Find a good thing and stick to it,' Faultless Starch."[9] *Sallie Short and Lillie Long* share the secret of all success in the home—Faultless Starch.[10] *Old Uncle Ritts* and the children went to sea only to be shipwrecked, but they floated home on boxes of starch. Their mother told them wisely—"And not only has Faultless Starch saved your life, but that of your mamma also. If through these years I'd ironed with other starch, I'd been buried long ago."[11]

Old Granny Grak gave the children some gladsome games, some jokes, some rhymes, and a box of Faultless Starch filled with gold.[12] You know it's worth its weight in gold. *Proud Tommy Tilt* has a silk hat that shines with starch.[13] Bin and Bun drank the starch and became so stiff they fell off their bicycles.[14] *The Four Little Sunbonnets*,[15] *Little Jack*,[16] *Mildred and Rosa*,[17] *Honey*,[18] and *Gentle Jane* have warm jokes, stories, interesting facts, Bible facts, trivia—enough to play Trivial Pursuit. And what is the eighth wonder of the world?—That everybody doesn't use Faultless Starch.[19]

His greatest tribute to this eclectic of "Ordinary People" is a clever section of curious epitaphs.

LINES ON A MAN NAMED OWEN MOORE

Owen, Moore has run away,
Owin' more than he could pay.

And another . . .

Sad was her fate, she met it thus—
She was run over by a bus.

And last . . .

LINES ON AN EDITOR

Here lies an editor,
Snooks, if you will!
In mercy, kind Providence,
Let him lie still.
He lied for his living, so
He lived while he lied,
When he could not lie longer,
He lied down and died.[20]

Arthur Brown recognized the importance of the *ABCs* for children, and he created his own poems to illustrate the alphabet. "*D* is for Dog, a fine, handsome fellow. He's a big St. Bernard, and is all white and yellow." If he managed a commercial, all the better: "*F* is for Faultless Starch, the very best. No ironer without it, In comfort can rest." And always he gave the children conundrums! "Do you know why a proud woman is like a music box? She is full of airs."[21]

Arthur Brown borrowed from the favorite tales of children, giving them a twist in the tradition of folktales—the storyteller feeling free to add his own interpretation. *The Owl and the Pussy Cat* went to sea in a beautiful pea green boat. "Oh Pussy,

The *ABC Book*.

Learning the abc's through the Faultless Starch Library.

oh Pussy, oh Pussy my love, Do you use Faultless Starch for your ha'r?" He added the fun of character reading in handwriting for all the hopeful fortune tellers. There are peculiar abbreviations and a little nonsense for gaiety.[22] *Little Red Riding Hood*, all done up with Faultless Starch, completely charms the wolf from his evil ways.[23] And who would need Faultless Starch more desperately than *Three Naughty Kittens*, who must wash their mittens?[24] How could anyone dare to consider "the washing—a dreadful sight, That looked as though it had suffered blight, Before it was starched with the kind of starch they used in *The House That Jack Built*?"[25] You'll *never* guess that brand. Mother Goose danced across the pages of the booklets in like style: "There was an old woman, who lived in a shoe. She had so many children, she didn't know what to do; So she starched all their dresses with Faultless so fine, And sent them to walk, for a long, long, time."[26]

Arthur Brown understood that fantasy entertained children as well as aroused their curiosity. He portrayed the job of ironing as enchanting and fun because work enriches life. "Once on a time I went to sea, In a sieve with a sail of silk," which could only happen in *Upside Down Land*.[27] There are starch ghosts, little frogs, mice, monkeys, bears, ants, and grasshoppers who find life much richer because they use Faultless Starch. He never forgets to add some sobering facts, such as one penny saved each day for fifty years at six percent interest will yield $950.00. And he speculated about how love would be for his grandchildren:

HOW IT WILL BE IN 1950

The coatless man puts a careless arm
'Round the waist of a hatless girl,
As over the dustless and mudless roads
In a horseless carriage they whirl—
Like a leadless bullet with a hammerless gun,
By smokeless power driven,
They fly to taste the speechless joy
By endless union given.
Though the only lunch his coinless purse
Affords them the means
Is a tasteless meal of boneless cod
With a "side" of stringless beans.
He puffs a tobaccoless cigarette
And laughs a mirthless laugh
When papa tries to coax her back
By wireless telegraph.[28]

Arthur Brown added fairy tales to his collection, knowing that everyone needs a pocketful of magic. Arthur told the story of *The Prince's Bride*, a Cinderella tale. Kelp, a fairy, found a magic potion—Faultless Starch—for a tired old dress that the bride wore to the ball.[29] *A Trip to the Moon* reveals what everyone knows to be true: fairies wash the moon with Faultless Starch and that is why it is white. Fathers were always remembered in the booklets in fanciful ways. "Breathes there a man with soul so dead that never to himself hath said. Faultless Starch my wife shall have."[30]

Some popular titles.

Arthur Brown did not forget the ethnic groups. In the tradition of one little, two little, three little Indians, Arthur subtracts pickaninnies for a lesson in math. The final line reads, "One little pickaninny, when with Faultless Starch she's done, Finds she's turned all over white, and so there are none.[31] *Hans and Gretel* are Dutch,[32] and Arthur remembers *The Indians*.[33] The Chinese are not forgotten. He spins a tale of love with its painful moments of competition, even suicide. Of course, there is a happy ending because of Faultless Starch. "Chin-chin married Chow, and they did live a long and happy life, upon the shelf behind the vase— Chin-chin and Chow, his wife."[34]

The Kansas City Historical Association sent a family record that listed D. Arthur Brown's children—four boys and a girl. Fortunately, I found a son listed in the Kansas City general information. The telephone call to Albert Brown became the first of many warm conversations with the Brown family, all living. The sons of D. Arthur Brown added a new dimension to the story of *The Faultless Starch Library*.[35]

Art Brown worked in the Charles E. Brown Printing Company when the firm printed *The Faultless Starch Library*. He remembers that the old engraving house, Teachenor-Bartberger, drafted the artwork. Located in the same plant as the Charles E. Brown Company (701 Central Street, Kansas City, Mo.), the engravers created the covers of the booklets by making half-tone engravings. First, the engraver made a photographic negative of the copy. Constructed of two glass plates cemented together, the half-tone screen is placed between the film and the lens. One is ruled with vertical lines, the other ruled with horizontal lines. Together they form a mesh of tiny squares. An arc lamp floods the copy with light. Dark areas on the copy absorb most of the light. Bright areas absorb little light. As it goes through the screen, the light is broken by tiny lines of the screen into thousands of separate beams "burning" tiny dots into the emulsion of the film. The negative is printed on a sensitized plate made of copper. Then, the plate is etched in much the same way as a line engraving. The dots transfer ink to the paper, blending in the viewer's eye to re-form tones of the original picture.

Art explained that the Charles E. Brown Printing Company printed the interior of the starch booklets and set the type by hand. Employees printed the pages in sheets and saddle stitched them with a Christensen machine, then used a power cutter to slice two hundred books per stroke. A child gained prestige in his neighborhood if he could own the booklets and a Sunkist orange spoon, both considered waste advertising.[36]

The eldest son, William R. Brown, joined the Charles E. Brown Printing Company first and handled the selling on the outside. After Arthur Brown died, William became president of the firm. When asked to comment about what he remembered most about his father, he said, "My father was a montage of many good things. He was a whole hearted, happy spirited individual—optimistic, attuned to others' problems. There were jovial times around the table. We were happy. Once a man asked dad why he had so many children. Dad answered, 'Which one of them would you have me do without?'"[37]

Charles Brown, the youngest son, became a writer and publicist. He remembers his father as, "Basically, very even tempered, very affectionate, thoughtful, a considerable character. This generation would say he was an authoritarian. Understanding what motivated people enhanced his ability to be a good businessman and a money-maker. He possessed honesty and integrity—a man of probity."[38]

Al Brown remembered that some of the ideas for the stories of the booklets came from family members. His sister, Rebecca, was the little girl who lost her hat. The family saw Rebecca's hat on a lake where the children played and believed "Becky" had drowned. Fortunately, she made her way home safely. Merwin Brown, son of Charles E. Brown who founded the printing company, posed for the picture of Little Jack, a cover with the photograph of a very important little boy with his feet propped on a desk.[39]

I treasure the thirty-six booklets found in my grandfather's trunk. The booklets gave me a very unique and special touch with the past. I encountered relationships with new and interesting people. Most important of all, the booklets gave me laughter—rich flowing, healing laughter. D. Arthur Brown's work demanded that I know him. The acquaintance with his story reveals that his children and readers remember him with warmth and affection.[40]

ENDNOTES

1. Faultless Starch/Bon Ami Company, 1025 West Street, Kansas City, Missouri 64101, correspondence.
2. Ibid.
3. Ibid.
4. Ibid.
5. *Kansas City Star*, [Kansas City, Missouri], December 20, 1944.
6. Brown, Charles D. 1721 Maxwell Ct., McLean, Virginia 22101.
7. Faultless Starch/Bon Ami Company, correspondence.
8. Brown, D. Arthur. *The Faultless Starch Library: Elisa May*, Vol. 25. Kansas City: Charles E. Brown Printing Co., 1900.
9. ———. *The Faultless Starch Library: The Tuttles Fourth of July*, Vol. 36. Kansas City: Charles E. Brown Printing Co., 1900.
10. ———. *The Faultless Starch Library: Sallie Short and Lillie Long*, Vol. 18. Kansas City: Charles E. Brown Printing Co., 1900.

11. ———. *The Faultless Starch Library: Old Uncle Ritts*, Vol. 15. Kansas City: Charles E. Brown Printing Co., 1900.
12. ———. *The Faultless Starch Library: Old Granny Grak*, Vol. 16. Kansas City: Charles E. Brown Printing Co., 1900.
13. ———. *The Faultless Starch Library: Proud Tommy Tilt*, Vol. 14. Kansas City: Charles E. Brown Printing Co., 1900.
14. ———. *The Faultless Starch Library: Bin and Bun*, Vol. 17. Kansas City: Charles E. Brown Printing Co., 1900.
15. ———. *The Faultless Starch Library: The Four Little Sunbonnets*, Vol. 6. Kansas City: Charles E. Brown Printing Co., 1900.
16. ———. *The Faultless Starch Library: Little Jack*, Vol. 30. Kansas City: Charles E. Brown Printing Co., 1900.
17. ———. *The Faultless Starch Library: Mildred and Rosa*, Vol. 29. Kansas City: Charles E. Brown Printing Co., 1900.
18. ———. *The Faultless Starch Library: Honey*, Vol. 26. Kansas City: Charles E. Brown Printing Co., 1900.
19. ———. *The Faultless Starch Library: Gentle Jane*, Vol. 28. Kansas City: Charles E. Brown Printing Co., 1900.
20. ———. *Mildred and Rosa.*
21. ———. *The Faultless Starch Library: A B C Book*, Vol. 14. Kansas City: Charles E. Brown Printing Co., 1900.
22. ———. *The Faultless Starch Library: The Owl and the Pussy Cat*, Vol. 9. Kansas City: Charles E. Brown Printing Co., 1900.
23. ———. *The Faultless Starch Library: Little Red Riding Hood*, Vol. 33. Kansas City: Charles E. Brown Printing Co., 1900.
24. ———. *The Faultless Starch Library: Three Naughty Kittens*, Vol. 24. Kansas City: Charles E. Brown Printing Co., 1900.
25. ———. *The Faultless Starch Library: The House That Jack Built*, Vol. 20. Kansas City: Charles E. Brown Printing Co., 1900.
26. ———. *The Faultless Starch Library: Mother Goose Rhymes*, Vol. 3. Kansas City: Charles E. Brown Printing Co., 1900.
27. ———. *The Faultless Starch Library: Upside Down Land*, Vol. 22. Kansas City: Charles E. Brown Printing Co., 1900.
28. ———. *The Faultless Starch Library: The Reformed Pig*, Vol. 23. Kansas City: Charles E. Brown Printing Co., 1900.
29. ———. *The Faultless Starch Library: The Prince's Bride*, Vol. 9. Kansas City: Charles E. Brown Printing Co., 1900.
30. ———. *The Faultless Starch Library: A Trip to the Moon*, Vol. 7. Kansas City: Charles E. Brown Printing Co., 1900.
31. ———. *The Faultless Starch Library: Ten Little Pickannies*, Vol. 21. Kansas City: Charles E. Brown Printing Co., 1900.
32. ———. *The Faultless Starch Library: Hans and Gretel*, Vol. 32. Kansas City: Charles E. Brown Printing Co., 1900.

33. ———. *The Faultless Starch Library: The Indians*, Vol. 33. Kansas City: Charles E. Brown Printing Co., 1900.
34. ———. *The Faultless Starch Library: Chin-Chin and Chow*, Vol. 8. Kansas City: Charles E. Brown Printing Co., 1900.
35. Biographical Data of Kansas Citizens, Citizens Historical Association, Public Library, Kansas City, Missouri.
36. Brown, Art N. 12630 Crystal Lake Dr., Sun City, West, Arizona 85375.
37. Brown, Charles D. 1721 Maxwell Ct., McLean, Virginia 22101.
38. Brown, William R. 439 W. 58th Street, Kansas City, Missouri 64101.
39. Brown, Albert V. 117 W 99th Street, Kansas City, Missouri 64114.
40. Pevehouse, Venus. "I Remember the Starch Booklets," cited in *Mature Living*, November, 1982.

SCHOOL DAYS

School days, school days
Dear old golden-rule days!
Reading and writing and 'rithmatic,
Taught to the tune of a hick'ry stick.

You were my bashful barefoot beau,
I was your queen in calico.
Oh, for those days, I loved them so,
When we were a couple of kids!

4

Day Care Oral Traditions and School Yard Games

by Tierney Untiedt

"Thumbkin"

Where is Thumbkin? Where is Thumbkin?
Here I am. Here I am.
How are you today, sir? Very well; I thank you.
Run away. Run away.[1]

Everyone remembers this song, but do you remember where you learned it? If you're like me, it was probably at home. My younger brother and I both recall my mother constantly singing around the house, teaching us not only the pop songs she loved, but also childhood standards such as "Thumbkin" and "Patty Cake." I remember learning how to do "Itsy Bitsy Spider," which I eventually taught to each of my children. I have fond memories of when I was a young girl growing up in Iowa and learning to play stickball and Kick the Can in the alley behind my house. My friends and I shared local urban legends, and I never tired of hearing my grandfather tell stories during family gatherings. Most of these memories are tied close to the home because that is where most of us once learned the songs and stories we all cherish from our youth. Parents told fairy tales at night, and songs, games, and local lore were shared throughout the day by all family members.

Of course, some of these songs and games were learned in social settings such as church or school, but most of it came from within the home. Before our society became so overrun with soccer moms and specialized classes for everything from dance to karate, the home was the predominant setting in which children learned. However, after the Second World War, economic and social changes caused many families to become dual-income households. Due to the increase in women entering the workforce, there was a sudden demand for child care outside the home. This demand has grown steadily, and now it is seemingly unusual for women to stay home. As a result, day care has become a booming industry. Licensed day care centers not only provide families with an alternative form of child care to allow them to survive in today's financial state, but they have also become instrumental in keeping alive traditional folk songs, games, and stories.

Learning the songs and games we all love has always had more of a purpose than just mere entertainment. Before children enter kindergarten, they need to develop basic learning skills to help ease their transition into a formal school environment. Many of the songs they learn to sing with their peers help foster these skills. The repetition and rhyming schemes in most children's songs help improve memorization and allow children to learn patterns of words, as well as musical skills. They learn language skills and proper enunciation in songs such as "The Name Game," where they sing a name with a series of words such as, "Hanna, Hanna, Bo Banna, Fee Fie Fo Fanna, Hanna." Some songs teach children tales that include hidden geography and history lessons, such as with "Johnny Appleseed." Most of these songs involve counting, teaching children basic math skills while they sing. An example of this is one of our favorites:

"THREE [OR FIVE, OR TEN] LITTLE SPECKLED FROGS"

> Three little speckled frogs, sitting on a great big log,
> Eating the most delicious bugs—Yum, Yum!
> One jumped into the pool, where it was nice and cool,
> Leaving two speckled frogs—ribbit, ribbit![2]

Childhood games play an important role in helping children improve their physical skills. They teach children agility and dexterity and allow them to participate in physical activities, which is

Ring Around the Rosey is still popular.

especially good because exercise makes children tired. Nothing can make a child ready for an early bedtime like a long game of "Ring Around the Rosey" or "Red Rover Come Over."

They can also learn coordination skills through games such as "Itsy Bitsy Spider," which requires children to sing and make corresponding hand movements at the same time. Occasionally, this type of play is nothing more than entertainment, but this could also be beneficial, if not for the children, then for the mother. While the kids are busy playing games and singing songs, it keeps them out of their mother's hair so she can work. For anyone who has had to clean the house or do laundry or prepare a meal, a few moments where the children are playing by themselves can be the only way to complete household chores in a timely manner.

Traditionally, the primary teacher of these songs and games in the home was, of course, the mother. But there were other members of the family who could be just as important. Some families had always been dependent on two incomes and both parents had to work. Other families had to get by with only one parent. In many cases, if the mother could not care for the children, other relatives filled in. Aunts, older cousins, or the old stand-by grandparents often were essential in these extended families, which sometimes even lived together to save expenses. Changing economic conditions eventually caused the disintegration of this type of family environment, and the aunts and cousins were also required to enter the workforce. Even grandparents began postponing retirement due to financial burdens. In the middle of the twentieth century, we began to see more mobile generations, with people moving farther from home to look for work, like us.

Hence, the widespread advent of day cares. Early day cares were referred to as "nursery schools."[3] They first appeared in the early 1920s with the goal of preparing children for kindergarten. These early nursery schools were overseen by the Board of Education with strict standards of operations, and they later evolved into "day nurseries," or what we generally refer to as day cares. There are four basic types of day nurseries. Independent commercial nurseries are where women provide in-home care for neighborhood children. My mother-in-law operated a day care in her home her entire adult life, providing care for children throughout two generations. She shared things from her childhood with the kids she "baby-sat." She also exposed them to unique Untiedt-family folk speech. Who knows how many children she taught to "poose" on their food if it was too hot. After some of the kids grew up, they chose to take their own children to her for day care services. In the small town where we grew up, most child care was of this in-home type.

A second type of day nursery or day care is called a philanthropic nursery. This type of day care is provided through charitable organizations. A third type is a public school-system-sponsored day care where children are offered after-school monitoring and activities. The last type of day care is the industrial nursery. These are independentlyowned day care centers and employer-sponsored programs. Some of these businesses operate numerous centers, locally, and even nationally. Kindercare is the largest, with over 1500 centers nationwide. All of these types of day cares are now closely regulated, as opposed to years ago when people could have dozens of children in their care each day with little regard to sanitation, nutrition, or educational standards. Day cares are now licensed—at least those that are operated legally—and they are regulated by individual state agencies. Here in Texas, it is the Texas Department of Protective and Regulatory Services or what day care administrators affectionately refer to as "Licensing."

I originally became involved in the day care industry when our oldest daughter Miché was an infant. I applied at the day care she attended for a job as an assistant director, a job which consisted mainly of duties similar to that of a bookkeeper or secretary. We viewed it as a chance for me to be close to her while I was at work, and I felt better being able to monitor the quality of care she received. Before I knew it, unexpected personnel changes landed me the job of temporary director. I eventually received my Texas Director's Certificate, and I ended up staying in the business for seven years. I worked in small, locally owned centers in Lubbock, as well as centers belonging to huge corporations in and around the Dallas area.

I worked in centers that provided care to all economic and social levels of families, and they all had the same responsibilities: to provide kids with a safe place to stay while their parents worked, and also to teach them the songs and games and stories that are vital to the growth and development of all children. These children obtained a rich variety of folklore in the process, learning as much about their own heritage as that of their peers and teachers. I witnessed countless teachers and staff sharing with the kids their family histories and personal folklore, in addition to traditional songs and games. I was very interested in the regional differences of what they learned. I found that my children and the others in the day cares where I worked were learning many of the songs and games that I had learned as a child in Iowa, but also some that I had never heard of. You may have heard this, or some variation of it, but it was new to me and all of our family in Iowa:

"Little Bunny Foo-Foo"

Little Bunny Foo-Foo, hopping through the forest,
Picking up the field mice and bopping them on the head.
[Spoken] Down came the Good Fairy, and she said,
Little Bunny Foo-Foo, I don't want to see you
Picking up the field mice and bopping them on the head.
[Spoken] Or I'll turn you into a goon.[4]

Day cares provide a service to parents in today's financially demanding world, and it is a service that is growing in necessity every day. More kids go to day cares now than ever before. According to Internet listings, there are currently close to one-thousand licensed day cares in the Lubbock region.[5] There are almost 1,500 in the San Antonio region, which Victoria belongs to.[6] In Texas, there are over twenty thousand day care facilities. As many as there are, there is still a shortage in many areas, and parents often must place their children on waiting lists before they're born in order to find a place where they can receive quality care.

As for us, Miché is no longer in day care at all, Brody attends an after-school program provided by a private entity through the cooperation of the school district, and Ashland is still in a regular, licensed day care center. We have found that the younger ones are learning new things that Miché is unfamiliar with now that she has been out of day care for so long. Where she once taught them what she had learned to sing and play, now they are teaching her new songs and games that are currently circulating in day cares. We rely on day cares to do what our busy lives prevent us from doing, at least while we are at work. They keep alive the songs, games, and stories that we treasure from our childhood.

Endnotes

1. Traditional.
2. Traditional. Continue counting down until you leave "no speckled frogs."

3. This summary regarding the history of day care centers in the U.S. is taken from the following source: Lascarides, V. Celia, and Blythe F. Hinitz. *History of Early Childhood Education.* New York: Falmer Press, 2000.
4. Traditional. This chorus is repeated until the Good Fairy *does* turn the child into a goon.
5. The data on numbers of day care facilities were obtained from the Internet site "Child Care Facilities in Texas." 18 Jan. 2002. 18 Jan. 2002 < http://www.Tdprs.state.tx.us>.
6. This paper was presented at the 2002 meeting in Victoria.

5

You Can Tell · A Scout From Texas

by Rebecca Matthews

eople have many different images of Boy Scouts—a boy in a funny looking hat and knickers helping a little old lady across the street, youngsters in sharp uniforms marching in a parade, or perhaps a group of scruffy guys telling ghost stories around the campfire. Though scouting still encourages outdoor skills, patriotism, and service to others, the ghost stories have gone the way of knickers and helpless little old ladies, while campfires are traditional, ceremonial occasions with songs and skits. Scouting has grown during its seventy-nine years in America. The Cub Scouts program is now open to boys in grades one through five, while the Boy Scouts program is for those between the ages of eleven and eighteen. Their uniforms and activities have changed to keep pace with the times, yet many of their traditions echo those of the fathers and grandfathers of today's scouts.

The opening flag ceremony in Lubbock, Texas.

For any scout gathering, a flag ceremony is the traditional opening and closing. The flagpole also provides a good place for songs and cheers. Throughout Texas, in Boy Scout camps and Cub Scout Day camps alike, singing "Squirrel" to recover items turned in to "Lost and Found" is a tradition. "Squirrel" is an action song. To begin, the singer holds his hands curled at chest level and bends his knees to imitate a squirrel as he sings: "Squirreley, squirreley." He then turns his back to the audience and adds: "Shake your little tail [providing the appropriate action.] Squirreley, squirreley, shake your little tail. Put your finger on your nose. Put your finger on your toes. Squirreley, squirreley, shake your little tail." Now if that's not enough to encourage a boy to keep up with his things, nothing is.

Scouts seem to have an appropriate song for every occasion. For any group left waiting in line, "Birds in the Wilderness" comes in handy (sung to the tune of "The Old Gray Mare"): "Here we sit like birds in the wilderness, birds in the wilderness, birds in the wilderness. Here we sit like birds in the wilderness, waiting on . . ." People who are not from Texas may wait for someone or something; we from Texas wait on a person or event. Another useful song is "Announcements, announcements, announcements. A terrible death to die, a terrible death to die, a terrible death to be talked to death, a terrible death to die. We sold our cow. We sold our cow. We have no use for your bull now."

At campfires and troop or pack meetings, action songs are popular. One favorite is "Singing in the Rain." In the Scout version of the song, people sing the traditional chorus, then pause and follow the directions of the song leader (who will, for example, say "Thumbs up"). They then wiggle their hips back and forth as they sing: "Chee-chee-cha, chee-chee-cha, chee-chee-cha-cha" [repeat once]. The "Singing in the Rain" chorus is repeated with additional directions added at the end each time. By the completion of the song, everyone must sing "chee-chee-cha" with thumbs up, elbows back, knees bent, toes together, buns out, head to the side, and tongue out.

Of course, not all songs are action songs. A hint of the Texas mystique is found in "Scout From Texas" (sung to the tune of "Yellow Rose of Texas"):

> You can tell a scout from Texas,
> You can tell it by his talk.
> You can tell a scout from Texas,

You can tell it by his walk.
You can tell it by his manners,
By his appetite and such.
You can tell a scout from Texas,
But you cannot tell him much.

The younger boys also enjoyed songs that are slightly risqué. For instance, "Oh, I wish I was a little bar of soap [repeat]. I'd go slippy, slippy, slimey over everybody's hiney. Oh, I wish I was a little bar of soap."

Now, Scout summer camps are not dedicated entirely to singing. Standard merit badge programs are offered at most camps, with special programs included as locations permit. Horseback expeditions into the hills are a big event at El Rancho Cima near Wimberley, Texas, while a backpacking trip into the Pecos Wilderness is offered at Tres Ritos, New Mexico. Theme camps offer an interesting variety of activities, as well. Many Texas scouts are treated to Cowboy Camps. At Camp C. W. Post south of Lubbock, boys can visit a Plainsman Camp and an Indian Village, while Tres Ritos offers a Mountain Man Camp. In these special areas, boys learn about the past by eating foods indigenous to the era and participating in activities such as roping or firing a black powder rifle.

Local historical legends often offer a unique focal point at the camps. A reproduction of Adobe Walls can be found at Camp Don Harrington near Amarillo. On special occasions, it is manned by costumed historians who explain that Adobe Walls was originally built by the Bent brothers as a Comanche trading post and later became the site of a famous battle between Indians and buffalo hunters. Camp Don also has a buffalo cliff on its grounds, a place where Indians in pre-horse days stampeded buffalo over a cliff in order to gather the meat. If the campers are lucky, the ranger may even include the story of an Indian lover's leap in his campfire tales.

Camp Post contains its own bits of history. The first road up the Caprock in that area is on the grounds, as is the first well and the grave of the first recorded death in Garza County. Campers have an opportunity to learn something about these "firsts" as members of the Sunrise Club. In this program, they hike up the Cap, camp overnight on top, and hear a short history of the area, which includes such items as cereal magnate C. W. Post's colonizing efforts and his "rain wars."

The highlight of any camp is usually the campfire conducted on the final evening. While parents watch, awards are handed out and entertainment is provided. In some instances, the lighting of the fire is a ceremonial occasion in itself. The announcer may display a jar of white ashes collected at a national jamboree, taken from the very hottest part of the fire. He explains that if the people around him have enough Scout spirit, the logs will burst into flames when he dumps the ashes on them. He empties the jar and leads the audience in a chorus of "I've Got That Scouting Spirit Down in My Heart." Sure enough, with a poof and a great deal of smoke, the logs burst into flame. The ceremony serves the dual purpose of creating an impressive display and getting rid of all the mosquitoes in the area in one fell swoop.

Once the fire is lit, the entertainment begins. Scouts usually rely on songs, jokes and skits for entertainment, with skits dominating the event. Boy Scout skits are fairly short and simple, requiring few or no props, and they take little preparation or planning. The skits seen at summer camp will filter their way back to the hometowns and show up again at troop meetings, courts of honor, and campfires later in the year. They may even metamorphize into jokes told on campouts or field trips. Some skits are merely short "run-on's." For example, a boy may walk by dragging a rope behind him. Someone will ask, "Why are you pulling that rope?" The boy replies, "Have you ever tried pushing one?"

Most skits have unknown origins, but their motifs are ageless. One such skit is "The Ugliest Man." In this one, a person stands in front of the audience with a coat or sack over his head. The announcer claims that he has the world's ugliest man here. He asks for volunteers to come forward and look at the ugliest man. The first two or three "volunteers" have been coached. They lift the coat or sack, peek at the man's face, then scream and run off. Finally, a real volunteer comes forward. When he lifts the coat—the ugliest man screams and runs away.

Another skit that is as common as mesquite across the state is "The Candy Store." To begin this one, a scout comes forward and announces that he has a candy store, but he needs some volunteers to help him out by being props. People from the audience are called forward to act as the doors, counter, cash register, and shelves for the candy store. Once these people are in place, other scouts walk through the doors and ask for different candies. The shop-keeper searches through the shelves but announces that he is out of that type of candy. Finally, a scout asks, "What kind of candy *do* you have?" The shop-keeper replies, "I don't have any candy." He waves his hands toward the volunteer props. "But just look at all these suckers."

Camp entertainment is supposed to be clean. One director warned his staff, "Don't do a skit unless you'd be willing to do it in front of your mother and your preacher." Yet, sometimes questionable skits slip through, much to the delight of campers. One example is an elaborate skit called "A Fairy Tale." This one is longer than most, requiring a script and mass audience participation. The viewers are divided into sections, and each section must respond with a phrase when they hear a certain word. For example, the word "king" elicits the response, "I *am* the king;" the king's "pretty daughter" is greeted with "Oo-la-la," while the "ugly daughter" hears "Oo-oo-icky-pooh. What a dog!" when her name is called. The script tells a common fairy tale with a knight saving the kingdom by slaying a dragon. After his brave deed, the knight stands before the king and is offered a reward. The king ("I *am* the king") asks whether the knight ("Bum-da-da-dum") prefers the hand of his pretty daughter ("Oo-la-la") or that of his ugly daughter ("Oo-oo-icky-pooh. What a dog!"). The knight responds, "Neither, my king. I want you." When the king asks why, the knight says, "Because this is a *fairy* tale."

The skit survived Boy Scout Camp with only mild complaints, but when someone tried to present it before Cub Scouts, the staff responded with a "blunder bust." They all walked into the council ring, making noise and creating confusion, until the skit's announcer was escorted offstage.

The audience is expected to respond to skits and award ceremonies with cheers or applauses. These are especially popular with Cub Scouts, and no one at a Cub activity would dream of simply clapping his hands. Instead, they may give someone a big hand (hold hand up, palm out) or a round of applause (clap, moving hands in a circle around the head). The most popular cheer is the "Watermelon." People pretend to hold a watermelon slice in both hands, eat it with a loud slurp and then spit out the seeds. An appropriate cheer for the aforementioned "Fairy Tale" might be the "Oil Cheer" ("Crude, crude, crude"). An unpopular announcement might meet with the "Cookie Cheer" ("Crumby, crumby, crumby") or the "Cactus Cheer" ("Yucca, yucca, yucca"). There are myriad cheers, and their ranks seem to increase daily, but these are the most universally known and best loved of them.

After the awards and entertainment at summer camps, the campfires are usually concluded with an "Order of the Arrow" (OA) tap-out. This is a solemn, long awaited occasion since OA membership is considered a high honor. New members are chosen by their home troops in yearly elections, but their identities are a closely guarded secret until the night of the tap-out.

On those nights, when the sky is black so that the campfire provides the only illumination, four OA members wearing Indian garb and war paint step into the circle of light. They ask that everyone remain totally silent and that no photographs be taken during the ceremony. Though there is room for improvisation, the ceremonies follow general guidelines. One Indian announces that the Great Spirit of Scouting will speak to him and tell him who in the group is worthy of OA membership. After a few moments of silence, he declares that he has found none; he must appeal to the Great Spirit again. Finally, the identities of the new members are revealed. In times past, the other OA Indians would circle the group and tap new members on the shoulder. Some say that a person was not properly tapped out unless his knees buckled under the impact. In the last few years, tap-outs have been banned by new laws against hazing, so boys are now called out. A voice from the darkness calls their names, and they move into the circle of light. The new candidates take a vow of silence and cannot speak until released from that vow the next morning. Other members of the audience are asked to return to the parking lot without speaking.

Those outside scouting circles may wonder where one learns these songs, skits, and cheers. Boy Scouts of America publishes reams of printed material, some of which probably includes every song, skit, and cheer imaginable—I've discussed only a small sampling. But very few people actually pick up ideas from these sources. Instead, in the best of folk traditions, they learn by observation and word-of-mouth. They exchange ideas at training sessions, camps, and other council-wide activities. Traditions travel as people move or visit, and they are recycled when ex-Boy Scouts become adult scout leaders. One suspects that the skits and songs existed long before they were frozen in printed texts. As one middle-aged Scoutmaster says, "They stay the same with only small variations for years. At least that's been my experience because the same ones I was doing when I was a scout are still being done now."

The author's sons, Joel, Jeremiah, and Josh as scouts in 1989.

6

It All Depended on the Teacher:

Classroom Resources in Texas Country Schools

by Lou Rodenberger

Resolved: Texas should be divided into two states.

W hen Carl Halsell suggested a debate defending or attacking that idea to the boys who had arrived early one fall morning in 1922 at their country school ground to practice basketball, most of them looked puzzled. Carl knew that the students, who seldom saw a newspaper and had no radios in their homes, would learn at least a few research techniques, as well as gain confidence from having to stand in front of their parents and friends and express opinions, whether they actually believed in their defense or not. When he laid out his plan, however, his pupils looked at each other with skepticism. How could they argue for something they definitely didn't believe in? To them, boasting that they were citizens of the biggest state in the Union set them apart from Yankees, Arkansawyers, and Okies. Finally, their teacher convinced them that the topic merited their thought. Two of the boys said they would argue the affirmative, even if they didn't believe it.

Soon, as their teachers, my parents Mr. Carl and Miss Mabel, had hoped, contestants were mailing letters to the governor, their legislator, mayors of several cities, and state agencies that they thought could provide information to support their stands. Parents, who stopped farm work to attend Friday literary society meetings already established by the two young teachers at the two-room school, took up the argument. The favorite topic at the post office in McCracken's Store was the future of Texas—as one state or two.

On the afternoon of the debate, the schoolhouse was crowded. Carl raised the partition between the two rooms—an operation not unlike raising a window, except that the wooden dividing wall was so heavy, several of his husky students had to assist the teacher. Three parents acted as judges, and after arguments and rebuttals were concluded, they huddled for several minutes. Their decision: Texas should be divided into two states. Carl remembered that those debaters on the affirmative side "knew their stuff." He later described what he saw as valuable about the debates, which he often sponsored wherever he taught:

> The constituents of most rural schools loved the debates. They were often heard, after a debate, discussing the pros and cons of the affirmative or negative side of the issue at the general store or in the post office. As teachers, we felt there was great profit in the students' participation in debates. For one thing, it was a great panacea for stage fright. It also broadened their insights into the research needed to present intelligently their side of the question.

As Mr. Carl's debate idea proved, providing resources for learning in rural schools between the two World Wars required ingenuity, know-how, and considerable knowledge of the art of make-do but most importantly, teachers with a passion for knowledge. My parents' stories, while not explicitly folklore in the narrow sense of that term, reflect what the respected folklorist Mody Boatright perceived as "customs of a group with a common body of tradition." In an introduction to *Mody Boatright, Folklorist* (1973), Ernest B. Speck calls Boatright "a historian of the folk" and adds that he saw folklore as "a basic expression of human belief, feeling, and practice." The folk history unique to rural school teaching no longer exists, except in the memoirs and oral history of storytellers who knew at the end of their careers that a unique era had closed in Texas history. Both on tape and in writing, my parents left a worthy heritage—a record of a now-lost culture.

Growing up in a tough West Texas railroad town, my father, Carl Halsell, learned early how to make sure his resources for

Carl Halsell, the author's father.

acquiring knowledge were assured. Once he had learned to decipher what at first looked like "chicken tracks across a freshly scrubbed porch," he read every book his hands fell upon. When his family arrived in Hawley, a raw West Texas frontier town in 1907, Carl and his sisters attended school crowded into the Methodist Church sanctuary. Soon, however, citizens, who exhibited considerable foresight, built a four-teacher school in the second year of their town's history. The new superintendent had a college degree, a rarity in those days of teacher certification by testing. Sharing his love of good literature with his rough-edged pupils, he insisted that a separate room in the new building be designated the library. With the help of study clubs in nearby Abilene and generous trustees, he provided one of the best libraries my father would ever enjoy, even later as a teacher in Texas' rural schools.

My father read and reread the works of favorite American poets, particularly Holmes, Longfellow, Whittier, Whitman, and Bryant. His imagination fueled by Edgar Allan Poe's poems and short stories, he decided as a creative adolescent that the tall blond man who came in from the country every week to mail a thick brown envelope at the local post office must be a writer. He never learned if his surmise was true, but years later, he remembered every detail of this mystery man's weekly appearances in town. Carl's curiosity teamed with vivid imagination fueled his desire to know more. When Carl reached high school, he began to sample

Lamb and Carlyle, and decided that Kipling was his favorite English author.

Gaining access to the books as he needed them—and finding time to read—required scheming. My father had several older sisters who considered him the chief errand runner in the family. Small for his age, young Carl discovered that he could squeeze behind the upright piano sitting "catty-cornered" in the living room near a window. He read there undisturbed long afternoons in the summer, ignoring his sisters' demands. When he reached high school, he took the job as school janitor, a duty requiring daily monotonous sweeping of the entire school house. It was worth it. The bonus kept my father on the job. He could take a book out of the library overnight, read it, and have it back on the shelf before a teacher missed it the next morning. Other students could check out books only over the weekend. His book source for the summer was guaranteed because Carl had the foresight to leave a library window unlocked. In summer dusk, he would stealthily crawl in and make his next selection.

My mother Mabel's love for reading found an early outlet in the serial stories that ran in the *Semi-Weekly Farm News* that arrived regularly in her home. The Art Literature Series, reading textbooks in which literary selections were illustrated with reproductions of famous paintings, fueled her budding appreciation of both art and good writing. In high school, her love for math and literature blossomed under enthusiastic teachers including Lexie Dean Robertson, the English teacher who would later become poet laureate of Texas.

Mabel Halsell, the author's mother.

The two young teachers, 23-year-old Carl and 18-year-old Mabel met in 1922, when they arrived at Romney in Eastland County to take positions in a two-teacher school. Right away, both Mr. Carl and Miss Mabel decided that the more involved the pupils and their parents were with the school, the more likely learning might take place in classrooms with no library except Carl's *World Book* reference works and the knowledge they had acquired along the way to earning teaching certificates. In 1923, they

A couple of young, dedicated—and innovative—teachers.

merged their lives as well as their enthusiasm as teachers when they married on December 1. For the remainder of their long careers, they demonstrated (as they had with their organization of a Literary Society where students could debate, recite poetry, sing, and participate in community plays) that if any learning took place, it would depend on the teachers to provide the resources for learning in those barren rural classrooms.

By 1936, the year Texas celebrated its Centennial, my father was teaching for a second time near the Brazos River in Palo Pinto County at a school called Lucille, a place where he said, "There was one road in and no roads out." When the two teachers told their charges that this year they would be celebrating the hundredth birthday of the "greatest state in the union," their students in the two-room school enthusiastically began planning how they could observe the occasion. My father asked the students to appoint a committee to work with the teachers. Two boys and two girls elected by their classes sat down with their instructors and worked out their plans.

The boys decided they wanted to make replicas of a Conestoga wagon, the Alamo, and a pioneer log cabin. My father knew a thing or two about the famed covered wagon that had brought pioneers to the area. His own family had traveled east out of drought-stricken West Texas in 1917 in a covered wagon, seeking a place to graze their cows and find shelter in Callahan County. He asked the would-be model makers, "Do you know what a doojin pin, rocking bolster, stay chain, neck yoke, tailgate, chuck box, coupling pole, ox bows, doubletree, and wagon sheet are?" Few had more than a hazy idea of how the wagon should look. Then, one boy volunteered that he knew of an old Conestoga wagon that had been abandoned on a nearby ranch. The teacher organized a field trip.

The would-be model makers soon learned that the doojin pin (probably properly spelled dudgeon pin) served two purposes: to attach the doubletree to the wagon and to function as a wrench when the wheels needed greasing. The wagon miniature would need a rocking bolster, or wheel-like mechanism, to turn the front wheels without torquing the wagon bed. The coupling pole held the wheel frame together and furnished the mechanism on which to attach the brakes. From the practical information the students gained on their field trip and under the tutelage of their knowledge-able teacher, they were able to build the wagon model authentically. Even the wheels were individually assembled from hub to outer rim, as the early blacksmith had fashioned wagon wheels originally.

The Alamo model was built to replicate pictures in their Texas history books. Most of the boys roamed around crumbling log cab-ins, many with dogtrot porches, still located on surrounding ranches and farms. Within a few weeks all three models were complete. Lucille school was almost ready to sponsor a community celebration.

Working from textbooks, the reference books my father fur-nished, and the well-known Pennybacker *History of Texas* from their teacher's personal library, each student wrote an essay about his favorite Texas hero. David Crockett, Stephen F. Austin, and Jim

Bowie proved popular subjects. The teachers chose the best of the essays. Each winning author memorized his essay to be presented as part of the program the school patrons had been invited to attend. On March 2, Texas Independence Day, maps, pictures, and the models were ready to exhibit. In addition to the essay readings, the program that evening included the pupils' performances of Texas songs, early Texas poetry, excerpts from speeches of early-day leaders, and several one-act plays depicting events in Texas history. My father summarized the celebration this way: "When all of this was finished, the students of the two-teacher school out on the owlhoot were not only proud of their accomplishments, but they were proud that they were citizens of the Lone Star State."

If rural teachers loved books as my parents did, they could usually persuade trustees to turn loose of enough money to buy a few storybooks and reference works. But my parents remember very few schools with more than a two-foot shelf of books. My mother's resourcefulness was tested to its limit when she became teacher at Cedar Bluff, often referred to as Last Chance, a one- room school in Callahan County. She taught there four years at the ragged end of the Great Depression, which tailed out into World War II before she finished her tenure there. With an average of eighteen students ranging in age from six to seventeen in grades one through seven, my mother conducted at least thirty classes a day. Although newly painted, the schoolroom offered few learning resources except a tin-lined sandbox on legs, then called a sand table, where pupils could lay out miniature gardens during free time. Alphabet charts and illustrations of the Palmer method of handwriting decorated the top of the blackboard across the side and back of the room. An old tin cookie display case on which an occasional book had rested completed existing resources. No books of any kind were shelved there, however, when my mother arrived.

Moving her piano into the schoolhouse came first. Then, my mother ordered a hectograph, a flat rectangular pan just larger than a sheet of legal-size paper, filled with gelatin. Drawings and class materials could be superimposed from a master prepared with a special pencil. Thirty or forty copies could be made before the ink disappeared into the gelatin. Sponging the surface repeatedly with cold water prepared the copier for the next job.

Willing students painted the make-do cookie display case a bright blue, converting its slanted shelves into a bookcase, which became the school library after my mother made a trip to Baird, the count seat, where the county superintendent kept a special collection of books for use in the county's rural schools. There in a dusty closet, she could choose about twenty books, mostly novels and biographies, to keep for a month. Students read them during free time or checked the books out overnight. Parents also occasionally took advantage of the check-out service.

Often on Fridays, near holidays, my mother planned a picnic as part of the celebration. Her pupils, who brought their lunch to school anyway, usually added a treat or two to share with friends. Before noon, all of the students set out with their teacher across the ranch bordering the school grounds to picnic in Devil's Hollow, a cool natural bowl formed in a nearby creek by years of erosion. After eating, many added their initials to those carved over the years on the sandstone walls. On their return to school, my mother slowed her rambunctious students in a holiday mood down to a walk by pointing out the fact that they could make their trip back a nature hike. She encouraged them to collect interesting rocks and plants along the way. Once back in the classroom, her students arranged their finds into a garden in the sand table.

No project those four years, however, generated more enthusiasm for learning than the exchange program with other schools across the nation. My mother initiated this program with a letter to the *Instructor Magazine*. She had always subscribed to this publication, even during the tight money days of the Great Depression. Lesson plans, seasonal patterns and pictures, and articles on teaching methods augmented the teacher's creative energies. Together, her pupils composed a letter requesting samples of products, information about local life and letters from students in other rural schools across the country. Their letter appeared in the

School Exchange column, a regular feature of the magazine, after a month or two of eager waiting. Within two weeks, the mailbox at the end of the lane began to furnish exciting surprises each day.

Samples of wheat arrived from rural schools in Kansas and Nebraska. Children in Minnesota and Wisconsin sent cheese samples. Booklets the children prepared to inform their correspondents included maps, product samples, state flowers, trees, birds, songs, and mottos. Soon several pupils were exchanging letters with pen pals across the nation. For many years, one of my mother's students, who became a school teacher herself, reported regularly on the activities of her New York pen pal.

For their contribution to the project, Cedar Bluff students, with encouragement from their teacher, made booklets in the shape of Texas. Explanation of state symbols accompanied their drawings of the pecan tree, the bluebonnet, and the mockingbird. Illustrated maps described the terrain and located regional products of Texas. For seventeen boys and girls growing up in an isolated community where newspapers were nonexistent, this exchange brought knowledge, new ideas, and the excitement children feel from anticipating daily the arrival of another package of surprises.

These experiences exemplify the ingenuity that my parents, as well as all Texas country teachers, needed to furnish even minimum resources for learning to their rural charges. In those years between World Wars, rural school teachers fought to give their students opportunities for learning and to encourage unity of community spirit. By 1950, most Texas rural schools would be consolidated into nearby small-town schools. Schoolhouses would become community centers exclusively. My parents' former students, now gray-haired retirees, often express their regard for the positive influence the rural school and their teaching had on their lives. Many completed college educations. If they learned little else under Mr. Carl's and Miss Mabel's guidance, they learned how to find out about the world for themselves.

[Portions of this essay appeared in an article first published in the *Texas Library Journal*, Spring 1986.]

7

Folklore in Schools:

Connections Between
Folklore and Education

Barbara Morgan-Fleming

Introduction

The relationship that I see between folklore and schooling has a great deal to do with my personal experience. I came to teaching by a rather circuitous route, beginning with the study of classical Chinese at universities in Taiwan and Kansas, through graduate study at the Folklore Institute at Indiana University, and after work in adult education and as a bilingual case worker for Indo-Chinese refugees. When I went back for elementary certification, I intended to teach for one or two years and then go into curriculum development. Two surprises stand out as I remember my first year of teaching: first, the class of fifth graders with whom I was to spend the year, was as complex and unique a culture as any I had ever experienced, and second, teaching was more intellectually taxing and fulfilling than any job I had ever had.

As I tried to make sense of my new environment, I drew upon my experience and knowledge base. I saw that I was having difficulty getting access to the floor and that I was struggling with other speakers for control of conversational topics. I began to notice myself using certain formulaic phrases ("We're reading") that I had not known that I knew. These phrases occasionally had magical properties, so I continued to use them though they often sounded strange even to my own ear. I noticed that there were day-to-day rituals, that some students seemed to step in and out of roles during the school day, and that I seemed to adopt roles in response, again almost unconsciously. I was caught occasionally between my past as a folklorist and my present as a teacher, as I admired the beautiful speech strategies students sometimes used to completely destroy my well-planned lessons.

I was struck by the methods other teachers used to help me learn how to teach. Individuals would show up in my room after school and tell me stories about their first year of teaching or about students they had had trouble with in the past. Sometimes a fellow teacher would come to my room with a piece of curriculum that I might want to use, and as we looked at the material, that teacher would tell me how she had used it and drop an advice phrase— "You've got to keep them interested" or "You've got to let them know they can't get away with anything"—that I would try to internalize and use to reflect upon my new practice. The advice was always oral, oblique, and placed in a social context. It reminded me of the women in my mother's diner advising a new mother or the women I grew up with teaching one another about the products described by Yocum:

> Most of the products of these (women's) labors are ephemeral. Paradoxically, they last for a brief period of time, but they are constantly re-created: dinner table decorations of multicolored flowers, dishes of roast beef garnished with onions and carrots. Yet these items as well as those that last longer live on in the women's storytelling sphere as women comment on their displays of table and food, of sewing and ceramics.[1]

I grew to realize that the type of knowledge and the ways in which that knowledge was taught were similar to those found in traditional crafts that I had investigated as a graduate student in folklore. Story and experience seemed much more informative than discrete recommendations couched in general theory and statistics.

I began to see teaching as a traditional oral genre performed primarily in contexts of women and children and was often reminded of Bauman's description of the oral composition of epics:

> The essential element of the occasion of singing that influences the form of the poetry is the variability and instability of the

audience. The instability of the audience requires a marked degree of concentration on the part of the singer in order that he may sing at all; it also tests to the utmost his dramatic ability and his narrative skill in keeping the audience as attentive as possible. . . . If he misjudges, he may simply never finish his song.[2]

Theoretical Underpinnings: The Enacted Curriculum

In researching teaching, I have found classrooms to be complex, oral environments in which the teacher must combine knowledge of curriculum, instruction, and management structures. The teacher must then orally improvise a means to meet the complementary and conflicting goals he or she may have, while other individuals in the classroom simultaneously attempt to meet goals that may be at odds with the goals of the teacher. Such a conception of classroom teaching has implications for the study of teachers' knowledge. Past conceptions of teachers' knowledge focused either upon discrete behaviors or upon, in Kathy Carter's words, "operations inside the teacher's mind."[3] Oral skills have not been highlighted; instead such knowledge has been embedded in categories such as instruction[4] and pedagogical content knowledge.[5]

Although, in the past, pedagogy, curriculum, and classroom management were considered separate fields within educational research, recent scholars such as Walter Doyle,[6] Catherine Cornbleth[7] and R. Weade[8] have pointed to the interdependence of these three aspects of classrooms and have called for attention to the curriculum that is enacted in classrooms. At the same time, other scholars including Frederick Erickson,[9] Courtney Cazden,[10] L. C. Wilkinson[11] and J. L. Green[12] have called attention to the social and oral nature of the enacted curriculum.

Scholars studying the enacted curriculum have much in common with folklore scholars, for both are attempting to capture oral performances of text. Although these performances show striking consistency across time and across performers, no two performances are exactly alike. Dell Hymes writes that "folklore is a special case of the ethnography-of-speaking approach" and makes an important contribution, "because it can direct attention to essential features of language that are now neglected or misconceived in linguistic theory."[13] These essential features include, "the social properties of syntax, semantics, and phonology as used in situation."[14] Because folklore is concerned with linguistic forms larger than the sentence, it can potentially explain not only grammatical norms but the underlying social rules that influence the choice of utterances available to particular members of a linguistic community. Hymes summarizes the potential contribution of folklore as a discipline in the following way:

> [In mainstream linguistics] there is no adequate conception of language as having organization beyond the sentence—and even the text—in terms of speech acts and speech events. . . . Folklore par excellence, understands the normal use of language as drawing on kinds of knowledge and organization that are parts of "competence" beyond the purely grammatical.[15]

Although I found occasional references to the oral improvisational nature of teaching in Erickson, Cazden, Wilkinson, Green, Robert J. Yinger,[16] and Doyle, most educational research I read ignored what I considered to be central aspects of teaching. In this paper, I use concepts drawn from performance-centered folklore to frame a discussion of those aspects.

An Example

I take Joseph Schwab's warning concerning the "vice of abstraction"[17] seriously, and so I return to my experience teaching fourth and fifth grade to explain the connections I see between folklore and teaching. I am thinking particularly about the last elementary class I taught. In that class, I kept the same students during their fourth and fifth grade years. I have described this experience at length elsewhere[18] and will give only a general overview here.

I had been on leave taking doctoral courses for a year when I decided to return to the classroom. Once I had made this decision, my way of looking at the world changed. I began hoarding supplies, looking for new ideas, activities, and contacts. I thought I would plan for months before I began teaching, avoiding what always seemed like a last minute rush to get ready for the new school year, but I found such planning impossible to complete in the abstract. During this period, my journal was full of goals and struggles and curriculum chunks but very little writing about how these chunks would be enacted. This was quite frustrating to me. In the end, the majority of my planning took place the week before school started when I was in my classroom and the other teachers were in theirs. At this point, the school seemed to come alive, and the coming year became palpable and real. Only then could I begin walking around in it, imagining what I would say and what the children would say, blocking out physical areas where certain pieces of curriculum might be enacted, creating a sense of where I wanted to go, and developing a set of initial events out of which I knew (or hoped) the year would emerge.

I knew that I was again a rookie because I was hoarse at the end of the first day and had almost lost my voice at the end of my first week. This brought home to me again the oral nature of teaching. While thinking and writing are certainly part of teaching, I realized anew that teachers live or die by the mouth. Even if one's teaching repertoire includes relatively little of what my colleagues and I sometimes called "full-frontal teaching," there is still a need for considerable conversational patter. Managing a classroom, asking and answering questions, telephoning parents, talking to other teachers in the lunch room, yelling to get a student's attention on the playground, all require the use of the oral channel. In studying my own practice, I found considerable moment-to-moment variation in what Hymes terms variety and register.

Although I knew I would be speaking much of the day, it was impossible to predict what I would need to say. As a first year teacher, I planned elaborately, but as my experience grew, I realized that the "script" was not mine to write—it would be constructed orally with my students as it was performed. I learned to jot down an outline, write down some concepts I considered major, and block out potential questions and activities, all the while understanding that plans, while important, never taught anything. A lesson was not a written text but an oral, improvisational performance.

I experienced anew the bonding moment when a class becomes a community. I was never able to predict when this bonding moment would occur or, in fact, see it when it happened. It was something I only recognized after the fact as I noticed myself give a relaxed internal sigh, knowing that these were now my children and I was their teacher. While conflicts and problems still occurred, they felt different to me—they were now family issues rather than conflicts with that strange child down the block. I explained this bonding experience as well as I could to a teacher whom I mentored. I told him that one couldn't predict when this event would take place but that I generally found that it arrived shortly after I had definite thoughts about leaving the field forever. The formation of community was fundamental to my ability to teach. It caused me to reject efforts to departmentalize and was responsible for my remaining in elementary school even though I liked working with middle school-aged children. I loved the self-contained classroom where I could enact the entire curriculum in one community. This strong feeling of community also caused me to move with these children to the fifth grade and was perhaps a reason why all the children chose to remain with me during that next year.

When I began to teach, I was conscious of being part of a tradition. I shared an occupation with Socrates, Mr. Chipps, and the teachers who had always made me sit in the halls or discuss underachievement with the guidance councilor. When I started reading educational research, it seemed to me that in teaching, if a practice had not changed for hundreds of years, it was considered negative; while in folklore that same statement would lead to an automatic, "it's precious and must be preserved!" I began to wonder what was a constructive relationship between tradition and innovation.

Dailies

The event "dailies" took place every day and were a major part of the morning structure of the classroom. The children would come into the room and begin work (individually and in small groups) on two sentences with grammatical errors and four non-trivial math problems I had written on the board. Later, papers were exchanged and graded.

Within this rather mundane event, there was embedded a strand of playful events termed "magic"—magic paper, magic chalk, and magic fingers. The "magic" element arose spontaneously as I interacted with the children. While I sometimes grew tired of these props, I came to realize how much the children enjoyed them. When talking to other students about how weird their teacher was (and I think they meant this as a compliment), they would tell them stories about what I did with my magic paper, chalk, and fingers. When I moved with the students to fifth grade, I did not intend to revive the magic traditions after summer break, but the students remembered and let me know that this was a part of our classroom's culture that they valued.

"Magic fingers" arose near the beginning of the year as I was trying to get the children to think first about what math problems with a complex appearance were asking. I also wanted the children to realize that "baby" strategies like counting on fingers could actually be quite powerful if applied in the right situation. I can't remember the problems we worked with, and I was not recording during the time this routine began, but I remember counting down from 1,000,000 while singing music which frequently accompanied sleight of hand tricks, showing the students there was nothing up my sleeve, etc. The students laughed and paid attention to what I was saying, two powerful rewards for a teacher.

"Magic paper" often involved the same music, as I showed the students how I could turn halves into fourths, eighths, and sixteenths. It was made possible by a serendipitous surplus of supplies. When I decided to return to the classroom, I began scrounging for materials. I happened to pass by as a secretary in the College of Education who was cleaning out a closet. Inside was a large amount of yellow mimeograph paper that the College no longer needed. The secretary said I was welcome to it.

This paper was available to the students in unlimited supply. It was used for scratch paper, for folding and coloring fractions, for clustering, drawing, and, at times, for paper airplanes. In a classroom where materials were in short supply, magic paper provided a feeling of sufficiency, almost affluence. It was not rationed, students did not need a good reason to use it, and if ten pages were needed to do four problems in daily oral math, no negotiation was necessary. This was also not "work paper." Assignments were usually written on lined or unlined white paper. Magic paper was for rough drafts, problem solving, private thoughts, and communications.

I wish I could claim credit for knowing how important an unrestricted supply of paper was going to be, but "magic paper" as a classroom artifact evolved through time and personal interactions in the classroom. I realized how important it had become when the students asked to have the name tags they would be wearing to the school's track meet made from magic paper. I don't think they believed that the paper would make them run any faster; instead, the paper had become a symbol of our class if for no other reason than it was unique to our classroom.

Magic chalk also began inadvertently. A student had done a division problem that I was about to check with multiplication. Knowing that the student's answer was correct, I began teasing that it wasn't correct until the teacher had checked it with her magic chalk. I began writing the multiplication problem with an especially shoddy piece of colored chalk that broke as I was doing the problem. The children laughed, and one said that the chalk had broken because it knew that I was wrong and they were right.

Magic chalk grew in importance as the children found that during this period they could break the discourse rules, which at other times were rigorously enforced, and shout at me statements such as "You're wrong!" and "Sit down!" At times the entire classroom would chant "Break, break, break, break" until the chalk would magically break. For Christmas, a student named Frank gave me a jar with my name in needlepoint on the lid that contained a selection of colored chalk. I later had to secretly replace the chalk he had given me with school chalk because the chalk he had given me was too difficult to break.

Ms. Morgan's Magic Chalk.

Applications of Folklore Concepts to Teaching

In this section, three concepts of folklore are illustrated with examples situated in the classroom context discussed above. For the purpose of this paper, I have restricted my discussion of teaching to teacher-directed lessons, although I believe this kind of analysis could provide insight into other types of classroom speech events, as well. The concepts to be discussed again are:

- The redefinition of linguistic competence and linguistic community.
- The view of text as emergent from the social structure in which it is told.
- The emphasis on locally determined norms and rules for linguistic conduct.

Redefinition of Competence and Community

If, as John J. Gumperz argues, linguistic communities are brought into existence by the speech events that they share,[19] can the classroom described above be considered a linguistic community, and, if it can, what speech events are shared? In order to answer this question, it would be useful first to define the term "speech event."

Hymes distinguishes three levels of speech: *speech situations*, which include non-verbal as well as verbal events, *speech events*, which are "restricted to activities, or aspects of activities, that are directly governed by rules or norms for the use of speech," and *speech acts*, which represent "a level distinct from the sentence, and not identifiable with any single portion of other levels of grammar."[20] For clarification, Hymes offers the example of a party (speech situation) in which, during the course of a conversation, (speech event) someone tells a joke (speech act). In the example presented above, the school day can be seen as the speech situation, dailies as speech events, and the various "magical" components can be seen as embedded sub-events because they occur only during dailies but involve different rules and norms. Various verbal components such as raising a hand and answering questions or taunting the teacher during magic chalk are speech acts.

The magic portions of dailies can be seen as context-specific rituals that served to define and delineate the classroom community. The students' request to use magic paper for their name tags, Frank's gift of a special holder for the magic chalk, and the students' references to my magic fingers and chalk when introducing me to classroom newcomers or when describing their class,[21] are evidence that these portions of dailies were instrumental in forging and maintaining the classroom's community and identity.

My individual classroom community did not exist in isolation. Instead, it was embedded in two other communities: the school and the neighborhood. A brief look at speech events that define each of these communities is presented below. This school had a close-knit community. An important component of this community was the sharing of oral and written stories in formal and informal settings. These stories were often similar to the kernel stories described by Jordan & Kalcik:

Most often a kernel story is a brief reference to the subject, the central action, or an important piece of dialogue from a longer story. In this form, one might say it is a kind of potential story, especially if the details are not known to the audience. . . . Kernel stories lack a specific length, structure, climax, or point, although a woman familiar with the genre or subject may predict fairly accurately where a particular story will go. The story developed from the kernel can take on a different size and shape depending on the context in which it is told.[22]

Many teachers' stories fit well into the kernel structure. When talking about difficult children or classroom violence, I might say, "Like Janet's kid with the scissors or the time Alice's kid threw the desk." Told to other teachers at my school, this kernel would be sufficient because it involved shared knowledge and narrative. In fact, shared knowledge of the situations underlying these stories played a major role in defining this community. On the other hand, in an audience made up of people who do not know Janet, Alice, or their classrooms, my telling of these stories can become quite elaborate. I told Janet's story to my preservice class, ending with the formulaic "someone would yell 'Scissors' and everyone would take cover." A student with a military background replied, "Like in the military we yell 'incoming!'"

Researchers interested in teachers' stories must be aware of these "kernels" and ask the questions needed to bring the story into full form. Kernel stories may also be a window into the common understandings and beliefs of a group of teachers in that they show what experiences are shared in story and what experiences are not.

My school and classroom were also settled within a neighborhood. The children's conversations and stories generally had more to do with home and neighborhood than with school. They told stories about jumping off the roof (into a mud puddle, onto parked cars), dogs that had died, puppies that had been born, and about various things they had eaten because someone told them it tasted just like chicken. I shared similar stories about my child-hood—about how my sister told me that I really could fly if I just took a running start off the roof, about my dog Toto who was in absolute control of my household, and about eating beef heart which, in the first place sounded like something it wasn't and in the second place definitely did not taste like chicken. Such stories helped us find common ground and share the laughter that is part of being human. Parents often mentioned that their child had re-told a story from the class, often responding with a similar story of their own.

While such sharing of stories and participation in shared speech events may appear more "noise" than "data," I would point to the foundational importance of creating and maintaining connections within and between these three communities. It was much easier to discuss a problem that a student was having when all those connected with the problem—the student, her/his family, school personnel—viewed one another as full-bodied individuals rather than as paper opponents, existing only in the problem situation. The creation of a community of learners is a real goal, and the oral means used to create and maintain that community are wor-thy of study.

Linguistic Competence

If teaching is viewed as oral improvisation upon curricular themes, and if the oral channel is of primary importance in the maintenance of community, what linguistic competence is necessary to teach successfully?

As discussed above, teaching is largely an oral activity. In one event studied by this author, ten written sentences and twenty written math problems involved over one thousand six hundred lines of transcribed speech.[23] While other forms of text such as print, film, and music are involved in teaching, it is the oral text that explicates, introduces, and connects new text to old. It is only the oral channel that requires the immediate proximity of teacher and student, and only oral texts that can be modified during composition to meet the needs of individuals or adapt to context-specific situations.

The ability of oral text to adapt quickly to context also points to one way in which curriculum writers and curriculum performers differ. Curriculum writers have a high degree of control over text. They can decide what topics to present and how to sequence those topics. The curriculum performer has some control of topic selection, but the maintenance of topic in face-to-face communication is more problematic. The curriculum performer, like the performer of epics, must improvise upon known text as he or she reacts to the varying attention and interest of his or her immediate audience.

Crafting curriculum performances requires specialized communicative competence on the part of the teacher. As will be discussed in more detail below, the teacher must key different frames within teaching, signaling students that it is time for recitation, or indicating that it is time for play. She must orchestrate the talk within a lesson to maintain students' attention and make the material that is central to her performance memorable to her audience. She must be able to follow a student's lead, asking questions that make the student's point clear, helping the student share his or her knowledge with other classmates. A teacher must decide how to use the public and private spheres of the classroom, deciding, for example, when a child's "off-topic" question should be fully answered during recitation and when such a question should be discussed with the student after the lesson.

Successful participation in dailies required specialized communicative competence on the part of students as well as teacher. In the event dailies, students had to understand subtle verbal and non-verbal cues that signaled changes in norms of interaction and interpretation. They had to know when it was acceptable to move around the room speaking to classmates and when they must remain seated, speaking one at a time after raising their hands. Upon hearing their name called by the teacher, students had to know whether this word signaled a request that they answer a question or whether the same word was being used as a desist, in which case, the correct response was silence. They had to know when magic chalk began and when it ended, obeying the very different rules that applied in and out of that playful frame. These complex rules were nowhere written and were rarely discussed overtly, yet research showed a strong degree of shared knowledge among the students about the signals used in this classroom.[24]

Emergent Text

Bauman describes emergent texts as middle ground between memorized scripts and completely novel forms.[25] Performances of emergent text, while recognizable across time and space, are strongly affected by local factors such as audience and setting. The teaching recitation fits this categorization well.

An important component of these curricular performances is the keying of what Gregory Bateson and others have termed "frames."[26] As previously described, frames are metacommunicative devices that carry information regarding how messages within that frame are to be interpreted. Signaling of key may be verbal or non-verbal and the signaling within a speech community may be extremely subtle and commonplace. In Hymes' words:

> The significance of key is underlined by the fact that, when it is in conflict with the overt content of an act, it often overrides the latter (as in sarcasm). The signaling of key may be nonverbal, as with a wink . . . but it also commonly involves conventional units of speech too often disregarded in ordinary linguistic analysis, such as English aspiration and vowel length to signal emphasis.[27]

Three levels of frames operate in the example being discussed. First, teaching itself can be seen as a frame. The physical boundaries of the classroom, as well as the strong cultural definitions of the participants' roles, operate as strong keys, and participants interpret messages within the frame differently than identical messages spoken outside of the frame. For example, another fifth grade teacher and I laughed over the implicit commands we found in our teacher speech. I asked her if she ever used statements such as "We're reading" as a reminder to students who were doing anything but reading. When she admitted using this kind of statement I asked her what her reaction would be if her students responded, "Actually, we're not reading. We're throwing spit wads and hitting one another." We both laughed (often a sign that the edge of a frame is being used for play: see Fry[28] and Babcock[29]) as we realized that such a linguistically true statement would be considered entirely inappropriate in the social context of the classroom. Within the frame of teaching, statements such as "We're reading" or "We're silent now" are to be interpreted as commands: "read," "be silent."

Within the frame of teaching, the performance frame is sometimes keyed. An example of this frame can be found in the recitation portion of "dailies." This event began when I walked to the front of the room and uttered the formulaic "Exchange your dailies. Who can do number one?" It ended with the students passing their papers to the recorders in their group. In open-ended descriptive writing, the students also used these cues in referring to the event "dailies."[30]

Within the event dailies, a playful sub-event called "magic chalk" took place. This embedded frame was keyed by my picking up a particular kind of chalk and saying in a loud and prolonged tone, "Oh yeah?!" (This is an example of what Bateson calls a "this is play" sign,[31] and can be found in several of the students' descriptions of the event). In this part of dailies, relationships were inverted. I was at the mercy of the students who shouted at me to "Sit down!"—breaking the hand-raising rule, which was at other times rather strictly enforced. The students taunted me with songs and chants, while I pretended to be oblivious to the taunts, returning to the original frame with the key, "Who can do number ___?" This is also mentioned in the students' writing as the conclusion of magic chalk.[32]

The inversion of roles in this event is similar to that described by Brian Sutton-Smith, who argues that play and other forms of inversion make existing social relationships tolerable and increase flexibility.[33] I have a powerful personality, and in my teaching I always had to worry more about over-control than under-control. Playful events in my classroom were therefore important because they allowed the children and me to relate to one another in a different manner.

Barbara Kirshenblatt-Gimblett and Joel Sherzer, drawing from Roger Callois,[34] list six characteristics of play. According to these authors, plays is free, separate, uncertain, unproductive, governed by rules, and involves make-believe.[35] "Magic chalk" fits this notion of a playful event. While participation in the individual work and recitation portions of dailies was required, students had some choice over whether or not to participate in magic chalk. The students were still required to be in the room during the time in which magic chalk took place, but they did not have to participate orally, and there was no requirement to "pay attention." Magic chalk was "bounded in time and space" and could therefore be considered separate. The well-recognized keys described above served to set this event off from other classroom events. In addition, magic chalk only occurred during dailies and was thus restricted to a regular time slot in the school day.

The third component, "uncertain," is less descriptive of magic chalk than the former two components, for all participants knew that the event would end with my breaking the chalk. This may have been a function of teacher control. While I was content to allow a certain amount of verbal play, I did feel a need to "keep a handle" on dailies. In this sense, dailies must be seen as constrained play. Left to their own devices, the children probably would have allowed dailies to develop in a variety of ways. My original purpose for magic chalk was to illustrate the way in which multiplication was related to division. I would have abandoned magic chalk when I felt it no longer served its purpose, but the children urged me to continue it long after this purpose was served. This event then became unproductive, the fourth component of play described above.

In describing the characteristic on play, "governed by rules," Kirshenblatt-Gimblett and Sherzer state, "ordinary laws are suspended and new ones established which are the only ones which hold for the time plays is in operation."[36] As stated previously, normal rules of classroom interaction dealing with things such as hand raising, turn taking, and acceptable volume of voice were suspended during magic chalk. Different rules prevailed during magic chalk, many having to do with the temporary restriction of teacher power. For example, a student yelling at me to "Sit down!" during any other event would have been reprimanded. If such behavior continued or spread, negative consequences would have increased. It would have been inappropriate for me to have responded in this manner to similar behavior during magic chalk.

The sixth characteristic of play is "make-believe," described as "a special awareness of a second reality or a free unreality."[37] I don't believe this characteristic describes magic chalk. The students were well aware that I broke the chalk, and the first reality of the classroom was never really challenged. Magic chalk could be described as constrained play, less uncertain and less situated in make believe.

The methodological problems of scholars wishing to study classroom curriculum events parallel those encountered by modern folklorists who became dissatisfied with studying decontextualized written texts of myths, legends, and other forms of verbal art. Many argued that classification and study of text were impossible without a strong understanding of the community in which the text was told, that the telling was as important as the tale. The unit of analysis became the performance of text, and interpretation of that performance was based on an understanding of the linguistic community in which the performance took place. In Hymes' words:

The essential element common to all these approaches is the movement from a focus on the text to a focus on the communicative event. The term "context" takes on a new meaning or new force in this regard. To place a text, an item of folklore, in its context is not only to correlate it with one or more aspects of the community from which it came. . . . It is not content to take folkloristic results on the one hand and results of other studies on the other, each independently arrived at and then try to relate the two after the fact. It wishes to study the relation between folkloristic materials and other aspects of social life *in situ* as it were, where that relation actually obtains, the communicative events in which folklore is used.[38]

Events within a community often have a symbolic meaning[39] that may be misunderstood by those outside that community. The seating arrangement in my room was one example. I liked to place the desks in groups of about four—we called these groups "pods." This arrangement made it easy to do group work, and was the easiest way to get thirty-two desks and four tables for centers to fit in the room. When two of my students were having trouble concentrating I asked them if they'd like to sit by themselves in an "office." I told them it was their choice, but they might find it easier to work. To my surprise, not only did these two students decide that they wanted an office, most of the rest of the class members decided that they wanted an office, too. We had a class discussion about how to arrange the room, and the children voted for eight rotating offices (the highest number of isolated places I could find in the room), with the rest of the students seated in straight rows with space between each desk. The decision having been decided by democratic methods, we arranged the room in the manner the students wanted, even though this arrangement was not particularly to my liking. Imagine my surprise when I heard that pre-service teachers called me "old school" and "authoritarian" because of the physical setting of my room.

The importance of understanding the symbolic meaning of classroom events was brought home to me even more clearly in connection with having students in the room with me at lunch time. One reason that students might be in the room with me at this time was that they were being punished. On the other hand, one of the most sought-after rewards in this class was having lunch with me in the room. Both occasions involved the same time and space. Both meant that the student could not play with peers during this time. Yet one was the most avoided event and the other the most sought after. The symbolic declaration of one as punishment and one as reward affected the meaning of this event.

Political Issues of Voice and Ownership of Story

One potential danger of the current interest in story is the creation of a caricature of teacher as "noble savage" or perhaps, "noble earth mother." This endangers not only research but teachers, as well. We do not need to substitute one stereotype for another. My purpose in bringing forward folklorists' work on story is to add a tool and a perspective for viewing teaching, not to make teachers sacred "folk."

Romanticism not only can blind the researcher, it can steal the individuality and humanity from teachers. When hearing a story we must always remember that there is a teller, an agent who has a purpose in telling the story. The purpose may be to share knowledge that she believes to be true, but the purpose may instead be to seek the opinion of the audience, to entertain, or to let off steam. Kathy Carter points out that teachers' stories are not video tapes, that stories are frames and interpretations of situations.[40] This is an important point.

One genre especially comes to mind when thinking about accuracy of stories. That genre is modern urban legends. These stories are told as true, although there is disagreement[41] in the literature about whether or not informants believe them. Delmont reports some of these legends she found in schools,[42] and I can remember one (part of a "crazy principal" cycle, I'm sure) that was told to me in my first year of teaching. I'll retell it here, but you must imagine yourself in a classroom as a senior teacher tells it with full voices and gestures referring by name and school to the particular principal he was describing. It was told in first person, so I will write it in the same way:

> I was in the principal's office after school and he was talking to me, just as regular as you please, about what we were going to do about this project. As he was talking he picked up an imaginary bottle of fish food (full gestures here, walking around the room), walked over next to the wall and starts feeding these imaginary fish—there's not even a tank there and he's goin' on about how "aren't these lovely fish swimmin' around" and I'm sayin' "yeah, very nice" backin' toward the door, tryin' to get out of there! He retired not long after that.

I don't know why this story was told to me, although I could make some guesses having to do with initiation of gullible young people into an occupation. The important point is that it can't be taken as automatically true.

Fieldworkers must avoid simple analysis. They must know who is telling a story and why. They must have a sophisticated awareness of the variety of purposes and functions served by story. Some possible functions of stories I would look for are first, for providing advice in an indirect manner. Norms of privacy and autonomy often preclude direct opinions and open exchange of information. Thus, advice might be embedded in the less-threatening story context. "You know I had a student like that and it wasn't until . . ." "My first year of teaching was terrible. I thought I had to grade everything and I ended up . . ." Second, for relieving stress or "letting off steam." These stories often contain a great deal of black humor. Taken out of context, they could give an inaccurate picture of teachers' regard for students. And last, for entertaining.

Teachers are not only teachers but are human beings as well. They may tell jokes, legends, or stories just for the pleasure of story-telling itself.

In closing, I would like to offer a final caution about folklore as a field of research. We must not assume that because we are moving into new forms of research that the history and power relations of teachers and researchers have substantially changed. Individual researchers are genuinely interested in what teachers think and the stories teachers tell, but research as an institution still has multiple agendas. If researchers enter the teachers' private sphere, take part in storytelling and then use the stories to prove teachers' moral and intellectual deficiencies, great harm could be done. Research in the past was often harmless because the worlds of teacher and researcher were remote from one another. Folklore research has the potential to bring those worlds into collision and must be done carefully and ethically, precisely because it is such a powerful lens.

ENDNOTES

1. Yocum, M. "Woman to Woman: Fieldwork in the Private Sphere." *Women's Folklore, Women's Culture.* Rosan Jordan and Susan Kalcik, eds. Philadelphia: University of Pennsylvania Press, 1985. 49.
2. Bauman, Richard. "Verbal Art as Performance." *American Anthropologist* 77 (1975): 302.
3. Carter. Kathy. "Teachers' Knowledge and Learning to Teach." *Handbook of Research on Teacher Education.* Ed. Houston, W. New York: Macmillan, 1990. 297.
4. Elbaz, Freena. "Teachers' Knowledge of Teaching: Strategies for Reflection." *Educating Teachers: Changing the Nature of Pedagogical Knowledge.* Ed. J. Smyth. London: Falmer, 1987. 45–53.
5. Shulman, Lee S. and Gary Sykes. *A National Board for Teaching? In Search of a Bold Standard: A Report for the Task Force on Teaching as a Profession.* New York: Carnegie Corporation, 1986.
6. Doyle, Walter. "Curriculum and Pedagogy." *Handbook of Research on Curriculum.* Ed. P. W. Jackson. New York: Macmillan, 1992. 486–516.
7. Cornbleth, Catherine. "Curriculum In and Out of Context." *Journal of Curriculum and Supervision* 3 (1988): 85–96.

8. Weade, R. "Curriculum 'n' Instruction: The Construction of Meaning." *Theory into Practice* 26 (1987): 15–25.
9. Erickson, Frederick. "Classroom Discourse as Improvisation: Relationships Between Academic Task Structure and Social Participation Structure in Lessons." *Communicating in Classrooms.* Ed. L. C. Wilkinson. New York: Academic Press, 1982. 153–181.
10. Cazden, Courtney. "Classroom Discourse." *Handbook of Research on Teaching* 3rd ed. Ed. M. C. Wittrock. New York: Macmillan, 1986. 432–436.
11. Wilkinson, L. C. "Introduction: A Sociolinguistic Approach to Communicating in the Classroom." *Communicating in the Classroom.* Ed. L. C. Wilkinson. New York: Academic Press, 1982. 3–10.
12. Green, J. L. "Research on Teaching as a Linguistic Process: A State of the Art." E. Gordon (Ed.), *Review or Research in Education* 10 (1983): 151–252. Washington, DC: American Educational Research Association.
13. Hymes, Dell. "The Contribution of Folklore to Sociolinguistic Research." *Toward New Perspectives in Folklore.* Richard Bauman and Américo Paredes, Eds. Austin: The University of Texas Press, 1972. 48.
14. Ibid.
15. Ibid.
16. Yinger, Robert J. "Research on Teaching: *Policy Implications for Teacher Education.*" Policy Making in Education. A. Lieberman and M. McLaughlin, Eds. Eighty-first Yearbook of the National Society for the Study of Education, Part I. Chicago: University of Chicago Press, 1982. 215–248.
17. Schwab, Joseph. "The Practical." *School Review* (November 1969). 310.
18. Morgan-Fleming, Barbara. "Dailies: An Enactment of a Curriculum Event." Diss. University of Arizona, 1994.
19. Gumperz, John J. "Sociocultural Knowledge in Conversational Inference." *Linguistics and Anthropology.* Ed. M. Saville-Troike. Washington, D. C.: Georgetown University Press, 1977.
20. Hymes. "The Contribution of Folklore to Sociolinguistic Research." 56.
21. See Morgan-Fleming.
22. Jordan, Rosan. & Susan Kalcik, eds. *Women's Folklore Women's Culture.* Philadelphia: University of Pennsylvania Press, 1985. 7.
23. See Morgan-Fleming.
24. Ibid.
25. Bauman. "Verbal Art as Performance."
26. Bateson, Gregory. *Steps to an Ecology of Mind.* New York: Ballantine, 1972.

27. Hymes, Dell. *Foundations in Sociolinguistics: An Ethnographic Approach*. Philadelphia: University of Pennsylvania Press, 1974. 62.
28. Fry, William. Sweet Madness: *A Study of Humor*. Palo Alto: Pacific Books, 1963.
29. Babcock, Barbara A., ed. *The Reversible World*. Ithaca: Cornell University Press, 1978.
30. See Morgan-Fleming.
31. Bateson.
32. See Morgan-Fleming.
33. Sutton-Smith, Brian. "A Developmental Structural Account of Riddles." *Speech Play*. B. Kirshenblatt-Gimblett and Joel Sherzer, Eds. Philadelphia: University of Pennsylvania Press, 1976. 111–119.
34. Caillois, Roger. *Man, Play, and Game* (M. Barash, Trans.). New York: Free Press, 1961.
35. Kirshenblatt-Gimblett, Barbara and Joel Sherzer. *Speech Play*. Philadelphia: The University of Pennsylvania Press, 1976.
36. Ibid.
37. Ibid. 4.
38. Hymes. "The Contribution of Folklore to Sociolinguistic Research." 46.
39. Turner, Victor. *The Anthropology of Performance*. New York: PAJ Publications, 1986.
40. Carter, Kathy. "Preservice Teachers' Well-Remembered Events and the Acquisition of Event-Structured Knowledge. *Journal of Curriculum Studies* 26 (1992): 235–252.
41. Brundvand, J. H. *The Vanishing Hitchhiker*. London: Picador, 1983.
42. Delmont, S. "The Nun in the Toilet: Urban Legends and Educational Research." *Qualitative Studies in Education* 2 (1989): 191–202.

BIBLIOGRAPHY

Babcock, Barbara A., ed. *The Reversible World*. Ithaca: Cornell University Press, 1978.

Bateson, Gregory. *Steps to an Ecology of Mind*. New York: Ballantine, 1972.

Bauman, Richard. "Verbal Art as Performance." *American Anthropologist* 77 (1975): 290–311.

Bauman, Richard and Américo Paredes, eds. *Toward New Perspectives in Folklore*. Austin: The University of Texas Press, 1972.

Bauman, Richard and Joel Sherzer, eds, *Explorations in the Ethnography of Speaking*. London: Cambridge University Press, 1974.

Brundvand, J. H. *The Vanishing Hitchhiker.* London: Picador, 1983.

Burke, Kenneth. *A Rhetoric of Motives.* New York: George Braziller, 1955.

Carter, Kathy. "Teachers' Knowledge and Learning to Teach." *Handbook of Research on Teacher Education.* Ed. Houston, W. New York: Macmillan, 1990. 291–310.

————. "Preservice Teachers' Well-Remembered Events and the Acquisition of Event-Structured Knowledge. *Journal of Curriculum Studies* 26 (1992): 235–252.

Caillois, Roger. *Man, Play, and Game* (M. Barash, Trans.). New York: Free Press, 1961.

Cazden, Courtney. "Classroom Discourse." *Handbook of Research on Teaching* 3rd ed. Ed. M. C. Wittrock. New York: Macmillan, 1986. 432–436.

Cornbleth, Catherine. "Curriculum In and Out of Context." *Journal of Curriculum and Supervision* 3 (1988): 85–96.

Delmont, S. "The Nun in the Toilet: Urban Legends and Educational Research." *Qualitative Studies in Education* 2 (1989): 191–202.

Doyle, Walter. "Curriculum and Pedagogy." *Handbook of Research on Curriculum.* Ed. P. W. Jackson. New York: Macmillan, 1992. 486–516.

Eisner, Eliot. *The Educational Imagination.* New York: Macmillan, 1979.

Elbaz, Freena. "Teachers' Knowledge of Teaching: Strategies for Reflection." *Educating Teachers: Changing the Nature of Pedagogical Knowledge.* Ed. J. Smyth. London: Falmer, 1987. 45–53.

Erickson, Frederick. "Classroom Discourse as Improvisation: Relationships Between Academic Task Structure and Social Participation Structure in Lessons." *Communicating in Classrooms.* Ed. L. C. Wilkinson. New York: Academic Press, 1982. 153–181.

Fry, William. *Sweet Madness: A Study of Humor.* Palo Alto: Pacific Books, 1963.

Green, J. L. "Research on Teaching as a Linguistic Process: A State of the Art." E. Gordon (Ed.), *Review or Research in Education* 10 (1983): 151–252. Washington, DC: American Educational Research Association.

Goffman, Erving. *Frame Analysis: An Essay on the Organization of Experience.* New York: Harper Colophon, 1974.

Gumperz, John J. "Sociocultural Knowledge in Conversational Inference." *Linguistics and Anthropology.* Ed. M. Saville-Troike. Washington, D. C.: Georgetown University Press, 1977.

Hymes, Dell. "The Contribution of Folklore to Sociolinguistic Research." *Toward New Perspectives in Folklore.* Richard Bauman and

Américo Paredes, eds. Austin: The University of Texas Press, 1972. 42–50.

———. *Foundations in Sociolinguistics: An Ethnographic Approach.* Philadelphia: University of Pennsylvania Press, 1974.

Jordan, Rosan. & Susan Kalcik, Eds. *Women's Folklore Women's Culture.* Philadelphia: University of Pennsylvania Press, 1985.

Kirshenblatt-Gimblett, Barbara and Joel Sherzer. *Speech Play.* Philadelphia: The University of Pennsylvania Press, 1976.

Lord, Albert B. *The Singer of Tales.* Cambridge, Mass.: Harvard University Press, 1971.

Morgan-Fleming, Barbara. "Dailies: An Enactment of a Curriculum Event." Diss. University of Arizona, 1994.

Schwab, Joseph. "The Practical." *School Review* (November 1969): 1–20.

Shulman, Lee S. and Gary Sykes. *A National Board for Teaching? In Search of a Bold Standard: A Report for the Task Force on Teaching as a Profession.* New York: Carnegie Corporation, 1986.

Stoeltje, B. "Feminist Revisions in Folklore Studies." *Special issue of the Journal of Folklore Research* 25 (1989): 3.

Sutton-Smith, Brian. "A Developmental Structural Account of Riddles." *Speech Play.* B. Kirshenblatt-Gimblett and Joel Sherzer, eds. Philadelphia: University of Pennsylvania Press, 1976. 111–119.

Turner, Victor. *The Anthropology of Performance.* New York: PAJ Publications, 1986.

Weade, R. "Curriculum 'n' Instruction: The Construction of Meaning." *Theory into Practice* 26 (1987): 15–25.

Wilkinson, L. C. "Introduction: A Sociolinguistic Approach to Communicating in the Classroom." *Communicating in the Classroom.* Ed. L. C. Wilkinson. New York: Academic Press, 1982. 3–10.

Yinger, Robert J. "Research on Teaching: *Policy Implications for Teacher Education.*" Policy Making in Education. A. Lieberman and M. McLaughlin, eds. Eighty-first Yearbook of the National Society for the Study of Education, Part I. Chicago: University of Chicago Press, 1982. 215–248.

Yocum, M. "Woman to Woman: Fieldwork in the Private Sphere." *Women's Folklore, Women's Culture.* Rosan Jordan and Susan Kalcik, eds. Philadelphia: University of Pennsylvania Press, 1985. 45–53.

High School
Years

Knowledge About Folk Medicine Among Students in Alice High School

by Elizabeth Galindo

[I found this article by searching our database for articles related to education; the words "High School" in the title jumped out. I read the paper and liked it, so we decided to include it. However, we could not locate the author, Elizabeth Galindo, and no one could remember how she came to present the paper at the 1989 meeting in Uvalde. Through diligent detective work, Heather and I tracked her down. Unfortunately, Ms. Galindo (1930–2001) is now deceased, but her daughter, who is also named Elizabeth, told me of her mother's interest in folk medicine and her involvement with the school system in Alice. We are thankful for her research, although not all of it could be located so as to be included with this piece. Perhaps, this will serve as an inspiration for someone to pick up where she left off, as was her wish.—*Untiedt*]

As part of a broad study of folk medicine and its use among all age groups in South Texas, during the fall of 1988, I conducted a survey of high school students in Alice, Texas. The purpose of the survey was to discover how many of the students were familiar with the different aspects of Mexican-American folk medicine, including *curanderismo* and the well-known illnesses among them, which are usually dealt with by family members or someone in the neighborhood and are not found among other ethnic groups. I wanted to know if the students knew any curanderos and if they had consulted them.

It is important to know the extent to which folk medical practices exist in South Texas because, as Moore and others have argued: First, "the incorporation of diverse cultural concepts and community factors is a means of achieving . . ."[1] good health care. Second, "The cultural belief system exerts considerable influence on the means and efficacy of the curative strategies available."[2] And third, "Culture—in the form of belief systems and their related

The 1948 graduating class of Eagle Pass High School. Elizabeth H. Galindo is in the second row on the far right. Her future husband, Carlos, is in the same row, fourth from the left.

systems of curing disease—has a significant impact not only on how disease is acquired but also on how it is treated."[3]

The question we are attempting to answer is this: "Is *curanderismo* still an important force in the lives of Mexican-Americans?"

Folklorists recognize three levels of culture. The *elite* level is the official culture and is obtained through the formal institutions of society. Medical doctors are, therefore, part of this level, along with institutionalized medicine and formal prescriptions. The second level, the *popular* level, is the mass culture expounded and transmitted by the mass media, including television, magazines, and newspapers. Advertising in these media promotes the use of over-the-counter medicines. The *folk* level of culture is that passed on informally from person to person and generation to generation within a closed group. The *elite* level of culture is passed on through academic training, the *popular* through media, and the *folk* level though personal contact.

Folk medicine is not a random collection of beliefs and practices. It constitutes a fairly well-organized and fairly consistent theory of medicine. As Lyle Saunders noted, "The body of 'knowledge' on which it is based often includes ideas about the nature of man and his relationships with the natural, supernatural, and human environments."[4] In the Mexican-American folk culture, folk medicine and religion are totally intertwined. Saints are invoked or used as co-supplicants or intercessors to God for everything in their lives. God and Satan are in constant combat for their souls.

The belief system in Mexican-American folk medicine is that certain people receive "*el don*," the gift from God to heal the sick, often through magical-religious activities, using objects and rituals, including prayers, in their manipulation of forces. The anthropologist Moore claims, "Magical world views regarding disease causation relate to beliefs that these result from human manipulation of the forces in the universe, such as through sorcery or witchcraft. . . . The religious views suggest that the events of life, including disease, are controlled by supernatural powers"[5] and can be influenced by supplication. The practitioner in this culture thus combines the belief in the human manipulation of forces with objects and rituals and the belief in the supplication to a supernatural deity. The *curandero* believes that he has received the gift of healing from God and uses many religious articles in his rituals. He relies on the faith of his patients to accomplish the healings.

As Graham and others have shown, the Mexican-American folk medical system consists of a hierarchy of healers, seen as a triangle.[6] At the base of the triangle are the housewives or grandmothers who dispense "*remedies caseros*" or home remedies. These remedies are designed to treat the more common ailments such as headaches, nosebleeds, cuts and scrapes, diarrhea, and so forth. Herbal remedies are the most common type of treatment used by this group. If an ailment is serious, the next step is to go to someone more experienced—a neighborhood healer. She may also be a partera or sobadora, and she is consulted for the well-known folk illnesses such as *mal ojo, susto, empacho*, and *bilis*.

Perhaps I should briefly define some of the terms which are common in Mexican-American folk medicine. A "*partera*" is a woman who aides in the delivery of babies. A "*sobador*" or "*sobadora*" is a person who heals sprains, strains, and sometimes broken bones. "*Mal ojo*" is harm caused by excessive admiration by someone with a strong gaze. "*Susto*" is caused by a very frightening experience. "*Empacho*" is caused by a ball of food lodged in the digestive tract, causing a blockage. "*Bilis*" is caused by excessive anger.

When ailments do not respond to either of these two levels of healers, those in the highest level of the hierarchy are consulted. These are the "*curanderos*" or "*curanderas*," the ultimate source of medical knowledge in the culture, who have received the gift of healing from God. They treat the most serious illnesses and are the only source of help against "*brujeria*," witchcraft.

My purpose in this survey was to determine the extent of the knowledge of the Mexican-American folk medical system among high school students in my hometown. The survey conducted at Alice High School consisted of a personal profile of each student, including age, religion, predominant language spoken at home, etc. There were:

- Forty-five questions to be answered Yes or No;
- Fifteen questions to be answered by degree: (Strongly Disagree, Disagree, Indifferent, Agree, Strongly Agree); and,
- Twelve questions to fill in the blanks.

These seventy-two questions were confined to illnesses in the Mexican and Mexican-American culture, including *mal ojo, empacho, susto,* and *bilis.* Other questions related to *curanderos, parteras,* and *sobadores.*

Thirty-eight students responded to the survey. Of these, seventy-nine percent were Mexican-American and twenty-one percent were Anglo. The majority of Mexican Americans, sixty-three percent, spoke mostly English at home (Appendix B).[7] The folk illness most familiar to these students was *mal ojo*; eighty-seven percent were familiar with it. Fifty-five percent had suffered *mal ojo* and had been treated for it (Figure 1). Familiarity with the other folk illnesses was as follows, in descending order:

sixty-eight percent had heard of *susto*, forty-nine percent had heard of *empacho*, and eight percent had heard of *bilis* (Figure 2).

Over half of the respondents, fifty-seven percent, knew of someone who could cure some of the folk illnesses; a third acknowledged that someone in their own families could treat these illnesses (Appendix B). Eighty-six percent of the Mexican-American students believed that a *curandero* could cure some illnesses, and fifty-two percent believed that a *curandero* could cure any illness (Appendix B). Sixty-eight percent of the total respondents, Mexican-American and Anglo, used household remedies, while forty-seven percent used herbal teas (Appendix B). Although thirty-five percent believed magic spells work, only nineteen percent knew someone who could perform them (Appendix B). In contrast, there were seventy-four percent who had seen a medical doctor in the last year, and eighty-four percent believed that a medical doctor could cure most illnesses (Appendix B).

Dr. Joe Graham states in an article published in *Western Folklore* that folk culture in general, and belief in *curanderismo* in particular, decline as Mexican Americans become better educated and better off economically.[8] Formal education challenges traditional wisdom. As Mexican Americans become more educated, there is a tendency on their part to reject folk medicine, particularly the belief in *brujeria*, or witchcraft, because it is more closely associated with superstition in the majority culture and is at greatest variance with medical science and what is taught in the schools.

With increased education they reject other aspects of folk medicine: the power of the *curandero* to cure all illnesses and even the ability of the neighborhood healer to cure the better-known folk illnesses, which they now also reject. The remaining level of Mexican-American folk medicine is the *remedios caseros*, or home remedies, usually herbal teas or poultices. These are the most likely to retain acceptance even among the most educated since the general culture, the popular culture, accepts them as efficacious. Although the survey indicates that *curanderismo* still exists, with eighty-seven percent having heard of *mal ojo*, the majority of this group seemed to rely on institutional medicine. Of those surveyed, twenty-nine percent had seen a *curandero*, while seventy-four percent had seen a medical doctor. This shows a strong acceptance of institutionalized medicine from the *elite* level of culture.

It is important to expand these surveys to include more respondents so that we can increase our knowledge about the use of folk medicine among the Mexican Americans, because as Moore has argued, "Future health care policies must take into account influences on health that stem from all levels of environmental influences as well as from the individual's adaptive capacity and means for coping and repair."[9]

ENDNOTES

1. Moore, Lorena G., Peter W. Van Arsdale, JoAnn E. Glittenberg, Robert A. Aldrich. *The Biocultural Basis of Health.* Prospect Heights, IL: Waveland Press, 1980. 261.
2. Ibid. 251.
3. Ibid. 19.
4. Saunders, Lyle. *Cultural Differences and Medical Care.* New York: Russel Sage Foundation, nd. 146.
5. Moore, et al. 184.
6. Graham, Joe S. "Folk Medicine and Intracultural Diversity." *Western Folklore* Volume XLV, Number 3, July 1985.
7. No Appendix or Figures can be located to accompany Ms. Galindo's research.
8. Graham.
9. Moore, et al. 258.

BIBLIOGRAPHY

Graham, Joe S., "Folk Medicine and Intracultural Diversity." *Western Folklore* Volume XLV, Number 3, July 1985.

Moore, Lorena G., Peter W. Van Arsdale, Jo Ann E. Glittenberg, Robert A. Aldrich. *The Biocultural Basis of Health.* Prospect Heights, IL: Waveland Press, 1980.

Saunders, Lyle. *Cultural Differences and Medical Care* New York: Russel Sage Foundation, nd.

Trotter, Robert T., and Juan Antonio Chavira. *Curanderismo.* Athens, GA: University of Georgia Press, 1981.

THE FABLE OF THE OLD POODLE
& THE YOUNG LEOPARD

A wealthy old lady decides to go on a photo safari in Africa, taking her faithful aged poodle, Cuddles, along for the company. One day the old poodle starts chasing butterflies and before long, Cuddles discovers that she's lost. Wandering about, she notices a young leopard heading rapidly in her direction with the intention of having lunch. The old poodle thinks, "Uh-oh! This could be my demise!" Noticing some bones on the ground close by, she immediately settles down to chew on the bones with her back to the approaching cat. Just as the leopard is about to leap, the old poodle exclaims loudly, "Boy, that was one delicious leopard! I wonder if there are any more around here?" Hearing this, the young leopard halts his attack in mid-strike, a look of terror comes over him and he slinks away into the trees. "Whew!" says the leopard, "That was close! That old poodle nearly had me!" Meanwhile, a monkey who had been watching the whole scene from a nearby tree, figures he can put this knowledge to good use and trade it for protection from the leopard. So off he goes, but the old poodle sees him heading after the leopard with great speed, and figures that something must be up. The monkey soon catches up with the leopard, spills the beans and strikes a deal for himself with the leopard. The young leopard is furious at being made a fool of and says, "Here, monkey, hop on my back and see what's going to happen to that conniving canine!" Now, the old poodle sees the leopard coming with the monkey on his back and thinks, "What am I going to do now?" but instead of running, the dog sits down with her back to her attackers, pretending she hasn't seen them yet, and just when they get close enough to hear, the old poodle says: "Where's that dang monkey? I sent him off an hour ago to bring me another leopard."

Moral of this story:

Beware of messing with old poodles or old people . . .
age and treachery can always overcome youth and skill!

Brilliant BS only comes with age and experience!

9

School Yearbooks:
Time Capsules
of Texas Folklore

by Jean Granberry Schnitz

No one is surprised that yearbooks reflect history, but some people wonder how yearbooks reflect folklore. For many years, definitions of folklore strictly adhered to the idea that folklore included such things as the traditional beliefs, legends, customs, songs, and stories of a people and specified that folklore must be passed on orally from one generation to the next. More modern definitions, however, give broader meaning, emphasizing the importance of the written record and even stating that "the scope of folklore is as broad as the folklorist has the imagination and intellect to make it."[1] That is my license.

During the past year, I have studied hundreds of school yearbooks from every corner of Texas. I have found that yearbooks contain much more than mere memories. When viewed as mirrors of history and of prevailing traditions, attitudes, and behavior patterns, they become time capsules of Texas folklore. By the early 1900s, many Texas schools produced annual yearbooks, the earliest of which used words and drawings but few, if any, photographs.

As technology developed, annuals included individual pictures of students and faculty, photographs of school buildings and facilities, classes and class officers, scholastic and artistic organizations and groups, social activities, sports events, teams, traditions, and favorites. Today, school annuals still include these basic requirements—with variations as numerous as Texas schools.

The 1916–1917 *The Plain View* of Plainview High School introduced its volume like this:

> . . . Do not in these pages expect to find a Plain View of the school year, for, like the mirage of our Plains, it reflects only the hours of sunshine—the shadows we have left behind. When the eyes are growing dim and the temples are crowned with locks of

gray, we trust this volume may bring back memories of friends long forgotten and days of youth and glee. We shall feel then that our task has been accomplished.

The 1978 *Chancellor* of Winston Churchill High School in San Antonio described the task this way:

Each year when the school year begins, the *Chancellor* yearbook staff sits looking at 312 blank pages—frighteningly blank, white pages. How does the staff fill those pages? Since this book should be a history of the year, the staff must wait for you, the students, to make that history. When you have begun to create the events that comprise a year, the staff members can work.

A rare color page from the 1917 Plainview annual.

Current Events

Each yearbook staff is expected to create a book that follows tradition and includes the required ingredients. Some deliberately include sections and/or language describing current events, but others almost inadvertently provide records of changing attitudes, hair and dress styles, customs, priorities, and behavior. For example, the 1977 *Monticello* of Jefferson High School, San Antonio, included several pages of current events. *Roots* by Alex Haley was big news that year. Life at school and current fashions were shown with stories pointing out what was the rage in 1977.

Yearbooks clearly reflect traditions developed by each school. Such traditions include school mascots, rivalries, celebrations, sports teams, presentations of school favorites, drill teams, band and choir activities, with endless variations. Some traditions—such as having an annual Sadie Hawkins Day based on Al Capp's comic strip *L'il Abner*—lasted only a few years during the late 1940s and early 1950s and reflected a portending change in social relationships. As traditions begin, they also end. The 1975 *El Rancho* of Texas A&I University in Kingsville presented its last Lantana Queen and Court, ending a fifty-year tradition.

Traditions change. For instance, in many schools, homecoming queens were displaced by homecoming kings during the 1980s. In the 1990s, many schools feature homecoming queens *and* homecoming kings. Proms have become major productions, requiring students to wear tuxedos and evening dresses, and travel in limousines to dance to the music of expensive orchestras—a far cry from the home grown decorations and record players of long ago.

Attitudes and behavior patterns have changed throughout the years. These changes are reflected in yearbooks. For example, the rebellious attitudes of the 1970s are reflected in the 1974 *Matador* from Seguin High School, which included a statement that this was the time for "Revolution and Reformation," equating events of the 1970s with the American Revolution—illustrated by the famous painting of George Washington when he crossed the Delaware.

History is reflected by school yearbooks—sometimes by omission. Many schools did not print yearbooks during the years of World War I and World War II and/or during the Great Depression. Yearbooks printed during the World Wars usually reflected patriotic themes and/or tributes to students and faculty serving in the armed forces. Little was said about the Great Depression, with the exception of an article in the 1934 *Longhorn* of Texas A&M College, as follows:

> I feel that The Student Body would like to have some appreciation shown to those men that have made it possible for a goodly number of the young men that are now attending the College to do so. . . . There are several hundred men that are now working and going to school that would not have even had a job much less be able to attend school if it were not for the fact that they have been given jobs as student janitors and other odd jobs around the campus . . . . These things have meant more to these men than mere words can express, but each and every one of them is thankful from the bottom of his heart for the chance that has been given him that he would not have otherwise had. . . . The people that are responsible for this are farsighted men who can see into the future and realize what will happen to this Country and to Civilization as a whole if the men that are to take their places in a few years have not had that education and social contact so necessary to the successful business man and political leader. . . .

Descriptive Verses

Almost all of the annuals I reviewed from 1918 to the 1930s included descriptive verses beside the picture of (usually) seniors. Some were flattering, but some were questionable or outright "catty." Many are quotations, though rarely (if ever) are citations given. Many were no doubt composed by the annual staff, which had the power to embarrass or embellish. This example in the

1912 *The Mountaineer* from Llano High School could be used to describe my grandson: "For even though vanquished, he would argue still." From the 1914 *The Mountaineer*, Llano High School: "When he begins to talk, everyone crosses their fingers;" and, "I am not the first that love has led astray."

Examples of such verses from the 1918 *The Westerner* from Lubbock High School were these: "He trudged along, unknowing what he sought, / And whistled as he went for want of thought;" and, "She's just as good as she is fair, / With light blue eyes and flaxen hair." The 1916-1917 *The Plain View* from Plainview High School uses short paragraphs such as these: "Thelma is the spirit of the Senior Class. She is lively, but not a very studious lass; / But when she studies she studies with delight, and in her Latin she is very, very bright;" "Elmer is not supposed to be a lady's man, and we think that he lives up to his reputation. . . ." and, "Beulah Lee . . is like the Irishman's goat: 'The more we see of her the better we like her.'"

The *Crest* of 1922 from San Marcos Academy (a high school) included the following verses under the names of senior students: "He is young and may reform;" "He has a tongue that all but sees;" "Dignity! May it never forsake her;" "She is given to appearing at breakfast after a hurried toilette effected between 6:59 and 7:00;" "Roll on, thou long and twisted tongue of woman, roll! / Ten thousand men stop up their ears in vain;" "Juel knows the use of a powder puff much better than she does her history;" "Some call her beautiful, some call her attractive, some call her sweet; / in reality, she may be called all of these; / and yet, when she sees this, she'll vow it's sarcasm;" and, "The boys have an excellent nickname for him, but the Crest is subject to censorship."

Consider these verses from the 1923 *Crest* of San Marcos Academy: "So tall and handsome that cupid has never yet reached his heart;" "An advocate of woman's rights, a suffragette and man hater;" "If a guy is pretty good with a pigskin, someone will see that he gets a sheepskin;" "A faint heart never won a fair lady nor filled a spade flush;" and, "It's not his fault he wasn't named Valentino." From the 1924 *Crest*: "Music is the medicine of a breaking heart;" and, "I fain would climb but fear I would fall."

Just when I thought that the use of verses ended in the 1930s or before, I found these from the 1994 *Jacketland* from Llano High School, Llano, Texas: "It is better to light a single candle than to curse the darkness;" "If it weren't for the rocks in the bed, the stream would have no song;" "If you're too busy to laugh, you're too busy, period;" "Face the facts; sometimes you're the windshield, and sometimes you're the bug;" and, "A boy is the only known substance from which a man can be made."

In the 1932 *Monticello* of Jefferson High School in San Antonio, pictures of seniors were accompanied by their names and a one-line saying or statement. These captions seem to reflect what students in 1932 might say:

> I'll swear!
> Now wouldn't that freeze you?
> Oh, yeah?
> That's keen!
> Great Caesar's Ghost!
> Aw Rats.
> Ain't that the snitz! [Now, that one got me!]
> Such is life!

The same formula was followed in the 1933 *Monticello*:

> Ye cats and little gold-fish!
> Jump in the lake.
> It's a great life if you don't weaken.
> The best defense is an offense.
> Oh, go sit on a cactus!

In the 1956 *Jackrabbit*, Graford High School, seniors had accomplishments listed by their pictures, but juniors had these sayings:

Real gone.
Go, man, go—
Absolutely zorch!
I'm hep.
Dig that.
Don't flip.

Jokes and Attempts at Humor

Early annuals usually contained several pages devoted to jokes and humor. The 1912 *The Mountaineer*, Llano High School, included an "Essay on Man":

Man is a queer animal. He has eyes, ears, mouth and nose. His eyes is to git dust in, his ears is to git the earache in, his mouth is to hatch teeth in and his nose is to get the sniffles in. A man's body is split half way up and he walks on the split end. The female man is called woman.

In the 1918 *The Westerner* there were several pages of what might have been new jokes at that time: "If no grass is grown in the frozen north, what then does the Eski-mo?" and, "Turn failure into victory. / Don't let your courage fade; / And if you get a lemon; / Just make some lemon-aid." From the 1917 *The Plain View*: "Mary Lee, a new comer to the Plains, rushed excitedly into the room one morning exclaiming: 'Girls, I just know there is going to be a norther. There is the awfullest cloud in the southwest!'"

The 1922 *Crest* of San Marcos Academy contains five pages of jokes. An example: "Mr. Smith (in history): 'In which of his battles was Gustavus Adolphus killed?' Elizabeth W.: 'I think it was his last one.'" From the 1929 *Crest*: "Student: 'Can a person be punished for something he hasn't done?' Teacher: 'Of course not.' Student: 'Well, I haven't done my algebra.'"

From the 1930–1931 Boerne High School yearbook, called *Junior Jargon*, predecessor of the *Greyhound*: "Did the play have a happy ending? Yes, everybody was happy when it was over;" "Q: How are you getting along since you went to the doctor? A: Terrible. He told me to drink warm water an hour before each meal, but after I drink water 35 minutes, I am so swelled up I nearly burst;" and, "If Indians didn't laugh, why did Minnie ha ha?" From the 1937 *Alcalde*, Sam Houston State Teacher's College, Huntsville, Texas: "A young man walked up to a young lady, saying, 'You look like Helen Black.' 'I know,' she replies, 'but you should see me in blue.'"

I found few, if any, written jokes printed in annuals from the 1950s to the 1990s, though sometimes sections of pictures meant to be funny are included.

School and Class Mottos

For many years, annuals included school or class mottos. Since the 1970s, however, mottos rarely appear in school yearbooks. In many cases, the mottos may have been "lifted" from another publication or from someone else's words. Sources are rarely cited. The Senior Class of 1917, Plainview High School: "Not Sunset, but Dawn." The 1918 Senior Class of Lubbock High School: "The elevator to Success is not running. Take the stairs." The Junior Class that same year was apparently less lofty in its ideals. Their class motto was: "We'll stick you if we can."

The 1922 *Crest* of San Marcos Baptist Academy indicated that the Junior Class Motto was:

> Let us, then, be up and doing,
> With a heart for any fate;
> Still achieving, still pursuing,
> Learn to labor and to wait.

From the 1932 *Monticello* of Jefferson High School, San Antonio, the Senior Class motto: "They can conquer who believe they can." The 1933 Senior motto was: "Look up! and not down, Out! and not in; Forward! and not backward."

Mottos from *La Yucca* of Comfort High School, one of the few schools to continue to include a motto for each Senior Class: "Out of the harbor into the deep" (1939). "The world steps aside to let any man pass if he knows where he is going" (1968). "Face the sun and your shadow will fall behind" (1970). And from 1974:

> I do my thing and you do your thing
> I am not in this world to live up to your expectations
> And you are not in this world to live up to mine
> You are you and I am I
> If by chance we find each other, it's beautiful.
>
> *Fritz Perls*

[This was one of the few mottos attributed to someone.]

For 1980:

> Do not follow where the path leads.
> Rather,
> Go where
> there is no path,
> and
> leave one.

In the caption for the picture of the 1987 Senior Class, all wearing sun glasses: "My future is so bright, I gotta wear shades!" The motto of Boerne High School appears in its yearbooks: "Everybody is somebody at Boerne High School."

Advertising

Most yearbooks have been financed in part by the sale of advertising space. The 1916-1917 *The Plain View* made an appeal to its readers to patronize its supporters:

Please bear in mind the fact that this annual would have been a mere pamphlet without the revenue derived from the space sold to our local business men for advertisements. Help us show our appreciation to them by giving them your trade. When you start to send an order to Monkey Ward or Shears and Sawbuck, please meditate if you will that these gentlemen never contributed one cent to our annual; they never payed [sic] for a drop of water to sprinkle our streets, and far be it for them to ever do anything of the kind.

Reading the advertising in older annuals reveals other changes in Texas culture. Gone now are many of the old general mercantile stores, the "undertakers," the tailors and dressmakers, meat markets, and others.

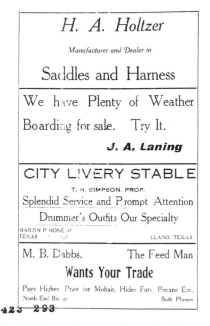
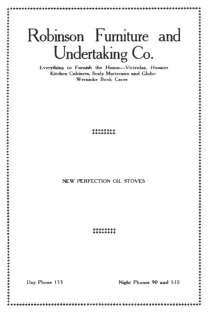

(Left) Advertisement from the December, 1910 *The Mountaineer*, Llano High School, Llano, Texas. **(Right)** Advertisement from the 1918 *The Westerner*, Lubbock High School, Lubbock, Texas.

Cartoons and Art Work

Sometimes interesting illustrations, cartoons, and other art work enliven yearbooks and portray contemporary attitudes and behavior, as well as exhibit students' skills. In the 1917 *The Plain View* of Plainview High School, one of the artists was Mabel Bohner. Here is an example of Mabel's work.

Mabel Bohner's take on faculty. *The Plainview* **1917 Vol. III. Plainview High School, Plainview, Texas.**

The 1926 *The Mountaineer*, Llano High School, used some interesting, timely art work from an unnamed artist.

Another depiction of students' perception of faculty by an unnamed artist.
The Mountaineer, 1926, Llano High School, Llano, Texas.

An unknown artist's rendering of the "popular crowd."
The Mountaineer, 1926, Llano High School, Llano, Texas.

Rachael Florez's illustrations. *La Cebolla*, **1950, Raymondville High School, Raymondville, Texas.**

The *La Cebolla* of Raymondville High School in 1950 used the cartoons of Rachel Florez as cover pages for the various sections of the yearbook. "*La Cebolla*" is Spanish for "onion." Raymondville is a center for growing and shipping of onions in the Rio Grande Valley of Texas.

"Venus and Apollo" by
Nancy Sue Everett.

Everett's use of Homer's
Sirens as ad material.

In the Beeville High School *Trojan* for 1953, Nancy Sue Everett drew very appropriate sketches for the yearbook sections.

The 1957 *Bobcat Chant* for Refugio High School displayed an interesting combination of art and photography.

"Cutting edge" technology for 1957.

Sketches by Howard Guthrie, Lee Duggan and Latimer Murfee highlight *The Westerner*, Lubbock High School, 1917–1918.

Howard Guthrie's conclusion to the 1918 *The Westerner*, Lubbock High School, Lubbock, Texas.

Lee Duggan's drawing for the section entitled Seniors. *The Westerner*, Lubbock High School, Lubbock, Texas.

Latimer Murfee's bucking bronc. *The Westerner*, Lubbock High School, Lubbock, Texas.

These illustrations by an unspecified artist come from the 1950 *The Flowsheet*, Texas Western College, El Paso.

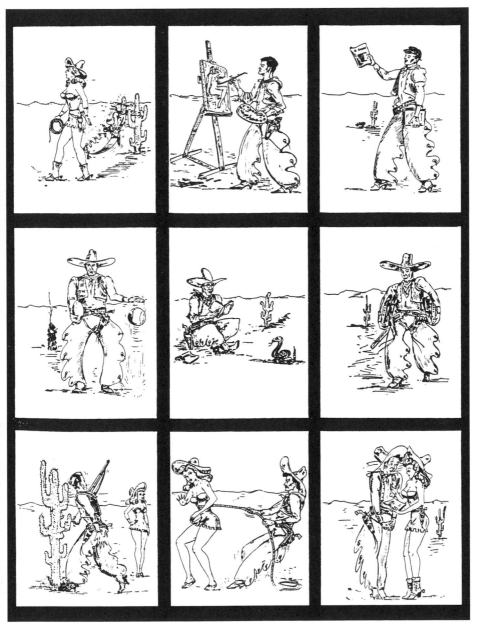

Several frames of unique desert scenes by an unnamed artist for *The Flowsheet* of 1950.

Autographs

Traditionally, as soon as newly printed annuals are distributed, students set out to get as many autographs of their teachers and classmates as possible. Many students sign their name by their pictures (as many times as they appear), and some write longer messages wherever space is found. I found several yearbooks with a signature beside *every* picture.

The autographs written by classmates and faculty members also reflect changes in manners of speech or customs and changes in the times. From my mother's 1920 *Senior Scrapbook* from Houston Heights High School:

> When you get old and ugly
> As old folks sometimes do,
> Just think of me, your classmate,
> Who is old and ugly, too.
>
> My friendship for you will always flow
> Like water down a tater row.
>
> In your chimney of remembrance
> Remember me as a brick.
>
> Beside the sea there is a rock
> And on it says "Forget-me-not."

Autographs from 1920s annuals from San Marcos Academy were at least a half page long, with others being hand-written on two or more pages. Most are eloquent treatises on friendship, thoughts of the fun and events of the past year, and hopes for the future.

From a 1970 *El Lince* from Gillette Junior High School in Kingsville: "My most favorite thing next to you is putting my mouth over a bus exhaust pipe and being dragged over a cactus patch during a wild pig stampede." The endearing comment: "Drop dead." From a 1974 annual: "To a dumb ass dude who really is what you call a freak. / To a funky dude, / May you get what you want in life." In the 1977 Churchill *Chancellor* was this little missile from a girl to a guy: "You are the weirdest and sweetest guy I know! . . . Come by and see me sometime. Love to one hell raiser from another."

The gentle, sentimental writings and verses from the early 1900s became the full-page, eloquent dissertations of the 1920s. Then came the matter-of-fact 1940s and 1950s, in which the autographs tended to speak to remembrances of good times with brief wishes for the future. The autographs of the 1960-1980s showed little of the sentiment indicated in earlier years. It is a disturbing reflection of the times that in the 1990s many schools have stopped allowing students to exchange annuals on school property because of obscene autographs.

Trends for the Future of School Yearbooks

Some Texas schools have stopped or curtailed the publication of annuals, citing lack of student interest and difficulty in finding students willing to spend the time and energy necessary to produce yearbooks, as well as excessive printing costs. Nevertheless, school yearbooks are alive and well at many schools. Photography and journalism skills continue to flourish.

Change, however, is inevitable. Recent news articles indicate a trend toward electronic, high-tech school yearbooks on videotape or on CD-ROM. School yearbooks as we know them may become another dinosaur facing extinction.

At the 1995 meeting of the Texas Folklore Society, Ab Abernethy distributed a document which summarized his definition of folklore. He based his definition on ethology, which is the study of behavioral relationships between animals and human beings. Quoting Abernethy, "My conclusion . . . is that behind every move that man makes is a wired-in behavior pattern which man holds in common with his animal kinsmen. This means that man has little control over what he does, only in how he does it. The 'how' is his folklore, his culture, his way of life." He based his conclusion as follows:

> . . . These behavior patterns—particularly sociality, dominance, territoriality, and sexuality—are modified by thought processes to fit the survival margin of his environment and are transmitted to the social group by symbolic language. The results are traditions and lore which the society establishes in order to promote a stable social union.

Look again at school yearbooks in light of this description of folklore. You will see *sociality*, beginning with the basic classes grouped from freshmen to seniors and in the propensity of people to join organizations and belong to teams. Sociality is also reflected in dress, hair styles, and activities.

You will see *dominance*, with some individuals assuming leadership roles, achieving status and recognition among their peers in sports, academics, music and art, and campus organizations. There is *territoriality*, defined by Abernethy as "that sense of space which an animal has which gives him a feeling of belonging to a particular piece of land. . . ." Students can say, "This is my school. . . . This is my class. . . . I am part of that group."

Though unanimously discreet in their treatment of the subject, Texas yearbooks clearly reveal *sexuality*. Hormones are "raging" during adolescence and early adulthood. Students of every generation think they invented sexuality, but photographs of school activities reveal that the pursuit of mates, playmates, dating partners, and sweethearts has always been a major activity at Texas schools. In Abernethy's words, "Folklore establishes familiar patterns of action—religion and rituals, customs and traditions—that bond a group together." Yearbooks document traditions important to each school. School traditions bond groups of people together. The yearbooks themselves are traditions.

By these descriptions, school yearbooks are the essence of folk-lore distilled into volumes which clearly reflect Texas culture. Take a fresh look at your school yearbooks. You will see more than history. You will see more than words, and pictures of people, places, and activities. You will see folklore.

Mabel Bohner's concluding cartoon for the 1917 *The Plain View* would probably not make the final cut today.

ENDNOTES

1. Utley, Francis Lee. "Folklore." *THE ENCYCLOPEDIA AMERI-CANA.* International Edition. Volume 11. Grolier, Inc.,1993.

10

Two-Bits, Four-Bits, or High School Cheerleading as a Lay Folk Ritual

by Ernest B. Speck

A few years ago the estimable Professor James Ward Lee regaled us with an account of the lore surrounding the Dallas Cowboy Cheerleaders, but when I learned that those seeming voluptuaries are actually a bunch of Dallas housewives who parade their persons for reasons I shall leave to their shrinks, I lost interest. But Lee did a dangerous thing; he started me to thinking. The result is what follows. My purpose is to point up and to describe some customary lore that no one, to my knowledge, has as yet delineated: high school cheerleading.

To prepare for this paper I have called upon some forty years of seeing high school football, off and on, returning last fall to observe one more game, and more especially, I turned folklorist in earnest and did a survey involving nine cheerleaders, who practiced their art at West Texas high schools in the last few years. They came from towns stretching from Hondo, just west of San Antonio, to Fabens, a suburb of El Paso. Their names are appended to this paper, and I'll refer to individual ones on occasion, but I'll name only one here, our own Karen Haile, who let Lee Haile, the toy maker, show his good sense by marrying her.

Before I get into some of the particulars of cheerleading, I should like to say that every

Karen Reinartz Haile, Head Cheerleader, 1975–1977, Hondo High School.

Sierra Chisos Haile, Bandera Middle School Cheerleader, with mascot, 2005.

girl I interviewed exhibited an ebullience of spirit that I found charming. Some showed an initial shyness at the sight of the tape recorder, but all of them would have been willing, after a minute or two, to lead me in a couple of cheers. They are vibrantly alive.

The pattern of Friday night football has become fairly well fixed in Texas high schools and, I suspect, nationwide. In only a few very small schools are the games still played after school on Friday afternoon, for want of a lightened field, but whether the school has both varsity and B teams or only a six-man team with no more than six others on the bench, certain factors are present. One such factor is cheerleading. And the girls I talked to all seemed conscious that they had performed a customary practice, and their desire had been to carry it out as well as, if not better than, their predecessors.

Let's begin with the first step, the way the cheerleaders are chosen. In most schools, there is a contest in which prospective cheerleaders display their abilities by cavorting about the auditorium stage or the gym floor exuding enthusiasm. There is then a vote by the student body, and the requisite number of girls is picked. The number of cheerleaders in the schools my girls represented ranged from four to thirteen. Two other methods of selecting the cheerleaders were mentioned: outside judges, often cheerleaders from a nearby university, are used at Lori's school;

Peggy said that judges on the faculty now select cheerleaders, although when she was chosen, the students still made the selections. However they are chosen, the honor of being chosen is enough to send the girls into paroxysms of joy and great fervor of labor that lasts throughout the year. Cheerleaders, by the way, are generally chosen in the spring for the following year so they can make preparations of the sorts to be mentioned later.

There are two concerns of cheerleaders once they begin to function: costumes and training. The girls call their costumes "uniforms." Each group of girls has at least two uniforms, one for indoor activities, such as pep rallies and basketball games and one for football games, consisting of sweaters, pleated skirts, at least mid-thigh in length, and over-the-calf sox. West Texas autumn nights, especially trans-Pecos ones, get chilly, and the girls wore pantyhose and bikini tights or leotards under their uniforms. Almost without exception the girls told me their uniforms were conservative. Lori said their indoor costumes were "interesting to look at," but Lori would be interesting to look at in any costume. Parental and official restrictions on their skimpiness prevented the indoor costumes from being overly revealing, but snug blouses or knit tops and shorts were the usual attire. When Dan Akroyd complained ironically a few years ago that high school cheerleaders' costumes were too revealing, he obviously had not watched cheerleaders in West Texas. On the other hand, there is no denying that watching energetic sixteen and seventeen-year-old girls vivaciously bouncing about can start masculine juices to flowing.

A wide range of elements is present in the training of cheerleaders. Typically, West Texas girls, whose parents have taken them to the Friday fracases since before they were weaned, have been eying for years either the majorettes with their batons and boots or cheerleaders with their megaphones and pompoms as occupying stations in life greatly to be desired. They have sought to emulate the actions and/or the words of their idols. When I wrote this, a typical pubescent daughter of a neighbor and five other junior high girls were practicing their routines on the front lawn. My survey showed that the girls' routines are generally worked out in just such sessions.

My informants cited two principal sources of schooling for their art: experienced cheerleaders and cheerleader camps. Local cheers and ways of doing things can be learned only from experienced girls; and again, I got the distinct impression that a sense of loyalty prompted the girls to want to carry on those traditions. Cheerleader camps, held on various college campuses in the late summer, instruct incoming cheerleaders in techniques in prompting crowd enthusiasm and elements of cheerleader sportsmanship. Nearly all of the girls I talked to had been to camp, but they generally could be no more specific (although they were a rather articulate group) than to say that they gained confidence by going to camp. Perhaps it would be well at this point to remind anyone who feels that such training is not folkloric in nature that Mody Boatright in 1958 (PTFS #28) said that if what is learned is a traditional practice, then it matters not if the practice is learned from one's grandparents or from a more regularized source, such as a book or a formal teacher. (May I inject here that Mody Boatright published this way of thought fifteen years before Richard Dorson picked it up and eight years before Alan Dundes did.)

But back to my lovelies. Hours of practice led the chosen few to the week of the first game. While there are similarities in what the girls did each week, there are three types of games for which the girls must prepare, each of which calls for a different type of preparation: the home game, the out-of-town game, and homecoming.

Let's look at the preparation for a home game other than homecoming. The three or four high school classes vied for recognition by decorating corridors, lockers, and giving other evidence of support for the team. Debbie's school, for example, allotted each of four main corridors to each of the four classes. In all schools, the class showing the most enthusiasm was awarded the "spirit stick" at the Friday pep rally; the spirit stick is a baton of varying length, up to six feet, painted in the school colors and embellished with streamers and other decorations. Cheerleaders act as judges and award the stick at the pep rally.

But cheerleaders have other duties each week. One is the preparation of a skit to be put on at the pep rally. Two variants on the cheerleaders' composing and doing the skits were reported: Crescella said their coach did not want skits, for he thought they detracted from the concentration of the team, and Rosemary said the drama club did the skits at her school. Although skits could be obtained from the Cheerleaders Association in Dallas, the girls preferred to make up their own and thus give them a more local flavor. The theme, of course, was some depiction of the mayhem the local warriors would inflict on their hapless opponents: how the Bucks would be dehorned, the Owls slaughtered, or the Golden Cranes thoroughly plucked.

Another chore is the making of "run-throughs." A run-through, for the benefit of those of you who are deplorably ignorant, is a strip of paper some twenty to forty feet long and four or five feet wide. It is attached at each end to poles, and painted with pictures and words calculated to raise the spirit of the team and the spectators, much in the manner of the skits. When the team comes onto the field just before the game, the cheerleaders and the players burst thought the stretched out run-through. The same routine occurs after the half-time intermission. Debbie said that the art club prepared the run-throughs during the summer and stored them for use in the fall. Karen told of being part of the beginning of a tradition at her school, as two cheerleaders held hands with the offensive captain and two with the defensive captain as they ran out on the field.

Another traditional duty of the cheerleaders at home games is to show hospitality to visiting cheerleaders. During the third quarter the girls bring the visiting cheerleaders from the opposite side of the field and introduce them to the home folks one at a time, and each is given a welcome cheer. The visitors then return the favor by asking the local cheerleaders to their side of the field. These hospitable actions have some overtones, for such a display of courtesy points up the fact that the contest is a sports event and not adolescent warfare. Karen told of feeling terribly rebuffed when her group was not invited by the hometown cheerleaders to come to their side of the field. Mary Kay, from a six-man school, said they did the hospitality bit during the second quarter, for six-man games are stopped at half-time, or anytime thereafter, if one team gets forty-five points ahead of the other.

I might inject here that such variations as there are in cheerleader practice are often the result of the preferences, and/or the efforts (or lack thereof) by the sponsors. Rosemary said they worked out their routines by themselves; Sally said their PE teacher sponsor gave them a rigorous workout in tumbling at every practice session so they put on quite a show.

Cheerleaders go to all out-of-town games, but the modes of transportation vary: Crescella said they rode with the band, Debbie said they traveled in a mini-bus, and Sally said their parents drove them. Since so many adults follow the teams to out-of-town games, transportation was generally no great problem. Practice varies as to what happens after an out-of-town game. The team goes to a restaurant for a meal, and cheerleaders and others go to the same restaurant to eat; in some instances, the cheerleaders go into the special dining room to eat with the team. Even after the shouting at the pep rally and during the game, the cheering at an after-the-game meal can be ear-shattering, even if the team has lost.

A part of the autumnal ritual is homecoming, that game day set aside to welcome back former students. Most homecoming celebrations include several of the following items in addition to the game: bonfire and pep rally, parade, barbeque, crowning of the homecoming queen, and dance. Cheerleaders have a role in most of these activities, but Ginger said that cheerleaders were in charge of all the activities, and even once succeeded in getting a band from Ft. Bliss at El Paso to come for their parade since the school had no band.

The bonfire and pep rally were held on Thursday night (often with another pep rally at the school on Friday afternoon). Cheerleaders usually had a hand in collecting bonfire wood, but Peggy said that the tradition of collecting privies for the bonfire ended just before her regime. Gathering wood at a place like Sierra Blanca or Eldorado poses a problem, unless one is willing to settle for greasewood or mesquite brush.

Parades were held when little more than the band, the cheerleaders, the students carrying banners or doing a snakedance, and some grade school kids on decorated bikes participated. Those who return to high school homecomings, by the way, are generally recent graduates; those of an earlier vintage come to class reunions, usually held in the summer.

Finally, homecoming gave the cheerleaders a special opportunity to display their abilities before their predecessors. It was a sort of test of how well they were carrying on the traditions.

A couple of other items need to be noted before we go on to the cheers themselves. Smaller schools often try to do nearly all that larger schools do but with many fewer people. For example, I have seen cheerleaders marching in the band at half-time wearing cheerleading uniforms. Crescella told of a quick change into band uniform and then back into cheerleader costume in time for the second half run-through.

Secondly, cheerleaders learn something of crowd control. While their primary function is to whip up enthusiasm, there are times when they calm over-agitated spectators. On one occasion, I saw the cheerleaders yell to the band to start the school song and then got the spectators to singing when some of the people in the stands were on the verge of attacking the officials for a ruling with which the local people did not agree.

And now the cheers themselves. If John A. Lomax were with us, he would no doubt record the cheers as anonymous folk creations, and then Jack Thorp or Austin Fife or John White would find the creators. My concern is simply to suggest that the cheers are universal in high schools (and colleges), that they are a part of American academic folk life (however little of the academic one may perceive in them), and that they are a part of contemporary folk custom.

Of the cheers the girls reported on, one cheer outranks all the others:

> Two-bits, four-bits, six-bits, a dollar;
> All for Sul Ross, stand up and holler.

After such an injunction, how could any red-blooded former fullback and his former cheerleader wife rest lethargically on their fannies? Virtually without fail the girls can get the congregation to rise and declare its allegiance to the boys on the field.

When I asked about the cheer that goes "Two, four, six, eight, Who do we appreciate?" informants said the cheer was little used in high schools, but the Democrats at a meeting last year chanted, "Two, four, six, eight, We remember Watergate," which indicates, at least, that the cheer is nationally known.

Second in popularity is the cheer in which the girls ask the spectators to shout back to them the letters spelling out the name either of the school or of the mascot. "Give me an L, give me an O," and so on through Lobos. Thus, some of the students learn to spell the names of their hometowns or the names of the creatures which served as mascots.

Also important are the chants which the cheerleaders start at crucial points in the game. When the opposing team seems to be making too much progress in moving toward a score, or has just scored, the cheerleaders will get the spectators to chanting, "Get tough, Lobos, get tough," or "Defense, defense, defense." If their team makes a first down on the way to what they hope will be a touchdown, the girls set up the chant, "First and ten, do it again; first and ten, do it again." As the team moves toward the opponent's goal line, the chant becomes, "We want a touchdown; we want a touchdown." Another chant that is used when the team is being particularly successful at scoring is, "All the way, one play; all the way, one play." Although there are locally used cheers and chants, these are the principal, widely used ones.

Thus far, I have concentrated on cheerleading at football games. Cheerleaders also function at other sorts of sports, but especially basketball games, although traveling to out-of-town games is less frequent. Debbie reported that her group also cheered at baseball and girls' basketball games and volleyball matches (practically everything except golf and track events), but Peggy said they did not cheer at girls' sports because they were participating themselves in her small high school. A chant that is often heard at basketball games is one used when the opponent is ahead in the score, has the ball, and is playing a sort of keep-away game. The cheerleaders then start the crowd to shouting:

> Get that ball,
> Get it, get it;
> Get that ball,
> Get it, get it.

Twenty minutes is hardly time enough to tell the whole story of high school cheerleading, its derivation from college cheering, and the cultural implications involved. So I shall quickly note only a few other things. Various groups of cheerleaders raised money to subsidize their enterprises by holding bake sales, car washes, and mum sales. They regularly did a lot of less spectacular things, such as standing at attention with pom-poms over their hearts during the playing of the national anthem. They learned the basics of the sports at which they cheered. They rendered various services to the coaches and team members, such as assisting when a player was hurt.

One question I asked the girls concerned their relationship with the team. All said the team was appreciative of their support, and many said the team was protective of them if anyone treated them unkindly or pestered them.

This paper has two conclusions. First, I hope I have shown that should an extra-terrestrial folklorist from Mars or Ork drop in on an autumnal Friday night Texas football game, he would be fascinated by the pageantry, the rituals, the incantations, and the human sacrifice displayed before him. Here, he would obviously say, is a folk ceremony being carried out in a prescribed fashion. I have sought to describe some essential parts of that ceremony.

Secondly, my inquiries into cheerleading led me to an amazing and titillating discovery. The Dallas Cowboy Cheerleaders are not cheerleaders at all. They are pom-pom girls. Let me explain. I also interviewed Kellie from a large high school in an affluent neighborhood in El Paso. Kellie is a honey blond who looks and walks as if she should be striding down the walkway of a Paris couturier, displaying the high fashion spring collection. She was a pom-pom girl; she was also Miss Davis Mountains in 1981. To allay any of your fears that I have interviewed a bubble-headed, minor league Miss Universe, let me add that Kellie is a bright political science major headed for law school. What Kellie said is that pom-pom

Karen Reinartz Haile at a Hondo High School Pep Rally.

girls are "dance oriented" and have nothing to do with football games except that they perform while the games are going on as an added attraction. Their costumes are definitely sexy, and their routines are dances and quite often have what some would describe as suggestive movements. And since they have no Tom Landry, nor anyone else with a Baptist computer for a brain and heart to deter them, they inspire males, but not those playing football, at least not while they are playing. Pom-pom girls are simply a latter day embodiment of the virtue, if that is the word, that was Minsky's.

The cheerleaders who served as informants and the schools at which they functioned are the following:

> Debbie Borrego, Monahans
> Peggy Clanton, Ft. Davis
> Sally Cauley Crawford, Eldorado
> Lori DeVolin, Fabens
> Ginger Tidwell Elliott, Sierra Blanca
> Karen Reinartz Haile, Hondo
> Mary Kay Kurie, Marathon
> Crescella Talley Rodarte, Van Horn
> Rosemary Sandate, Alpine
>
> And the pom-pom girl:
> Kellie Hudson, Eastwood High, El Paso

11

Seeing Red over Varsity Blues

by Ty Cashion

L ast year I had the occasion to speak to a group of students at Stephen F. Austin State University, in Nacogdoches. Having just written a social history of old-time Texas high school football coaches, I was curious to poll the students about the perceptions of their own head coaches back home. On my informal scale of 1 to 3—one being Fred Flintstone with a gimme hat and whistle and three being their favorite uncle—all but a smattering of about seventy students said their coach was like that favorite uncle.

So now, MTV brings us *Varsity Blues*, with Jon Voight playing Coach Bud Kilmer, the stereotypical troglodyte. The first view of Voight left no doubt about where this film was heading. It was at a pep rally, full of excited high schoolers—band blaring, cheerleaders screeching—who fell into a reverent silence at the mere outstretch of the coach's hand, outstretched, that is, in a not-so-subtle Nazi salute.

Here was a man who had brought the fictitious West Caanan two state titles and twenty-two district championships in thirty years. And this season, he boasted, he was gonna bring 'em number twenty-three. If there was any doubt that the town worshipped their coach, you had only to look past the corner of the end zone to see his graven image standing sentinel over—you guessed it—Bud Kilmer Stadium.

In real life, Texans don't deify active coaches. What would boosters do if their hero had a losing season? The last thing they would want is to look like a bunch of Russians pulling down statues of Stalin.

No, a good lynching is the way we do things here in Texas. That's exactly what disgruntled fans at Wichita Falls did to Joe Golding, when his Coyotes lost the first four games of the 1950 season. All right, I admit they hanged him in effigy, but I bet it still had the old coach tearing at the top button of his shirt.

The rub here is that the lynching came right in the middle of a two-season "stretch" in which Golding brought Wichita Falls back-to-back state crowns. Reflecting on Golding's career, his methods, his philosophies, you might think Bud Kilmer pales like a piker in comparison. In nine fewer seasons than the fictitious coach of West Caanan, Golding doubled Kilmer's output, winning the state championship four times. On two other occasions, his boys went all the way to the finals. Even at a time before district also-rans could wrangle a spot in the playoff brackets, it was a rare December that found the Coyotes sitting at home.

The program that made champions out of Golding's boys sounds barbaric today. Water breaks were unheard of, but there always seemed to be plenty of salt tablets available. And coaches felt like their boys weren't hitting unless they were bleeding. Workouts routinely lasted four hours and unfolded on a parched Wichita-river-bottom practice field that the players had dubbed "The Hell Hole." Coyote star and future coach Bill Bookout nevertheless insisted that the players took it all in stride: "Joe Golding was tough, but it didn't seem that way because we were used to it."

Offering no apologies, Golding himself stated: "If we worked them unreasonably hard, it was our effort and our philosophy that this is what was required for the rigors of combat and football." Of course, Golding coached through a time when boys could find themselves going straight from the gridiron wars to real battlefields. Texans, moreover, were still clinging to agrarian folkways, and life after high school often meant working outdoors in the sunshine.

Perhaps more of an eyebrow raiser than Golding's coaching philosophy was his unabashed view on education. In a 1975 interview, he said: "Being connected with competitive sports for as long as I can remember . . . I do have this profound feeling that our [coaches'] objective in education is perhaps the responsibility of developing young manhood and young womanhood, even more important than developing academic excellence. Both are important, but I don't think you can have academic excellence without having developed character."

That's not to say that Golding took education lightly. Rare was the old-time coach who hailed from a family with a tradition of higher education, but no group of men understood more keenly what an education could do for their own children. In fact, you wouldn't have to dig very deep to find that the old coaches sired a disproportionate number of doctors, lawyers, Ph.D.'s, and professionals —including many teachers and coaches.

This game program cover from a WWII era contest expresses society's belief that football provided an appropriate training ground for the times.

The experiences that shaped Golding's outlooks were typical of his times and his profession. The vast majority of old-time Texas high school coaches had grown up on red beans and rice during the Great Depression. Overwhelmingly, they were Southern in background, had religious roots in evangelical churches, and had experienced brutal physical regimens as high school and college players themselves. They were also first-generation college students at a time when the rigid social barriers that separated Texans by economic class were second only to those that kept the races apart.

In the couple of generations that separate the real-life Joe Golding from the fictional Bud Kilmer, Texas has changed dramatically. For one thing, high school football is not nearly as important as it once was, even though it is "bigger" in some ways than ever before. "Cheerleader Moms" and daddies living through their sons notwithstanding, ours is no longer a child-centered society. As for kids themselves, there are more distractions competing for their affections. And Texas today, buoyed by Northern migration and a high-tech economy, is more sophisticated than Golding's agricultural society.

In the popular perception, however, the one thing that seems to have remained constant is the football coach. The granite-tough image of men such as Vince Lombardi, Bear Bryant, and legions of Joe Goldings dies hard. Recast in today's terms, their progeny are "win-at-all-costs" caricatures of our collective imaginations. Manifested in Bud Kilmer, an even darker portrait appears in the form of a misanthropic racist, a child abuser, and a self-absorbed redneck.

In the five or so years that I spent interviewing high school football coaches, I didn't run into many Bud Kilmers. In fact, one of the questions I always asked was: "Tell me about a man who had no business coaching kids." Surprisingly, the same "short list" came up time after time.

On the surface, if the old coaches left hard, unyielding impressions, it was because they were products of an age when manliness meant that you did not show weakness, pain, disappointment, or sometimes even mercy. Yet coaches, declared Golding assistant Bill Carter, "always had feelings, but they just didn't show it. This 'my way or the highway' type of attitude was just a projection of what they had gone through themselves in just about every aspect of their life. As society has changed, so have the coaches."

The biggest change, according to Eddie Joseph, former executive director of the Texas High School Coaches Association, "is that you can put your arm around a kid's neck and tell him you love him." Most coaches today, said Commerce's Steve Lineweaver, "have taken courses on child psychology and on the dynamics of how people interact. Nowadays at coaching school they'll tell you that you need to take sociology classes and pay as much attention to your people skills as your 'X's and O's.'"

Standing on the sidelines at some important Texas high school football games in the last few years, I have seen that "kid-sensitive" approach in action—especially at critical moments when the scoreboard read in the other team's favor. It's easy to be gracious when you win, but nothing brings out true character like a close loss. As Mike Sneed's guest the night his Grapevine Mustangs lost to archrival Southlake Carroll recently, I saw his boys snatch pearls of defeat from the jaws of victory several times. If you'd guess that Sneed and some of the assistant coaches met the offending players coming off the field, you'd be right. But the coaches weren't berating them, they were there with pats on the back, admonishing their boys to shake it off and do better next time. And they did. When the season was over, Sneed rode home on the bus with the 4-A state champions.

Earlier, at Commerce, when the Tigers' six-foot-three, 225-pound "Super-Teamer" Mitchell Scott, Jr. came up with a lame knee, he ended up watching his last thirteen high school games from the bench. Coach Lineweaver told him there would be other seasons when he got to college. And it's not like the coach couldn't have used him. Their season ended at the Astrodome, where Mitchell Scott might have made up for the few points that kept his team from taking home the big trophy.

If you buy into the proposition that coaches "win at all costs," then it would stand to reason that the greatest number of human casualties would lie in the wake of the biggest winners. I'm here to tell ya': "It just ain't so." Most of the time it's the coaches who are standing between their players and boosters who would do anything to win.

I've watched some of today's most successful coaches at close range—the recently deceased Duncanville's Bob Alpert, Lewisville's Ronnie Gage, Midland Lee's John Edd Parchman, and the list goes on—and all of them have won a state championship. If they share one common denominator, it's that I wouldn't necessarily tag 'em for coaches if I met them on the street—well, nobody but John Edd.

And he, like the rest of them, seems just like, well . . . somebody's favorite uncle.

CRAZY WOMEN IN THE RAFTERS
Memories of a Texas Boyhood
By Paul Patterson
Sam McGoo and Texas Too
By PAUL PATTERSON
Illustrations and Foreword By ELMER KELTON
PECOS TALES II
III. "A Tribute to Paul Patterson"
• Ernestine S: "Jes Sir, Meester Patterson"
• Elmer: "Paul Patterson"
• Evelyn Stroder: "P.P.: Master Teacher"
• Lawrence: "Prose Narratives"
Notes on Paul
Occupations: cowboy, writer, poet, storyteller, teacher
Joined TFS: 1958!
Paul and the kids— El Paso 2005

A Tribute to Paul Patterson

PECOS TALES II

PATTERSON

Lydαy

Kathleen

Paul and
the kids —
El Paso
2005

tes on Paul

tions: cowboy, writer, play

poet, storyteller, teacher

1958!

Women,

'Jes Sir, Meester "Patternson":

The Legendry of a Master Teacher

by Ernestine P. Sewell

I t is possible for a Master Teacher to become a legend. Mr. Chips, for example, though he is out of fiction. Miss Dove. There are others.

This paper undertakes to show how a potful of folklore attached itself to the Pecos River Pilgrim Paul Patterson, erstwhile cowboy, and how that folklore, given a little time, has made legendary his reputation in West Texas education.

As a rule, we know a person first, by what he says about himself, second, by what others say about him, and third, by what we observe from what he actually does.

Paul tells that he plunged into a "poverty-plagued profession" in 1935 at the "darkest depths of the Great Depression." The place was Marfa, his assignment to Jesse Blackwell Elementary School, exclusively Mexican, this being "pre-desegregation, pro-discrimination days." Armed with an ego, over-sized for a fellow his size (by his own admission), thirty hours of education classes at Sul Ross State University and his text on child behavior in hand, Paul entered a classroom only to be met with "planned pandemonium and contemplated chaos." Where in his textbook were the recommendations for countering misbehavior? Probably in Volume II, which Paul had not got. What to do? First, throw away the book. Second, resort to motivation

The cover image from the *Southwestern American Literature* issue dedicated to Paul Patterson.

135

by intimidation, though the paddling arm suffer the agony of total exhaustion.

As the principal escorted Paul to his number five classroom that first day, he had one word of advice: motivate. Hateful word, that, the bane of all teachers: it slips so facilely from the tongues of smug administrators. Just how does one motivate? Impel, incite, provide with motive, says the dictionary; in Paul's words: *ignite.*

Motivation by intimidation had achieved the results he expected, and he had the cooperation of the parents. Take the case of Librado, who insisted on calling Paul by his first name. Paddling did no good, but Paul was not one "to turn purple and give up." Librado's grandfather was of the old school, and though short of stature, he demanded obedience and was a man to be respected. "Librado," said Paul, "you live with your grandfather?" "Jes Sir." "Good," said Paul, "when your grandfather gets home tonight, you call him Shorty. If you can get by with calling him Shorty just one time, you may call me Paul from now on."

"Jes Sir," Librado answered.

Next morning Librado hailed Paul from half a block away. "Oiga, Meester Patternson, I no call my grandfather Chorty no more."

It comes as no surprise to those who know Paul that he did not have the temperament—I should say heart—to continue motivation by intimidation. "By year's end," he says, "I would not have struck one of them in self-defense." He had to find another technique. He would try motivation by inspiration. Now Benito Juarez and Abraham Lincoln were both inspiring leaders, whose humble beginnings and poverty his students could easily identify with. In Paul's class, there was one Tony Dutchover who had "the energy of two A-bombs," but Tony never seemed to be able to direct his energy to his arithmetic homework. "Tony," Paul said to him, "Remember I was telling you all about President Lincoln and how poor he was when he was a little boy?" "Jes Sir." "And how he did his arithmetic with a piece of charcoal from the fireplace on a wooden shovel? And every time he started a new problem, he had to scrape off the old problem to make a clean shovel?" "Jes Sir,"

Tony responded again. "Then why didn't you do your homework last night?" Paul asked sternly. To which Tony answered, "But, Meester Patternson, I don't got no wooden chovel." So much for motivation by inspiration.

Obviously, another strategy was in order. Perhaps what his pupils would respond to would be motivation by innovation. Paul hit upon the idea of bringing what they had in their limited store of knowledge to bear on whatever problem the lesson for the day posed. For example, to impress upon them the difference between common and proper nouns, Paul combined geography with grammar. He would say, "Give me a proper noun for this common noun: city." They would shout "Marfa," or "Bachimba." Bachimba was an isolated village in Chihuahua, and this response was always accompanied by a derisive "Yeeee. . . ." as they pointed to a classmate they had nicknamed Bachimba because of his countrified ways.

Then he would reverse his question. He would say "Rockies," and they would answer "Mountain." Thinking to make it easy for them, Paul proceeded: "Now, students, the next one is going to be something not far away at all. You tell me what the common noun is when I give you this proper noun: Chisos." Gilberto Garcia was first to shout an answer: "Chisos Christ," he yelled.

Not one to give up, Paul continued, "State." Everyone joined in the answer, "Texas." Except William, who always yelled "Indiana!" His father, a soldier at Fort Davis, had married William's mother and had taken her back to Indiana where William was born. To remind his fellow classmates that he knew geography better than they, he opened every geography lesson by proudly marching up to the map, placing his finger carefully there and announcing: "Mr. Patternson, I born een Eendiana." The derisive chorus of "Yeeeee. . . ." never discouraged him. At last, Antonio Rojo did what the class failed to do: he shut William up forever. One morning, imitating William's mannerisms, his walk and his talk, he went up to the map, placed his finger on Marfa and proclaimed: "Meester Patternson, I born een the bed *here*."

There were times when even "Meester Patternson" would be so discouraged as to yield to his baser nature to get even with the young 'uns. That is, he would resort to motivation by aggravation, though this technique is useful, he says, only with the little ones inasmuch as it "triples one's troubles even as it quadruples one's fun." It goes like this: the teacher dictates a very long sentence "riddled with punctuation hazards." Then as they watch, horrified, he slaps a great big zero on each paper as it is turned in. The voices ring out after each round zero takes effect, "What's wrong with it?" "It's wrong is what's wrong; take it back, check it carefully, wait your turn, and I shall be happy to remove your zero after you show me where each and every error was," is Paul's command. It is a tall order, he says, "to see order restored, orders obeyed, and order kept." However, since this technique inflicts some injury upon the innocent, Paul kept motivation by aggravation in File Thirteen and let it lie for those times in the classroom when all else failed.

All the foregoing techniques succeeded more or less here and there as the Master Teacher attempted to impel, incite, and *ignite* his students to greater achievement. But when it came to grammar, nothing worked. To quote Paul, "The students look upon grammar like the kid who swallowed the golf ball. It is just something that has got to be passed, which entails pain as well as strain." Mindful that money is a powerful motivator, our Master Teacher warned his eighth graders a day in advance: "I strongly advise you to read the chapter 'Money as a Prime Mover' tonight." Next morning, he gave them a quick quiz, graded their papers carefully right before their eyes and awarded fifty cents for the best paper, thirty-five cents for the second best, and fifteen cents for the third. There was an uprising. "That ain't fair," they shouted. "All right, Miss Lorraine," Miss Lorraine being the self-appointed spokesperson for the class, "you tell us what is fair." Then, without giving her time to answer, he continued: "Take for example me and the Fonz. Whereas the Fonz is young, handsome, talented, rich, and working steadily, I am old, bald-headed, cross-eyed, poor and soon to be unemployed—and unemployable—forever. Is that fair?"

Miss Lorraine chose not to respond but to come back with a question, "How was we supposed to know we was gonna have a test?" The Master Teacher carefully repeated for the benefit of the whole class, "How were you suppos*duh* know you were going to have a test?" Then he continued, "You would not know if you were not paying attention yesterday when I said, 'I strongly advise you to read the chapter "Money as a Prime Mover" tonight.'" To which Miss Lorraine said, "That don't tell us nothin' 'bout no test. Besides tonight ain't last night." Now, a Master Teacher would know that to argue with an eighth grader is to make "headway on a treadmill—uphill." Regardless, Paul found motivating by inspiring the students to win money "soul-soothing and satisfying. It makes one feel clever and generous." And it really worked. Every so often, one of his students asked, "Meester Pat, when we gonna have 'nother one of them test contests?" The Master Teacher never failed to answer such a question with another question, "When are we *going* to have *another* one of *those* test contests?" And then, with a smile of pleasure, he added, "No man knoweth the day or the hour," bringing in the scriptures for a show of authority. "And when is that?" Miss Lorraine would demand, thus causing the teacher some difficulty to stifle the quick quip she deserved.

Paul found his technique worked better with the little ones. They were less insolent and less insubordinate—and much cheaper. He could get by with fifteen, ten, and five cents instead of the exorbitant sums the eighth graders expected.

Since the test contests were likely to empty his pockets, Paul continued to look for other ways to motivate. This brought him to Number Five: motivation by participation. As Paul tells it: "Motivation by money is as sounding brass as compared to motivation by participation, total participation whereby the pupils are co-workers in the writing, producing, directing, and acting in plays and skits, said works to be grammatically and technically correct before said super-colossal goes into production. To commemorate Uncle Sam's 200th birthday, each of my fifth graders at Sierra Blanca chose his or her most admired predecessor in the making of America. Then he or she was assigned that particular role . . . all in rhyme. The play was titled *In the Land of the Free Include Me*. Even though many were faced with as many as forty lines, every one—save one, Arvin—had committed every line to memory by morning. And Arvin, of all people, chose George Washington—of all people—as his idol, which meant that Arvin would not only be the leading character, he would be the lead-off character, meaning, as goes Arvin, so goes the show.

"Now I cannot tell a l-i-e, but it was my deep, personal conviction that Arvin was the most UN-motivated, DE-motivated, DIS-motivated, MIS-motivated child in the annals of child psychoanalysis. Give Arvin a cold, I surmised, and he wouldn't even sneeze; give Arvin a chill and he wouldn't move a muscle. Right up to within an hour of curtain time . . . not one sign of reaction, much less action."

"Mr. Pat, throw Arvin out of here. He's gonna disgrace us all."

"No. Arvin will not disgrace anybody . . . but Arvin. And his poor mother." (This in Arvin's presence, of course, in a desperate bid to impel, incite, and *ignite*. It was motivation by insinuation.)

"Oh, me of little faith. Came curtain time; came Arvin's moment of truth and hour of triumph all rolled into one. Triumph, that is, over himself and over a seizure of stage fright of such magnitude as to leave him totally paralyzed—with the exception of lips, finger tips, eyes, and vocal chords, all of which did his bidding this one time." Yes, Arvin came through.

True, Paul's experiences, as he relates them, are the stuff of legend. But the more documentary evidence the better. Someone said a legendary figure is one who is different; he or she will have some physical characteristic that is distinguishing, or the behavior of the person differs from the expected. Insurance agent Doug Chrane, whose career began along with Paul in the classroom, tells these stories that truly set Paul apart. "When Paul greeted a new group of students, he would remind them that he was able to see both sides of the classroom at the same time. Since Paul's eyes were somewhat crossed, one eye would check one side of the room while the other eye would check the other side. Paul would assure them that one or the other eye was on each of them all the time, but they would never know which eye. He had better discipline than most of us."

Elmer Kelton, topmost novelist of Texas history, lore, and legend, attests to Paul's ability to discipline his students, too. Elmer studied Spanish with Paul, and he says, "Don't you be mistaken. There was no horseplay in Paul's classroom. We were there to learn and learn we did."

About Paul's enthusiasm for teaching, Mr. Chrane writes: "Paul taught Spanish. Each summer he would attend school in Mexico City, but on the way to and from the city, he would stop in every little village to speak with the natives. When he returned, he would tell us of the mixtures of Spanish, Mexican, Tex-Mex, and farm labor tongues that he heard. I could see that a zealous teacher would do such a thing, but when Paul put business before pleasure on our faculty trips, it was a little too much. When we made trips to ballgames during the fall harvest time, we would stop at regular times for meals. But Paul would leave us to seek out the Mexican laborers and talk Spanish, Mexican, or whatever with them. I guess this sort of thing led us to say about Paul, 'Oh, he'd rather work than eat any old day.'"

"But Paul would never make the big time for having the best filing system," Mr. Crane continues. "His file cabinet was his shirt pocket. He never used a folder. Information was just scribbled on little bits of paper that were then folded, wadded, or stuffed in his shirt pocket, that is, except for those that sometimes fell out of his pocket and lay on his not-so-neat desk. Now, you can imagine the minds of those high school students busy at figuring ways to mix up the filing system, or insert some juicy love notes, or some very secret information about fellow students, or possibly an interesting picture or two. Some of these things did happen, but Paul never admitted that there were faults with his filing system."

Perhaps some of those original thoughts that found their way into his filing system would account for Paul's becoming an outstanding creative writing teacher. Mr. Chrane says, "Paul was one to encourage students to do creative writing and present articles for the school paper. Once, Paul let me read a story written by a student, which, he admitted, was the best story he had ever received, but he had to tell the student it could not be published. Why? Maybe Paul was afraid it would cost him his job. (In those days, complaints about administration and school facilities were taboo.) Or, it may have been that Paul did not want to hurt the feelings of the cafeteria manager, who was a lady with a tender heart.

"During the late 1940s the government had surplus foods for school cafeterias. One food they had plenty of was potatoes. We had potatoes every day—mashed. Mashing those potatoes must have been the easiest way to fix them for so many. The students hated those mashed potatoes and would not keep their feelings quiet but voiced their dislike loudly as they went through the serving line. Even threats from the teachers would not keep them quiet about those mashed potatoes. (We thought the same things but could not say so, of course.

"Paul's student wrote a story about the potatoes. One day, a student, Jerry by name, came into the cafeteria, smiling. The other students were puzzled, expecting the usual frown and usual string of gripes. They did not know that he had a plan to break into the cafeteria and smash the mashing machine. When night fell, Jerry did just that. He broke into the cafeteria and began beating on the machine. He was so carried away that he did not notice when he hit the button that turned on the machine. It was too late. He was caught in the machine and it was about to make mashed Jerry of him. However, as fate would have it, a bag of potatoes fell off the shelf and into the machine, jamming the works. Jerry was saved. The next day Jerry appeared in the cafeteria smiling, much to the puzzlement of his friends again, for he had made a solemn vow never to say anything against mashed potatoes ever again. Paul's encouragement of his students to be creative backfired that time!"

Mr. Chrane tells this story about Paul's ability to motivate his students' creative talents beyond the classroom: "One of his classes decided they would like to present a program for the high school assembly. They called it 'The Below Parr Show,' not as in golf, but as in Jack Parr. The students really put on entertaining shows. To cite one example, a rather timid boy opened the show with a number wherein he played the piano and sang. He had never done either before. We were all stunned when he beat the piano with both hands, stood up and yelled a few words that no one could understand, sat down again and repeated the banging and yelling for a few minutes—in imitation of some of the TV entertainers. If only I could have recorded that number, I could have retired with the income from the sale of a new hit song. Paul just had a way of bringing out the best in his students."

A further report from Mr. Chrane reveals Paul the Trickster: "During Paul's first year of teaching school, he met the girl of his dreams. She taught in the same school. They wanted to get married, but there was a problem. Husband and wife were not allowed to teach in the same school in the city. They decided to get married and keep it a secret. This they did for the remainder of the school year. Now, Paul's wife did not know until after their marriage that she would inherit a debt that he had made prior to their marriage. However, after thinking it over, she decided that to make such a catch as Paul, the debt was a minor problem. So the marriage lasted.

"The next year Paul and his wife were each hired to teach in Crane. Superintendent Lealand L. Martin did not know they were married. After about three months or so, Mr. Martin saw that Paul and his wife were really sweet on each other, so he suggested that they get married, take off a few days, and go off for a honeymoon. Paul thought this was a very good idea, and all worked perfectly until someone discovered they had been married earlier. When Mr. Martin was told, Paul almost lost his job. He had had a second honeymoon—with pay."

Thus far, we know what Paul says about himself in the classroom; we have found what others say about him; now the disinterested observer sums up.

Even the worst dry-as-dust theorists of educational methods would be moved to applaud Paul Patterson for his approach to teaching. Administrators, too. It is doubtful, however, that they would give him much credit for his folk heroic tactics in the classroom, their top priority being to move lots of papers across their unpolished walnut (or mesquite?) desks.

No doubt, Paul had deadlines for daily objectives, daily lesson plans, implementation of daily lesson plans, monthly objectives, semester objectives, daily tests, weekly tests, mid-term tests, final examinations, and final results. And no matter what the final results may be, they all had to be put to the curve, for to have results conform to the curve was the absolute measure of good teaching. There were attendance records, student conference records, and parent conference records (this writer recalls daily milk records and a potful of pennies to account for). Paul may or may not have escaped climbing the ladder for bracketed salary increases, encumbered by student evaluation, peer evaluation, administrative evaluation, etc., etc. But Paul probably satisfied administrative demands for all the paperwork, else he would never have arrived at his retirement dinner.

Ultimately, we have to ask, How did Paul achieve results in the classroom? What went on in those classrooms that enabled those Mexican students to acquire the skills that would place "Meester Patternson" among the ranks of Master Teacher?

Try your own skills at these ordinary fifth grade grammar problems taken from copies of Paul's lesson plans:

> Change the nouns to pronouns in these sentences:
> Jason jumped John.
> Elsa eats elephants.
> Kiki kicks kittens.

Can grammar be fun? Continue with these sentences, which are to be punctuated:

Bring back Bensons book Barbara bellowed
Are all anteaters angry Arvin asked
Look Danny cried Manny theres a wolf after your granny
Big deal cried Camille five thousand grasshoppers for
    a meal

So punctuation might be entertaining? Next question: Draw a line between the subject and the predicate; then put a V over the verb and an A over the adjectives:

Sabrina saw six sick snakes.
Benson buys big bags of bagels for his beagle.
Arvin asks Abel about Alicia's awful alligator.

It can be done, but just try your skills at changing this direct quotation to an indirect quotation:

"Ned," said Fred, "your head is pure lead."

His lesson plans indicate that the eighth graders were challenged by questions like these:

Punctuate the following:
Gorilla growled Gary get gone or you get got and got
    good get it
Courageous Clara calmly called in a cougar and coolly
    clipped its claws
Mrs. Mitchell mad at Micheles mischievousness made Miss
    Michele mount her motor bike and move on

Next, label the nouns and verbs in these sentences:

Lovely Lorraine's long lashes lashed lazily at Lancelot's
    lingering looks.

Daring Daniel drove deeply into the dark dungeon to rescue his darling Dorothy from that dreadful dragon.

Eventually, students must confront the dreaded tests. One of Paul's exams was concluded with a limerick for which the students were to furnish the last line. The best ending would earn for its composer fifty cents. Paul gave the students all night to work on this problem:

A dashing hotrodder was Irv,
Renowned for his cold, steely nerve;
His eyesight was super,
His reflexes duper

_____

The winner of the fifty cent piece brought in this line:

Poor Irv, he died hugging the wrong curve!

The point is, how could the children not learn? To which some stuffy, tradition-bound, be-spectacled schoolmarms and -masters may scream "Non-professional," their disapproval aimed at what appears to be excessive alliteration and rhyme.

But let us resort to the advice of experts. There are truly linguistic experts who say the most effective way to teach word recognition and language facility is to play with minimal pairs, that is, to change one sound at a time in a word. Paul was teaching Chicano children, and the big problem he faced was teaching the English language. So, he wisely may begin: "sad-mad-cad-bad-dad-fad-gad-had," and so on. Or, he may have a lesson on vowels: "mad-mid-mod-mud," and so on. His emphasis on rhymes is yet another method for gaining proficiency: the verses and limericks teach the contours of the language, the rhythms, what is often called erroneously "accent."

Yes, Paul Patterson was a Master Teacher. Let his name stand alongside Hercules' Centaur, Telemachus' Mentor, and Mr. Chips.

Like each of them, he was cast in a different mold, the prerequisite for a legendary figure. And, ultimately, the wisdom of this Pilgrim from the Pecos River Valley, erstwhile cowboy, poet, storyteller, folklorist, writer, dramatist, friend to man and woman, sums it all up in common with those other Master Teachers of yore with these words of advice:

"Mastering schoolmastering is so very simple—merely a matter of knowing when to wheedle and when to needle; that is, when to lean down and hug, and when to draw back and slug!"

[Author's notes: All quoted materials are from miscellaneous papers of Paul Patterson of Crane and Pecos, and correspondence with Doug Chrane, Crane.]

Ernestine Sewell in 1990.

ENDNOTES

1. This paper was presented as part of a special session dedicated to honoring Paul at the 1990 meeting in Kingsville. It was also published in *Southwestern American Literature* Special Edition: Paul Patterson-Writer, Folkloreist, Volume 15, Number 2, Spring 1990.

13

Paul Patterson[1]

by Elmer Kelton

I am pleased to have a part in a well-justified tribute to Paul Patterson. My friendship with him goes back more than sixty years, to his arrival in my hometown, Crane, Texas.

I grew up on the McElroy Ranch near Crane. My father, Buck Kelton, was the foreman, and Paul's brother John was a cowboy there. Paul had been teaching school in Sanderson and signed up to teach in the Crane school system beginning in the fall of 1939. He came a bit early, so to earn a little extra money, and to while away the time, he day-worked for Dad until school started.

It was at the time of the late-summer roundup. Dad always timed the branding for the last week or so of August to get the free use of us kids just before school closed in on us. I had known John for a long time, so I felt comfortable with his younger brother. I knew him first as Paul the cowboy, just one of the bunch. That lasted perhaps two weeks.

Then suddenly, he was *Mr. Patterson*, one of my teachers. His clothes and his situation made a drastic change. So did my attitude, out of necessity.

It was not that Paul was a formidable presence in the class-room; he never was. He was always a friend to the students, and if you ask anyone who studied under him who was his favorite teacher, the answer would usually be Paul Patterson. It was certainly so with my class, which was graduated in 1942. Paul has been a fixture at our class reunions ever since.

I would not want to give the impression that he was easy. He did not award grades that had not been earned. In that respect, he reminded me a great deal of Dr. DeWitt Reddick, of the school of journalism at the University of Texas. They were both likeable teachers. They smiled a lot and never raised their voices in anger in the classroom, though God knows they had reason enough at times. To get an A from DeWitt Reddick was like pulling your own teeth. Paul was no pushover, either.

In my case, he taught me Spanish and journalism. Paul is bilingual. He studied in Mexico and Spain. I say he taught me Spanish. Let me recant. He tried to teach me Spanish. I learned just enough to get me in some embarrassing situations whenever I have tried to use what little residue of it remained.

But the journalism took root.

J. Evetts Haley said once that a grandson asked him if he knew the difference between a fairy tale and a Texas tale. He said a fairy tale starts, "Once upon a time . . ." A Texas tale starts, "Now, I know you s.o.b.'s ain't goin' to believe this, but . . ."

I know you folks won't believe this, but I was ashamed of my writing ambitions in those days. It did not seem a respectable thing for a boy to be doing in the environment in which I grew up. I was winning spelling bees and making A's in English when other red-blooded boys my age were trying to break arms and legs playing football or roping and riding calves. In an oil-patch town like Crane, a boy who was good in English class and even beat the girls at spelling bees was automatically suspect.

I hid my writing from public view and hoped no one would ever find out until the day I burst upon the literary world with a best-selling novel better even than *Tom Sawyer* or *Huckleberry Finn*. I figured that was unlikely to happen until I was at least eighteen or nineteen years old.

But here was Paul Patterson, a certified cowboy, teaching us how to write. It gradually dawned on me that I might not be such a square peg as I had thought. It might be at least half respectable to admit that I wanted to become a writer someday.

Paul helped open that door for me, and he gave me the idea of going into it through journalism. He supervised the school newspaper. I found that working on it was a lot of fun. I began to feel that working on a newspaper, and being paid for it, would almost be like having a license to steal.

I have always felt that had it not been for Paul Patterson, my professional life might have taken a much different turn. My father was not keen on the idea. He had given up on trying to make a good cowboy of me, but he thought I might become a lawyer. He said I always talked too much, so I ought to be a good one.

But there was Paul, quietly encouraging, and I stuck by my original ambition to become a writer. I had another ambition in those days, too: to become an artist. Paul encouraged me in that, as well. I drew cartoons for the school paper as well as writing for it.

When we both got home after World War II, Paul wrote a couple of books and asked me to illustrate them. He published *Sam McGoo and Texas Too* in 1947. Doing the cartoons for that book took up a lot of my spare time that first summer I was home from the service.

Paul wrote another, a sort of fictionalized autobiography. I drew a set of illustrations for that one too, and I suspect it was those that prevented the book from being published in its original form. Paul rewrote the book some years later, removing the fiction. Published by the University of Oklahoma Press, it bore the title *Crazy Women in the Rafters.* My pictures did not make the cut.

Despite Paul's good intentions and encouragement, my art career went the way of my Spanish. My entire career earnings totaled $205. Of that, $200 came from Paul for *Sam McGoo.* The other five dollars came from a magazine that bought one cartoon out of a batch I sent them.

Ace Reid, the cowboy cartoonist, said when he was just getting started he used to draw up a dozen or so roughs and drive all the way from his home in Electra to Fort Worth to show them to Ed Bateman for his horse magazine. Bateman would pick out perhaps one. Ace would drive back to Electra, ink it in, then drive to Fort Worth again and deliver it for five dollars. That easy money almost killed him, he said.

It killed my art career. I gave up the drawing board for the typewriter. And there, always, was Paul Patterson, helping, encouraging, telling me to stay with it despite the many, many rejections I received.

Teachers have a special kind of immortality, for the work they do lives on in their students and in later generations influenced by those students. Even Paul probably does not know how many students he taught during all his years in Sanderson, Crane, and finally in Sierra Blanca. They must run into many thousands. If he touched their lives a fraction as much as he touched mine, he has left a legacy beyond price. No amount of money could ever buy it.

He has been my teacher, my mentor, and best of all, always, my friend.

I thank you, Paul Patterson.

ENDNOTES

1. This paper was presented as part of a special session dedicated to honoring Paul at the 1990 meeting in Kingsville.

Elmer Kelton, Evelyn Stroder, and Paul Patterson at Horsehead Crossing, February 1995. (Photo by Joe Allen)

14

Paul Patterson, Master Teacher[1]

by Evelyn Stroder[1]

Soon after I retired from teaching, Paul Patterson gave me my first membership in the Texas Folklore Society, with the admonition that he wanted me to "write something" for the Society. He knows I love to write, and I love history and folklore. But, much as I like to do research and be around other writers, I seldom go much farther than a news story or a newspaper feature with those loves. But Paul, who has a wonderful way of encouraging and motivating his friends just as he did his students, has perennially questioned me about whether I'm working on anything.

Now it serves you right, Paul, that I get to write about you.

I know I'm speaking to folks who already know about, and have often shown appreciation for, Paul Patterson the writer, the humorist, the storyteller. So how do I, having known him for only about half his life, have the audacity to tell this group anything about Paul Patterson? Simply by being one of the fortunate few having taught school with him, and the only person to succeed Paul in the journalism classroom.

We've spent some wonderful hours in what Paul calls the "clearing house"—the teachers' lounge. We've swapped tales over the copy machine and the coffee cups, discussing everything from education (on which we mostly agree) to politics (on which we mostly don't), and I was a better teacher for that, as well as for other, more specific helps which I will tell later.

But though I have learned a great deal from Mr. Pat, the school teacher, I never sat in his classroom. So for this research I got to do something I love best—talking with some of our old (well, former, but they're getting old fast) students and fellow teachers.

Call this an exposé, Paul, of your day job.

From those former students and fellow teachers I learned that his writing and storytelling skills—sense of humor, feel for drama, gift of words, understanding of people, and the like—served as well in teaching. And his good citizenship, love of country, and empathy for fellow man were conveyed to, and remain in, the hearts of his students.

That sense of humor was often self-effacing. Early in the year in Spanish class, according to K. V. Murphy, "Mr. Pat" referred to his "gotch-eye" and said the students would never know for sure when he was looking at them. Then he told a story from his army days, about a sergeant who was also gotch-eyed and how Paul and that sergeant were never sure when each other was looking. "He made us laugh," K. V. said, "put us at ease, and made a good point, too."

In another jibe at himself, Paul made a point about honest decision-making. This story was relayed by Gary Edmiston: Lawrence Welk, on concert tour, hired Paul to haul a piano to the Rankin Hotel and paid him in concert tickets for all three nights. The third night was Sunday, and Paul had enjoyed the first two so much that he decided to flip a coin to decide whether to go to church or the concert. "I had to flip several times before I could attend the concert," he said.

Fun and dramatics were often a classroom element. In journalism class, tests were in the form of contests, and students wrote and produced occasional plays relating to issues of the school paper, with their teacher giving enough leeway for all kinds of creativity to surface.

Word choices were made important to his students. Eddy Smith tells that he will always remember not to use the word *cabron* carelessly, as he learned in Spanish class that this word for "old goat" could get one into trouble. This use of humor to make lessons stick in students' minds was reported to me many times over. Marva Lee Taylor Hughes said that she wishes she had taken better notes.

"The wit and tall tales would have made a wonderful souvenir," she said. "What could easily have been a boring lesson on verb conjugation became fun and therefore memorable." She hasn't had much occasion to use her Spanish these last thirty years, but said, "I still can say the Pledge of Allegiance in Spanish—and remember Mr. Pat with it."

The Pledge of Allegiance. Of course. Citizenship and love of country are themes flowing through any subject taught by Mr. Pat.

Crane's loss was Sierra Blanca's gain when he and Marge moved down there for the last nine years of their teaching careers. His writing skills were of direct value to fifth through eighth graders there, as he wrote plays for the students to present. Students portrayed historical figures in the Bicentennial play, *In the Land of the Free Include Me*, in which historical truths are interwoven with modern democratic concepts. Here is a portion of the Molly Pitcher monologue, and I'm sure student participants, as well as the audience, learned some history, plus—well, just listen for the subtle acknowledgment of an equal rights principle:

> I was born in a period way back when
> The breaks, the honors all went to men.
> We realize now that it wasn't fair,
> Which didn't keep me from doing my share—

Is that not a teacher for you—building character with the implication that having things "not fair" shouldn't keep one from doing her share?

And this couplet from the same play conveys the poignancy of our continuing emigration enigma. Kids at Sierra Blanca would understand this:

> It takes the U.S. Border Patrol to know what America is
>   all about
> They catch thousands slipping in but not one slipping out.

Another value along with subject matter was the importance of education. Martha Bullock said she knew education was important to the Pattersons when Mr. Pat told the class how he and Marge put aside twenty-five cents a day (the price of a pack of cigarettes then, though they didn't smoke) for travel. "They went to Europe and all over with the money," she said. "When he taught us world history, we felt as though we had been to those same places."

I heard but ONE negative comment about Paul Patterson; ironically, it was passed on to me by Paul himself with, as you might know, a chuckle. The comment did not apply to his mistakes, or even to faulty techniques, and I tell it here only because it is ludicrous beyond insulting.

"To Paul Patterson, the person who inspired me to write," was inscribed in the front of the self-published, spiral-bound book. Then, in the text, the author said the fact that his journalism teacher, Paul Patterson, had published two "not very good" books had inspired this person—whom I will not name here—to try to have a book published, also! The former student also said that he doubted Paul's books sold many copies. I wonder whether he knows that my copy of one of them is now valued at $250. And I was of course reminded of several successful writers who give Paul credit for inspiring/leading them into the field.

People like Jeff Henderson, assistant dean at Southwest Texas State College at San Marcos, who is the author of many magazine articles. Jeff still remembers Paul's remark in the cafeteria line at Crane High School: "Jeff, I'll make a writer out of you yet."

And Elmer Kelton, who says Paul was a primary influence on him. "I had always wanted to be a writer from age eight or nine. Paul gave me the idea that a practical way to get into it was through journalism," Elmer said. He recalls that Paul was always gentle natured and easy to get along with, but was no "snap" teacher.

"At the University of Texas I found much the same style in journalism prof DeWitt Reddick," Kelton said. "But he did not give away good grades, either. You had to work for them." No coincidence. Just another of life's interesting cycles. Soon after

Paul had begun teaching in Crane, feeling himself underqualified, he set about studying in the summer—in Austin—with Dr. Reddick, whom he greatly respected. Takes one to know one, wouldn't you say?

It is significant that these examples, fresh and clear as they sound, are coming from years after the fact. Some of the folks who talk with animation about what Mr. Pat meant to them are grandparents themselves now (Paul, remember, left the regular classroom in 1977), but the effectiveness of a good teacher remains forever in one's makeup.

I had some good teachers in college, and other good teachers/mentors on the job. Paul was one of those. In forty-seven years, Crane had two journalism teachers. Paul Patterson led the program beginning in 1940, when he and Clint Carroll showed up looking for jobs in the oil field town where all the teachers except two had been fired—for being seen at a bar in town.

That's another story one of us needs to research some time, Paul.

When L. L. Martin, superintendent, mentioned that a journalism teacher was needed, Clint said, "Paul's a writer. He can handle that without any trouble." Handle it he did, but Paul says it was only with the help of the students, who gave him "on-the-job training," beginning with headline writing. The next summer found Paul in Austin, in that workshop I mentioned earlier.

When Paul eased out of the job in 1962 and 1963, I moved into it with mixed feelings. I was excited to be teaching my first love, but I knew I could not measure up to such a beloved institution as he already was. And I had known what it was like to follow a great teacher, especially when that teacher was going to stay around. I had seen disappointment and maybe belligerence in the question, "Why is Mr. Pat quitting?" So I explained that he was needed in the same school for an unusually high enrollment in Spanish and Texas history.

Oh well, I was already fond of Mr. Pat and, knowing he would not deliberately discourage or undermine me, I simply hoped for the best. I didn't know how lucky I was. Some students who had worked on the yearbook the year before were quite proprietary of their project and did not like for the new teacher to make ANY changes, however small. In fact, a few even went to their old sponsor to talk about me—just once. I don't know what he said, but those students found that, while he still loved them—in fact, because he still loved them—he would have nothing but support for their new teacher. Whatever I was able to accomplish in that position for the next twenty-six years got its jump-start from Paul Patterson, his presence and his precedents.

From the first day I appreciated his presence, and not only because of his confidence in my abilities. He was just down the hall, physically and mentally, whenever I had a question to ask or a woe to express. And his precedents—ah, he left such a trail of tradition that was not stick-in-the-mud, fun that provided for serious accomplishment, and a lightheartedness that still demanded student accountability!

For that trail he also left a guidebook and a map. The guidebook was Dr. DeWitt Reddick's *Journalism and the High School Paper*, autographed by Dr. Reddick and annotated by Paul Patterson, from those summer workshops. The map was in the form of highly detailed lesson plans—meticulously choreographed, step-by-step—for the first six weeks of Journalism I, the only "J" course offered in Crane then, with word-by-word scripting, even for lectures.

Those Patterson notes did wonders for a too-stiff, too-prim, green young teacher. The witticisms in his clever illustrations were such that I could, with a few adjustments such as changing of names in the examples, come out with some successful class lectures and illustrations. These were first-year journalism students, thank goodness, and if they thought I was very clever as I introduced them to the world of newspapering, well—how were they to know my lively wordage had come from the master teacher?

For example, focusing on thoroughness as a quality of a good reporter, the notes would say: "*Mary Anne* [I would fill in a name in my class] here is going to make her first parachute jump. Does she care whether the person who packed her 'chute had skipped only one part of the directions?" Or, in presenting elements of news value, the notes would say, with regard to nearness: "Which story would you read first—'1,000 in Asia on verge of starvation,' or '*Mike Jones* and *Martha Smith* faint in cafeteria line?'"

Paul, you do forgive me for plagiarizing, don't you?

Journalism isn't the only one of my classes to benefit from Paul. For a few years during which I taught world history, he was one of four wonderful resource persons, all high school teachers who had been in service during World War II. Those four days of presentations, with questions-and-answers between the students and the former servicemen, were some of my most inspired teaching days. Each one—all great teachers themselves—observed a particular theme in his experiences.

Paul, do you remember that your theme was "getting the big picture," the concept that, no matter how pointless any particular mission or activity seemed at the time, the day came when you saw that the activity had its part in ending the war?

And I am not the only fellow teacher Paul helped along the way. His "Timely Tips for Teachers" presentation at the meeting of the Texas Joint Council of Teachers of English inspired hundreds of us to love our students one by one, to encourage them, and to believe in and demand the best from each one.

Retirement or not, Paul has never quit teaching. His storytelling captivates audiences of all ages in many places; and, as we all know, to hear a well-crafted story is to learn—in the most painless way possible—about human nature, about words, and about the world. Mary Anne Bullard Reed, Paul's student in Crane some fifty-five years ago, often attended the Texas Folklife Festival in San Antonio to hear his Old West tales. This is her account of one scene:

The temperature in San Antonio in August was over 100 degrees, there was very little breeze stirring, and shade was sparse. This didn't seem to affect Mr. Patterson or his listeners. Seated in a large wooden rocker, he spun story after story to a gathering crowd of all ages. Children in particular were mesmerized and let their ice cream melt while they watched him like Saturday morning cartoons. I stood back under a shade tree and held back tears. I couldn't help wondering who will be the storyteller when people like Paul Patterson are gone. It's scary to think that, by his own declaration, Paul might never have made it to the classroom except for the relentless pursuit by his high school principal/coach/teacher, whom he calls "Old Prof."

Soon after graduation from Rankin High School, Paul—"vowing never to look another schoolhouse in the door"—took a job forty miles from town, cowboying. But Old Prof hunted him down to coax and help Paul go to Alpine to work AND go to college. Who knows the long-reaching effects of Old Prof's diligence? I think there must be many of us who would like to thank him for that. I wonder who gave "Old Prof" his nudge into education. Teachers really do, as astronaut Christa McAuliffe said, "touch the future." The chain of a teacher's influence is the original "never ending story." Just as it has no identifiable beginning, it has no end while this earth lasts. We are privileged to know one of its most sparkling links.

Not that Paul wouldn't have been a good cowboy. John Webb tells that one thing his father, "a cowboy's cowboy," had in common with the others was their admiration for Paul Patterson. As a child John always looked forward to the Sunday ropings, where Paul the announcer "added a great deal of class with his quick wit and good sense of humor."

But in high school John found Paul a different type teacher who treated the students as if they were equals, and—well, in John's own words: "He was much more athletic than I had imagined. He could walk on his hands better than any of my classmates and was one of only two people I have ever known who could lie flat on his back and jump to his feet without using his hands or a rocking motion, in a movement we called a 'kip.'"

Later, John had Paul in to participate in a special program for former POW's at the VA medical center where John works. He told them that when he had been cowboying, friends said, "Paul, you ought to be a teacher." Then, when he became a teacher, some of the same people said, "Paul, maybe you ought to be a cowboy."

And I'm glad Paul Patterson never quit being either one.

ENDNOTES

1. This paper was presented at the 2001 meeting in San Angelo; Paul Patterson was in attendance. It also appeared previously as "Paul Patterson, My Master Teacher" in the *Permian Historical Annual*, Vol. XLI (December 2001).

15

A Pecos
Pilgrim's Pilgrimage:
The Prose Narratives
of Paul Patterson[1]

by Lawrence Clayton

The vast, rough stretches of the Pecos River region epitomize West Texas to many people. Despite its being sometimes labeled "the graveyard of many a cowman's dreams" because of its droughts, it has produced a number of distinctive individuals. Paul Patterson is the son of this trans-Pecos region and knows its rough landscape, thorny flora, outlaw fauna, and strong and colorful people firsthand. Although perhaps best known as a cowboy poet and oral storyteller, Paul Patterson has produced a number of informative and humorous prose pieces detailing life in West Texas from early days to the present. Some of these tales deal with his experience with cowboys and livestock, but others are classic tales adapted to the West Texas scene.

Patterson's prose efforts to communicate the life he has studied are marked by a distinct style. His quick wit and skillful use of double entendre and innuendo for comic effect rank alongside his use of outrageous comparison and hyperbole. His interjections are among his best comic devices. The rhythm and pattern of repetition of his speech growing out of his remarkable gift in oral language are as evident in the patterns of prose as they are in his poetry.

His prose is subject to exaggerated description and linguistic embellishment by alliteration and allusion. Although the life of the cowboy on the frontier is the grain from which he derives the flour of his loaf, it is his yeasty humor that produces the staff of life—the humor of the cowboy on the frontier when that frontier was Upton and Crane counties in the 1920s, 30s, and 40s. Although Patterson's efforts reflect personal experiences with the life he is depicting, his style is punctuated with evidence of his formal education through allusions and outright references to classical or "respectable" literature. For example, in one of his essays, "The

Old-Time Cowboy Inside Out," he alludes to Gray's "Elegy Written in a Country Churchyard." He echoes Faulkner in the preface to *Crazy Women in the Rafters* when he says, "We not only survived but thrived." And in his balanced, alliterative style he describes his father thusly: "Some said it was a lack of savvy; a shortage of smart. Not so. It was simply a case of two soft a heart in too hard a time."[2]

In addition, in *Crazy Women in the Rafters* he refers to Kipling's Tommy in "On the Road to Mandalay." The following quotation shows the broad culture of Patterson, who simply preferred the life of the cowboy, which his father referred to as "the only calling on God's green earth worthy of considering at all." Following his first look at Upland, Texas, with a population of slightly over fifty including, as he says, "the cow ponies and one lone hound dog," he goes on to say, "The chimes of London's Big Ben, the deep-voiced bonging of the ten-foot bronze Mori of the torre dell' Orlogio on Saint Mark's Square in Venice, the tolling of temple bells the length and breadth of Spain and Old Mexico—all 'as sounding brass and tinkling cymbals' compared to the ring and sing of cowboy spurs in Upland that day. Ditto for the rest of the world's sights and smells."[3]

In remarks in *Cuttin' Beddin'*, folklorist Jim Byrd, a close friend to Patterson, says that the material is "humorous family history, centered around a peculiar folk custom of the past, told with unique humor and verve."[4] Byrd is correct. The material is what we have come to call family folklore. Mody Boatright, in "The Family Saga as a Form of Folklore," had earlier called this kind of material family saga, "lore that tends to cluster around families, or often the patriarchs or matriarchs of families which is preserved and modified by oral transmission and which is believed to be true."[5] He says further that this material is "not concerned with a type of tale, but with clusters of types, not with a motif, but with many motifs."[6]

In his first published volume, *Sam McGoo and Texas Too* (1947), Patterson set the pattern for his later work as he relates tales of the McGoo family: Sam, Yulick, Oglesby, Yancy, Absalom, Rumsey, Hankinson, Tewksberry, Ellick, Seaburn, Pendergast, Sappington, Fleecy, Shackelford, Ostrow, Plunkham, and Sandhill (the narrator). The volume, illustrated by Patterson's former student and long-time friend, novelist Elmer Kelton, contains outrageous tales from the "family" history. For example, Sam was a fancy dresser: "For a belt, he wore a rattlesnake skin with the rattler still in it—alive. No other snake would do, Sam says, because anybody knows no other kind of snake has a button. Since Sam didn't have the heart, he says, to take an innocent life he left the snake alive. He had to admit a live rattlesnake had its disadvantages. For one thing, it was always crawling off his pants. For another thing, and the main thing, it was too slow. Some mornings, Sam says, he'd have to nag at the snake five minutes before he could get it to sink its fangs into Sam's stomach and thus secure his pants. The snake's other end, the button, of course, was fastened into a belt loop of Sam's pants."[7]

Particularly is Boatright's definition of family saga applicable to Patterson's *Crazy Women in the Rafters*, subtitled *Memories of a Texas Boyhood*. Patterson's father, J. D. Patterson, is the patriarch; lesser satellites include his mother, brothers, and sisters. In a larger sense, the luminaries of his other tales, especially in *Pecos Tales*, are his extended family—cowboys he has come to know on such ranches as the Booger Y, Hoover, and others. Patterson's affections for and affinity with these members of a folk group, to which he himself also belonged as an integral part in his younger days, is evident in the care he has taken to record anecdotes, and incidents about interesting personalities. I have tended to think of this kind of material in the framework of "front porch tales," since most of the ones I have heard were told in that setting or one similar to it—around the kitchen table after meals, or in the living room around the stove in the winter. I have also heard them told by men huddled in the darkness on horseback on the backside of a pasture as they wait for enough daylight to ride off on a roundup, or sitting in a saddlehouse waiting for an infrequent rainstorm to blow over. Even though in "The Old-Time Cowboy Inside Out" Patterson decries the tendency of cowboys to gather at the local Dairy Queen, I know that in Albany, as local historian Morris Ledbetter says, "There will be more bad horses ridden and wild cattle worked in the 'Queenie' on a Sunday morning than on any range in West Texas." Even Robert Reinhold, writer for the *New York Times*, found that bit of wisdom to be true, for he wrote an article on the "Queenie" for the *Times* of June 18, 1987.

The purpose of these tales, when told by cowboys, is to reinforce their verve and bolster their courage for the demanding life they lead. They derive catharsis by telling and retelling the anecdotes. They are thereby able to retain their humor but still be reminded of what can happen to them if attention wanders—a broken arm or leg, a fractured collar bone, or worse. Many a cowboy has died under a fallen horse. Humor is a great healer, but it is also a useful tool to teach the newcomer—the greenhorn—of the danger of a foolish act without the uninitiated having to undergo the experience himself.

Even a casual examination of Patterson's various works convinces one of the broad and perceptive nature of the man's insights. *Pecos Tales* is a finely printed book by Bill Wittlif, one distributed as an extra volume to the members of the Texas Folklore Society in 1967. The material, according to the preface, "consists of anecdotes, accidents, and incidents that occurred to west Texans when people in progress advanced at a slower rate."[8] These pieces are relaxed, mostly short anecdotes of the sort lost in the loom of time as the years go by and oral tradition loses its storehouse by loss of memory and death. Anyone who would understand the cowboy, however, should study his humor. Patterson has done so firsthand and documented time, place, and individual. The earthy humor and outright laughter share time with the realization of loneliness, hard times, and demanding, dangerous work with cantankerous people and stock.

In "Night Horse Nightmare" Patterson depicts the fate of three cowboys, one of whom is himself, in a line camp, set afoot when Buster, the night horse, manages to escape on a romantic venture for a herd of mares in a nearby pasture and leaves the three men to a fate worse than death—afoot and in danger of having to walk into the headquarters to tell the boss of their plight. The shame prompts the three to risk life and limb and to sacrifice an old Dodge car to the chance that ends only when Buster is starved for water and finally trapped, thus saving the men from the ultimate humiliation for a cowboy. This humorous episode based on Patterson's own experience is also set in verse and is one of his best informative and entertaining tales.

In an unpublished paper read to the Texas Folklore Society in El Paso, Patterson explained that the cowboy is "in no ways wise, sex wise," and he followed the presentation the next year with "The Old-Time Cowboy Inside Out," in which he reveals the heart and soul of the cowboy and recounts at the same time some of his experiences after high school graduation in 1929, when he went to work on a ranch at the "foot of King Mountain in Upton County."[9] A fall from a can-tankerous horse convinces Patterson that his future lies in a more educated direction, and he leaves that life to enroll in Sul Ross College, now Sul Ross State University, in Alpine.

In *Cuttin' Beddin'*, a small collection published by his friend Art Hendrix, Patterson relates some of the humorous but hard facts of life perpetuated by the necessity of sharing one's bedroll or other couch of repose with a stranger or friend, or even a "perfect" stranger, as did the

The cover of Paul Patterson's *Cuttin' Beddin'*.

farmer's daughter who shared a roll with a traveling salesman. Her defense is simply that this could be "that very angel it speaks of in Hebrews 13:2,"[10] that is, an angel unaware.

For a collection entitled *Texas and Christmas*, edited by Judy Alter and Joyce Roach, Patterson wrote out a localized tale of entertaining an angel unaware by the family of Uncle Bud Roark's niece, who find themselves "four miles northwest of the pump station on the Southern Pacific Railroad in Terrill County, Texas."[11] Out of a snow-shrouded landscape, a stranger appears to share a meal of fried venison, gravy, hot biscuits, tomato chow-chow, red beans, and vinegar pie. He leaves no tracks as he departs, a puzzle for the family in the house.

"Cowboy Comedians and Humorists" in the *Golden Log* sketches several men Patterson knew. Lee Reynolds, cowboy humorist around Upland in the days of Patterson's youth, was accustomed to being alone—not the same as lonely—and often lived for months without seeing another human being. He sought various ways to break the boredom. He once resorted to roping a Texas and Pacific train in Odessa. Patterson also includes Bud Colbaugh, a San Angelo cowboy who told famous bronc rider Booger Red Privitt that if he was as ugly as Privitt, he would shoot himself. Harry Wade, from a ranch in Irion County, and Mose Rucker, from the 6666, also impressed Patterson as humorists. He concludes that cowboy humor is not quite what it was in the good old days, especially those represented by these old time humorists.

In "The Cowboy's Code," found in *The Sunny Slopes of Long Ago*, Patterson gives a humorous and anecdotal explanation of the twelve rules of cowboy behavior ranging from never letting go of a horse no matter how bad or snakey it was, to avoiding petty thievery. The anecdotes make the piece both informative and entertaining. "Hit's Tough Bein' a Texan," in *Horsing Around: Contemporary Cowboy Humor*, explores how difficult it is to be a tough Texan, especially in the eyes of those from out of state who don't really care for Texans at all. "Showdown at Sun Up" is an anecdote about how Fush Patterson triggers a trap and catches a bedeviling

Bob Harlen, half-Mustang gray horse, that has dealt the family misery, especially by leaving them afoot, "five miles from water and twenty miles from home."[12]

Patterson wrote several anecdotes involving Ace Reid, the cowboy cartoonist. In "Well, Well, Well," he relates how Ace and his old buddy traveled to the Cross S Ranch in Arizona looking for excitement. Ace finds he's riding on the one forbidden horse of the hundred and seventy-five he is helping to herd—a Roman-nosed roan outlaw. When Ace tries the brute, the two end up down a well. Ace manages to escape by tying onto several buzzards that come to eat him and old Roany, but in walking back to camp, Ace falls in the well again. He escapes this time on his own when the boss tosses a rattlesnake down the well, and both he and Roany ascend from the depths.

"Rags to Riches to Rags" is another Ace Reid story, this time about how Ace becomes rich from his cartoons and changes his lifestyle. Ace stocks his ranch with good cattle and begins to live the good life, with the narrator going along for the ride and riches. Then Ace sells out, moves "down-state amongst sheep-persons," and begins to economize or miserize and cut back on his old buddy. Then he fires his old buddy, who goes through outrageous efforts to get his job back and concludes that anyone cheap enough to keep sheep is too cheap to work for. The piece is given in classic Patterson dialect.

Patterson is interested in American cowboys, but from a trip to Australia, he wrote a number of unpublished papers contrasting the life of the American cowboy in West Texas with that of the Australian cowboy. "The Texan That Thunk Small" in *Horsing Around* is a result of that experience. Patterson discovers that the Australian notion of "big" in the Territory makes a braggart Texan ashamed and embarrassed at the smallness of things in Texas.

One of the highlights of Patterson's career was the production of his play *Ups and Downs of Crane Town*, which played to a full house, he says, "on a hot August night with the air conditioning gone out" on the occasion of Crane's fiftieth anniversary.[13] The action opens as Adam and Eve approach a sign on a hot, sandy landscape. The sign points to Crane city, a place which Adam announces is "as far away as we can possibly get from Paradise" (Act I, Scene I). Adam changes the arrow pointing to Crane Town so that it points down, a fact Methusalah agrees with in the next scene. Just being around town causes the old-timer to feel as if he's aged seven hundred years over night. Additional biblical characters in the play include Moses, Job, and a number of others.

Patterson includes as well several personalities of the area: some Booger Y cowboys, Bill and Ardeth Allman, Tom and Jewell Hogan, Buck and Beal Kelton, and George Teague. The latter is roping stock and dragging it aboard Noah's ark. It is Jewell Hogan who doubts the notion that when Noah's flood came, Crane County got half an inch. She prefers to believe it got none at all. The hard times depicted in the play show the verve and vigor of frontier humor. The people laugh at adversity and push on, whether it is in Crane or on the Booger Y. The badinage and humor reflect the work of a serious, perceptive humorist. Although Patterson's published prose tales are relatively few in number, his oral performances at such places as the Folklife Festival in San Antonio, the gathering of South Plains poets and storytellers in Hobbs, New Mexico in 1989, his poetry recitations at Alpine at the Texas Cowboy Poetry Gathering, at the Centennial Cow Camp in Kerrville in 1989, and a host of others as well as papers read at the annual meetings of the Texas Folklore Society have left us all richer for the experiences. We know more about life in West Texas and life in general from the humor of Paul Patterson.

In a sense, these stories are universal. They are adapted to a particular setting—the time and place—but they hold in common the same theme of adventures, tragedies, hard times survived, and dedication to carry on found in many literatures. This element of the culture of any folk group must not be lost. Thanks to Paul Patterson, those of Upton County in the early decades of this century are recorded—safe and sound—for posterity to enjoy and learn from. Here is the primary source material of the cultural historian.

These are not political wars and include no bank records or ranch account books. Here instead are the lives of people who give the west the golden aura that we see in retrospect. We glamorize and glorify those lives, but one can see beneath the humor the hard times, laughter, tears, and heartache of pioneer ranch folk who "not only survived but thrived."

ENDNOTES

1. This paper was presented as part of a special session dedicated to honoring Paul at the 1990 meeting in Kingsville. It was also published in *Southwestern American Literature* Special Edition: Paul Patterson-Writer, Folklorist, Volume 15, Number 2, Spring 1990.
2. Patterson, Paul. *Crazy Women in the Rafters: Memories of a Texas Boyhood*. Norman: University of Oklahoma Press, 1976. 4.
3. Ibid. 16.
4. Patterson, Paul. *Cuttin' Beddin': More Pecos Tales*. Ed. Art Hendrix. Commerce, TX 1987. 14.
5. Boatright, Mody. "The Family Saga as a Form of Folklore." *The Family Saga and other Phases of American Folklore*. Urbana: University of Illinois Press, 1958.
6. Ibid.
7. Patterson, Paul. *Sam McGoo and Texas Too*. 1947. Commerce: CowHill Press, 1994. 33.
8. Patterson, Paul. *Pecos Tales*. Austin. The Encino Press, 1967. vii.
9. Patterson, Paul. "The Old-time Cowboy Inside Out." *Sonovagun Stew: A Folklore Miscellany*. Ed. F. E. Abnerthy. Dallas: SMU Press, 1985. 76.
10. Patterson. *Cuttin' Beddin'*.
11. Patterson, Paul. "An Angel Unawares?" *Texas and Christmas: A collection of traditions, memories & folklore*. Judy Alter and Joyce Gibson roach, eds. Fort Worth: TCU Press, 1983. 35.
12. Patterson, Paul. "Showdown at Sunup." *Hoein' the Short Rows*, Ed. F. E. Abernethy. Dallas: SMU Press, 1987. 127.
13. Patterson, Paul. Letter to the author. 10 December, 1989

IV.

College Years

16

Small-Town Texas Wisdom

by J. G. "Paw-Paw" Pinkerton

When I was old enough to drive legally, Mister Barney Ragland asked me to come and work in his store with him and his wife, Mis' Mattie. They owned a Mom & Pop grocery at the east end of Main Street in my hometown of Junction, Texas. It was a small, rectangular, stucco, cinder block service station and grocery store painted white, with *Raglands Grocery* in black letters across the front. My folks bought most of their groceries and gasoline from Mis' Mattie and Mister Barney. The year was 1942, and I worked there after school and on weekends, except for Sunday mornings when I attended church with my parents.

The Raglands taught me all the things I had to learn to serve the customers who drove into the service station or came in the grocery store. In those days you waited on everyone. I already knew how to service a car, but I had to learn how to slice, weigh, and price meat and to wrap it in white butcher paper. All fresh foods were wrapped in paper and tied with string. People didn't go around the store with a basket gathering up the things they wanted to buy. They'd stand in front of the counter that divided the store and tell you they wanted a can of peas and you'd go over to the shelf and get a can of peas, and so it went. I liked waiting on people and I really liked working for Mis' Mattie and Mister Barney.

Mister Barney was a medium sized man. He always wore khaki pants and a dark shirt with an old blue, narrow-brim felt hat pulled down low on his forehead. While he was courteous enough, he never made small talk. He left that to Mis' Mattie and me. I noticed early on he'd rather either Mis' Mattie or me waited on the customers. Though, if a lady came in and he had to wait on her, he was always careful to first remove his hat. I soon learned that if

Mister Barney didn't take off his hat, he was making a comment about the woman standing in front of the counter.

Mis' Mattie was slightly shorter than Mister Barney and a little rounder. She'd formerly been a school teacher and wore her hair in a bun at the nape of her neck. Usually, she'd have a yellow pencil poked through the bun and when she couldn't find her pencil, we'd have to remind her where it was. Most often, Mis' Mattie wore some plain cotton print dress covered in front with a bib apron in a dark color. Over that, if it was cool weather, she'd have on a dun colored sweater. She hustled about energetically and eagerly smiled as she waited on customers. She enjoyed chatting away at some news of the day. If she was working alone in the back storage room, I'd hear her softly whistling to herself. Both of the Raglands were fine people with good hearts and no pretense.

Mister Barney had tried to be a rancher, but it hadn't worked out. He'd lost his ranch in the Depression and they'd gone to Old Mexico and worked for several years in The American Grocery, owned by Mis' Mattie's brother in Mexico City. Consequently, both of them were fluent in Spanish and about half of our customers were of Mexican descent. But Barney was not one to be living out of the country. He had served in World War I and he was a true American citizen and soldier. They came back to Junction, borrowed money from a local bank, and started their little store in the mid-1930s. Like I said, when I was old enough to have a driver's license, I went to work for them.

Mister Barney had a problem. He drank. When I was working for him I would say he drank a fifth of whiskey each day. The amusing thing was he didn't think anyone knew, and it was the worst kept secret in town. You could always tell when Mister Barney was about to take a nip. He would go and find the bottle from some place he'd hidden it, tuck it under his coat and go around the corner of the building to the men's restroom. There he'd have a nip. Most often, as I remember it, he drank bourbon. Then he would rinse his mouth out with Listerine Mouthwash. I figured some days he drank just about as much Listerine Mouthwash as he did bourbon.

On the rare days when he'd have a little too much, Mis' Mattie would say, "Barney, are you coming down with a headache?" That was her signal that he'd overindulged. I would drive him home and come back and Mis' Mattie and I would run the store until time to close. Then, Mis' Mattie would drive home in their black 1939 Chevrolet two-door coupe, and I would ride my bicycle across the South Llano River bridge to the house where I lived with my parents.

On occasion, when I was driving Mister Barney home and he'd really had too much to drink, he'd want to spend a little time thanking me for working for him and Mis' Mattie. Then, he'd say he was going to raise my pay by five dollars a week. At first, I doubted he'd remember what he'd said, but he always did. Mister Barney was a man of his word, with or without too much bourbon.

Mis' Mattie was a kind, generous woman. All over Junction there were people who needed help, and Mis' Mattie helped them. She would send me out with basket after basket of groceries to deliver to poor people who couldn't possibly pay. Sometimes, if a person was sick and Mis' Mattie knew about it, she'd have me stop at the City Drug Store and pick up some patent medicine to help them recover.

When I'd make a delivery, many of the people would say, "Now, son, you tell Mis' Mattie that we'll pay her just as soon as we can." After a while I came to know that they weren't ever going to be able to pay Mis' Mattie, but that didn't stop her from giving them food.

Every few days, she would send me by to see about one old woman and her retarded grown daughter. They lived in two rooms of an old house that was half-burned-out. In my mind's eye, I can still see those old scorched rafters black against the blue Texas sky. Mis' Mattie would tell me I was to go right on in the house and see if those people had any food. She said if I knocked at the door and asked, the mother would always say, "Now, son, we're just fine. We don't need anything. Tell Mis' Mattie thank you, anyway." But Mis' Mattie said, "You're not ever to let her stop you at the door.

The author, looking very young, at seventeen.

You're just to go right on in the house and look around and see if they have anything to eat." One day I went to that half-burned-out old house and there was not one thing to eat anywhere in the house except a shriveled up head of cabbage on the bottom shelf of a refrigerator that wasn't working.

People were poor but, even in their poverty, they had a lot of pride and did the best they could. After I'd been working for the Raglands about a year, I turned seventeen and was old enough to join the armed services. World War II was on and I kept begging my father until he finally agreed to sign my enlistment papers so I could join the Navy. Mister Barney was proud of me for going away to help fight in the war.

I was gone about two years before the war was over. When I came back, nothing would suit Mister Barney except for me to come back and work for him and Mis' Mattie. He already had two people working there but he just insisted I come back, so I went to work for them again. Only, now things were different. Mister Barney had me doing the ordering and pricing of the merchandise. I was soon in charge of all stocking of the store. I began to see that if Mister Barney kept on, I was going to be running everything.

One October day, Mis' Mattie said to me, "Son, I want you to stay back tonight and help me with the books." Helping Mis' Mattie with the books was something I did about once a month. We'd add up what people had charged on credit and send out statements so people would come in and pay what they owed. A lot of people ran up sizeable accounts with the Raglands, and I didn't think some of them would ever be able to pay what they owed. Mister Barney was just too softhearted to press for payment.

That night, I drove Mister Barney home and when I came back, Mis' Mattie and I closed the store. We turned out the lights in the front of the store and went back into the little office. I got out the charge books and the manual adding machine, ready to add up the accounts and write out statements. For a few moments, Mis' Mattie busied herself doing something in the stockroom. Then, when Mis' Mattie entered the office, she said to me, "Put the books away. That's not really why I asked you to stay back. There's something I want to say."

I put the books away and sat down facing her, wondering what might be about to happen. Business had slacked off lately. My heart began pumping hard. I tried not to show how concerned I suddenly felt that maybe I was going to be let go.

Mis' Mattie started by saying, "Son, there are some people who can live in a little town like Junction all their lives and find it quite satisfying, but I don't think you're one of them. If you stay here, Barney is going to go on giving you more and more work and pretty soon, you're going to be running the whole store. You'll like that because you like learning new things and you like being in charge. That'd be good for Barney and me, but it won't be good for you. I want you to go down to The University of Texas in Austin and get yourself an education.

"If you stay here, after a while you'll find you're not satisfied. Like most young men, you'll find a young woman and fall in love and get married. Then, the two of you will start having children. About the time you're in your middle thirties you'll come to realize you have never fulfilled the promise that lies within you. And you'll become restless with your life and maybe start drinking like Barney does. Or, even worse, start chasing after women.

"So, I want you to go down to The University of Texas. You've got the G.I. Bill and that'll pay for your books and tuition. You study whatever you want to be, only just make sure you can earn a living with it once you have your degree. Later on in life when you feel like you have fulfilled the promise that lies within you, you may decide to come back to Junction to live the rest of your life. Right now, the thing I think you should do is get an education."

She reached into her apron pocket and pulled out three hundred dollars in cash. She handed it me and said, "Now, you go down to Austin and enroll for the Spring semester. I want you to buy all the room and board you can with this money. Then, by the time this money is gone, if you're as smart as I think you are, you will have figured out how to stay there."

I took the money. I went down to Austin and enrolled in The University of Texas. Coming from a small town like Junction, I was scared, but Mis' Mattie was right—it was where I belonged. I knew that shortly after I got there. She was also right about something else. By the time the three hundred dollars was gone, I'd found a job working after hours and had figured out how I could stay there.

The years went by. I graduated from The University of Texas. I got a job and married. The three hundred dollars was always a secret between Mis' Mattie and me. She said it was her money. Mister Barney was never to know anything about it. After I married I would say to Mis' Mattie, "I can pay back the money now. I have it in the bank." She would say, "No, son, you keep the money. You keep it. One of these days, I'll find someone who needs the money more than you do and then I'll tell you where to send it." It wasn't until after our third child was born that I got a letter from Mis' Mattie. She wrote to say she had a friend down in Nixon, Texas who was sick and in a bad way and could sure use that money if I could afford to send it. Of course, I got the money together and sent it off.

Sometime after that I learned Mister Barney and Mis' Mattie had lost their store. They couldn't meet their loan payments, so the bank took over their store and sold it. I didn't know the couple who bought it, so I never went back.

Mis' Mattie and Mister Barney lived on a few years, but they are both gone now. When I'm back in Junction on a visit I always go by the cemetery where Mis' Mattie and Mister Barney lie buried under a great big mesquite tree and pay my respects. They only have foot markers on their graves. For some reason the family never raised headstones. But then, Mis' Mattie and Mister Barney never had any children.

Mis' Mattie and Mister Barney loom large in my life. Their small-town Texas wisdom still serves me well as I try to help others fulfill the promises that lie within them. Someday I'll be going back to Junction for good. My wife and I have bought burial plots not far from the mesquite tree that shelters their graves.

17

Aggie Incredibles

by Palmer Henry Olsen

Mortified & Demoted

I don't really know why I went to Texas A&M in 1912, but I enrolled with very high expectations. So, when I received my first scholastic schedule, I was shocked and mortified. Solid geometry and physics were the same texts I had finished in high school. I knew both thoroughly. Dean Puryear refused my strong plea for more advanced courses. He even laughed as he told me that a review would do me good. I was so disgusted I debated going home.

Hazing saved the day. I was quick, agile, and strong. Also, maybe strangely, I was blessed with an unusually tough hide. After a couple days, the hardest blows, with heavy leather belt or with bayonet, produced only temporary pink stripes. There was no pain. Running the gauntlet I would have made Daniel Boone or Kit Carson envious. I had a ball! In fact, any honors I received at A&M must have come because of my freshman speed, my tough skin, and my ready laughter.

In my first physics class, I explained to Prof. Skeeler about my hassle with Dean Puryear. He examined me thoroughly and had an exciting job waiting for me. It was my most pleasant experience at A&M.

Bonner Frizzell was my English teacher. Without ceremony, at our first lesson, he called the roll and told us to get a pencil and paper ready. Twenty simple words were given us to spell. *College* work? My God, I thought, am I now demoted to fourth grade? In one week all my hopes and dreams had been shattered. I had never cried, "I want my mamma," but now I needed help.

Again, hazing saved the day. There was something new and different every night. And considerable hope was renewed in my second English lesson. Frizzell explained why he had given a spelling quiz. Only two of us had spelled all words correctly. Five students from prestigious Ball High School had each missed more than ten words. All five were in "L" company, my company. For two weeks I had marveled at and maybe envied their city sophistication. Now, I had something to brag about.

To stay at A&M, I had to earn most of my expenses. At first only one job seemed available—juicing cows. But four a.m. and one good look at twenty Jerseys in a row was too much. Knocking over or digging stumps in a large field, where Highway 6 now traverses College grounds, was not bad but disgusting. Why should a thirty-five-year-old agricultural college have stumps and cultivate with a one-mule plow?

Dr. Bolton gave me hope. He wanted all windows in the new Electrical Engineering Building cleaned inside and out. Painters had splattered them. The building was next door to Austin Hall, my dormitory. Also, Dr. Bolton,

Cadet Palmer H. Olsen. The following description is found under his senior picture in the Texas A&M 1916 *Long Horn* yearbook: "A record which will hardly be equaled at A. & M. College has been made by this man, who is one of the strongest ever produced by any senior class of the school. His popularity among his classmates is shown by the fact that he has been president of his class for three consecutive years, his athletic ability by his truly wonderful baseball playing, his academic ability by the fact that he is a distinguished student, and his military ability by the high ranks which he has held. His amiability, his high moral standards, and his character as a real man, have created for him a reputation among his classmates that will live in their memory forever."

pleased with my work, allowed an hour for my fifty-minute vacant periods. Windows finished, I drilled countless three-quarter-inch holes in large marble slabs for switchboards in the basement.

Doomed To Die

On January 15, 1913, we had some of the most shocking and stunning events I have ever witnessed, peace or wartime. It was petrifying. Basketball season had just begun. Archer Koons had practiced the day before, eaten supper, was stricken ill and died in a few minutes. Cause of death was diagnosed as meningitis. W. C. McBirney, a freshman in Austin Hall, who had practiced with Koons, had eaten several big, juicy T-bone steaks. They had probably tasted too good, his stomach couldn't handle the overload, and now he was having a hard time riding his nightmare. His action was so loud and violent that all of Austin Hall was awakened. Some cadets already knew of Koon's death and, never having witnessed a wild nightmare, concluded that "Mac" had meningitis, too. He was rushed to the hospital, but everybody concluded that he was a dead duck. Uncertainty and fear ruled the roost.

At breakfast speculation was rife and ominous when a corps meeting was announced. No death march was ever more solemn than our trudge to Chapel. Even after we were seated, a morgue couldn't have been quieter. Shortly, Dr. Ehlinger, the lone College physician, appeared on the stage and began an effort to reassure and calm the students. He looked terribly tired and haggard. Hardly a word had been spoken when his talk was interrupted by a loud and desperate cry from the entrance of the Chapel, "Doctor, come here quick!"

Never have I witnessed such silence, awe, and portent of disaster. Our company was seated in the balcony; I sat next to the middle aisle. When Burl Cooper, a Clifton boy and friend, sitting two rows behind me suddenly slumped unconscious at my side, I suffered the most trying time of my life. Freshmen had no rights; could start no action. But when, for eternity, nobody made a move, I thought, "Well, come Hell or high water, I'm going to help Burl." Then, his captain and two sergeants picked Burl up and carried him downstairs. I learned later that he had merely fainted.

After a few minutes—moments of incredible suspense—Dr. Ehlinger appeared in a door at the back of the stage, leading a cadet by his ear. Doc made his point; fear was the greatest danger. Yet, one other cadet died that morning.

The Doc as Patient

Dr. Otto Ehlinger was an amiable and very competent college physician. But, he could be crusty and intolerant. Car owners in that time had no liberties or rights, though sometimes, when irked by some old farmer, they attempted to assert them. To the old hayseeds, the auto was an interloping hog that served no purpose but to scare their horses half to death.

One day, Doc, in somewhat of a hurry, was coming from Bryan on the very narrow and deep-sandy road along the railroad tracks. There were no paved roads around College at the time. Small hills of sand bordered the buggy-width road. Honking his raucus horn only scared a farmer's team, angered the old country coot and stiffened his neck. He yielded not an inch.

Doc, frustrated and furious, couldn't stand the strain. He'd show the old rustic a thing or two. But the loose sand was more of an obstacle than Doc had figured. Though silent, it had plenty to say. A small pile flipped his light tin lizzie touring car onto its top. The bows crumpled and the back of the front seat pinned the furious doctor face down against the fabric top and the ground. He couldn't move, his arms locked. To add insult to injury, the wagon master calmed his team, took a good look at Doc, gave him some indelicate advice and drove away. Doc had to wait some time to be rescued.

Lathes & Ladies

H. E. Smith was a very young man, maybe only a country bumpkin, I thought when I first saw him. So we were kin. Though not an impressive speaker, his earnestness and knowledge seemed above reproach. But he was easily embarrassed and would blush the easiest and reddest I ever saw.

On a very hot and sultry Saturday morning at eleven o'clock near the end of school in June, 1913, Prof. Smith had the lathe as his subject. The very large class filled the room but seemed half asleep.

After going over the speed gears, the chuck, and other exposed parts at the top of the lathe, Prof. Smith came around to the front. "This," he said, touching the plate below the bed, "is what we call the apron of the lathe. Now, let's lift the apron and see what we can see."

I'm sure that none of you has ever witnessed or heard so tumultuous an explosion as burst upon Prof. Smith. His face seemed aflame with embarrassment. Only after several seconds could he find the voice to dismiss the class. We never saw or heard or learned exactly what was under the apron.

As The Case Might Be

Hugh Cassidy was one of the younger, more affable professors, but he had one fault. At the beginning, after every pause, and always at the close of every sentence, he'd say, "As the case might be." It became ridiculous and distracting. I decided to try something.

Cassidy's lectern was in a corner near the entrance. Benches reached across the room to a blackboard. I decided to sit at the end of the second bench so, unnoticed, I could keep score. In no time at all, I had a flock of x's, domino scoring fashion.

After twenty-five x's, the class became unusually alert; a few couldn't hide their smiles. Prof. Hugh became suspicious. Puzzled, he began slyly examining his person. Nothing seemed awry. However, with each new "as the case might be" the merriment became more obvious, the laughter less controllable, and the professor's puzzlement more unbearable. When the score on the blackboard showed forty-five tell-tale crosses after only a few moments, the class exploded. Professor Cassidy exploded too. "Get the Hell out of here," he barked.

At our practice session a few days later, Hugh and I were early. He promptly asked me what had been wrong. I pointed to the board and my x's. "That's a domino count of your 'As the case might be,'" I said. Startled, he paused, but then gave me a hug and said, "Thank you." He was a true sport.

Ticks & Tact

In my days at A&M, tick fever was a serious problem for farmers. Dr. Mark Francis of our veterinary department had discovered the cause and cure, and was already recognized world-wide as an authority. However, many farmers and stockmen still doubted. One group came to College to argue. Francis was a closed-mouth operator; he wouldn't argue, he'd show them.

The Electrical Engineering Department was persuaded to build a table to specifications. I was one of the two-bit helpers. A 600 lb. calf, full of ticks, was strapped to the table. I missed the party, but heard from the rooftops that when the switch was thrown, the calf flung feet to the four winds, gave an earsplitting bawl, and breathed his last. Dr. Francis snorted and went home.

Unexpected Triplicates

In 1914, when Dr. W. B. Bizzell came to A&M from a sissy school, he was subjected to some trying moments. We loved the sissies but had doubts about their male overseer. However, his practice of getting prominent preachers of the state for compulsory Sunday services met with favor.

One Sunday the preacher began his hour by relating the tale of the city boy visiting his country cousin. The boy was an eager beaver and wanted to do most tasks alone. Near the close of day he was allowed to bring in the lambs from a nearby pasture. When darkness began creeping over the land his uncle became worried because neither his nephew nor the lambs were in sight. He found his nephew chasing jackrabbits and crying because he couldn't drive the lambs home. Most of the audience smiled, and the preacher felt that he had made a good point.

The next Sunday, a different preacher from a far different area and a different denomination began by telling the same story with hardly a change. The audience was truly amused this time and gave the preacher some honest smiles.

On the third Sunday, a still different smiling and jubilant preacher again began with the innocent little city boy. The roof nearly flew off the

Dr. W. B. Bizzell, president of Texas A&M, 1914.

chapel. Anyhow, if the preacher had suddenly lost his pants, he couldn't have been more surprised. The laughter continued so long and raucus and unabated that the preacher was shattered. Dr. Bizzell had a hard time explaining.

My Electric Necktie

In my days at A&M we could have some very violent electric storms. In 1916, about six o'clock one morning, we suffered the worst storm I had experienced since a boy. I had just dropped the *Dallas News* on Dr. Ball's porch and was running full speed along the walk toward the Chapel. The rain poured and the wind howled.

Suddenly, a blinding flash of lightning and a deafening clap of thunder stopped me. Something struck my throat and sparks flew all about me. I froze. I had run into some live electric power lines, downed by the storm. I couldn't see and didn't dare to move. It was a most frightening experience.

A Fool & His Running

I was chosen to run two races in a track meet of classes at A&M in 1916. I had never jumped a hurdle, even a low one, but agreed to run the 220 yard high hurdles with the aim of winning fourth place and one point. I also agreed to run the anchor lap in the mile relay. Can you imagine how crazy or stupid I must have been? Probably, maybe surely, I was the original "dumb Aggie."

When the pistol fired for the hurdle race I took off at full speed but, never having run a hurdle race, I got too close to the first hurdle before I jumped. I cleared the hurdle easily but nearly fell on my nose. The second hurdle appeared too quickly, but my nose cleared it as my extended arms, my body, and my trailing legs made the dive. Somehow I landed on my feet, paced my steps and won my one point.

I had never run a quarter mile race, but I had seen batons passed. So, when my turn came, I took the baton with ease and opened my throttle wide. About half-way, a most strange feeling came over me; I thought I was going to burst. But suddenly my breath was normal. I took off and hit the tape in first place. My legs crumbled and I slid several yards on the sharpest cinders I ever saw. I looked like I had just emerged from a fight with a dozen wildcats in a small cage.

We won the tack meet, but you might have trouble finding the record. Only page 303, 1916 *Longhorn*, contains this meaty news item: "Mar. 11 Seniors win first Class Track Meet ever held at College Station."

Seemingly, it was the last class track meet.

Hell and Damnation

About noon on June 13, 1916, my graduation day, the campus was agog over a small slick magazine that contained short life-sketches of all prominent college officers and teachers. When I made quick visits to say goodbye, all of the homes were roaring in laughter.

The stories were very humorous and portrayed their subjects in most unusual and comical roles. Everybody was pleased.

But when I reached my room, there was an urgent message to report to the Board of Directors in Gathright Hall. I took time to rush by Mitchell Hall to take my mother and my sweetheart to the mess hall. I expected to join them for dinner. At the Board meeting, I found Dr. Bizzell in a rage. Mrs. Bizzell was under the care of Dr. Ehlinger. They had found their story to be highly scurrilous. We had thought it exceptionally well written and extremely funny. Nobody thought it evil.

I was drafted as messenger and missed my dinner. Dr. Bizzell was so furious and so determined to find the "culprits" that he had me seek witnesses all afternoon and evening. I did manage to take time to escort Mother and Esther to supper with the Connors. For the Final Ball I turned them over to "Doiter" Daugherty, a classmate who had no company. I finally rebelled at ten o'clock, rushed to my room to clean up and spend a few minutes with my guests. My R. V. uniform, cleaned and laid out, had been stolen. I now barely had time to pick up Mother and Esther and catch the train for home. I could have murdered Dr. and Mrs. Bizzell.

Two years later, on October 30, 1918, I met Johnny Garitty, my classmate and close friend, on a road near the war front in the Meuse Argonne. He had his orders as a machine-gun platoon leader to cover my platoon of engineers, which would cut and clear the barbed wire on our front for the infantry advance in the proposed final drive to end World War I. We both knew it might be our final day.

Johnny had married before going overseas and now had a son. I learned for the first time that he had been the author of the Bizzell story. He had been denied his diploma. Now he wanted Dr. Bizzell to relent, accept his apology, and clear his name for his son. He thought I could change Dr. Bizzell's mind.

I rushed to my tent and wrote Dr. Bizzell the truth about the reaction of the student body and the college staff. I pleaded Johnny's case but couldn't have been more stupid. Dr. Bizzell

John P. Garrity, the author's friend, and party responsible for a humorous sketch of A&M's president, Dr. Bizzell.

wrote me a two-page, single-spaced typed letter calling me every foul name in Webster's Unabridged Dictionary. He wasn't about to pardon Johnny. His letter was received in Germany after the Armistice.

The Board of Directors held two meetings. The record of Dr. Bizzell's hassle is blank, but the meeting is recorded and signed by Ike Ashburn, Secretary. Ike was a very astute man, and probably showed the Board that considerable damage to the College could result if the whole story of Bizzell's violent anger were recorded.

Fortunately for Johnny and me, the French artillery support for our division did so magnificent a job that Johnny and I were relieved of our dangerous mission. Though both of us had some tough jobs around Dun-sur-Meuse, we came through unscathed.

Dear Bubba,

How are things at Texas A&M? We were so proud when
we got your latest grades—all C's. That is a quite
an improvement!

Things are the same here. Your daddy got arrested again
for hunting possums out of season. I tried to find work at
the Walmart, but I missed the #44 bus that was supposed
to take me there. By the time I took the #22 bus twice, it
was too late for the interviews.

They are talking about putting in a Taco Bell down the
street. I don't know what's wrong with the phone company
we already got. This NAFTA stuff has us all messed up.

That's all for now. Keep up the hard work.

Love,
Martha (your mama)

P.S.
We were going to send money, but we already sealed
the envelope.

xo (whatever that means)

18

Peas in the Family

by Charles Chupp

The first noteworthy Texas New Year's celebration was observed in 1851 at Fort McIntosh near the present location of Laredo. The menu consisted of black-eyed peas, corn dodgers and all the water you could drink. Only one discouraging word was heard, and the owner of the voice that said it went to bed hungry.

"I hate black-eyed peas!" was what he said.

"We're lucky to have black-eyed peas," a burly celebrant responded. "So we'll just split your helping amongst the rest." That quick response caught on, and from that date Texans believed that good luck would befall the consumer of black-eyed peas, if a batch was partook of at year's beginning.

The first organized resistance to the superstition was led by college students of Texas institutions. The hint of rebellion was first heard on Thanksgiving Day of 1939. The spokesperson for the group was stuffed with turkey and arrogance.

"The gorging of black-eyed peas on New Year's Day is a foolish practice. We, the collegians of Texas are flat footed opposed to the ridiculous tradition, and we'll not be a party to its perpetuation. And you can put that in your pipe and smoke it!"

The older and wiser Texans were outraged by the audacity of their rebellious sons and daughters. With tears in their eyes and sorrow in their hearts they pleaded for reconsideration by the youngsters.

"We ain't eatin' no black-eyed peas on New Year's Day!" the students responded. "So what are you gonna do about it?"

"We ain't gonna let any Southwest Conference team play in the Cotton Bowl!" the selection committee responded. "No peas, no play!"

True to their word, teams from outside the conference were invited. Not one native Texas son suited up for the Cotton Classic. Boston College and Clemson were invited, came, and Clemson pounded Boston College by 6-3. The substitute selections were logical in a way. Bostonians love beans, which the black-eyed pea actually is, and them good ol' boys from Clemson love that cornbread.

When 1941 rolled around, there was little resistance to black-eyed peas, and so far as I know, there are no native enemies to them today.

Cotton Bowl   1940

Clemson   6
Boston College   3

No Black-eyed
       Peas!

           South West
        Conference

19

College Rodeo Cowgirls:
from Queen to Contestant to Coach

by Sylvia Gann Mahoney

A little blond six-year-old cowgirl rode her stickhorse every morning from the ranch house down the dirt road to the little one-room schoolhouse. One afternoon the teacher heard her crying. Someone had taken the little girl's stickhorse. The teacher explained that they would make another one tomorrow; however, she kept crying. The teacher asked her why she was still so upset. The weeping child responded, "Now, I'll have to walk home." This mind-set framed a new role for women in the American West that has taken many twists and turns as it moved from the western frontier in the late nineteenth century to the college rodeo arena in the twentieth century. With the independence that ranch life afforded them, the first cowgirls enjoyed a freedom of expression and competition that women had seldom experienced. When cowgirls moved from the ranch to the rodeo arena, some of them gained a status equal to that of a movie star. However, when the cowgirl went to college, she practically had to start over again in her attempt to be recognized for something more than a pretty face. Over a fifty-year span, the college rodeo cowgirl's status has changed several times. She started as a queen, became a rodeo contestant, was, finally, elected to the national college rodeo board and, eventually, returned as a rodeo coach.

As the western frontier was being settled, many women became more comfortable in the saddle than on foot. Death and disaster on the frontier demanded that many women step outside their roles as wives and mothers. On the ranches, many young girls grew up on horseback because they had to be the ranch hands that helped with everything from roundup to branding. An early cowgirl, Tad Lucas, stated, "I rode all my life. I can't remember when I didn't ride. I rode three miles to school and back every day. I always had horses and rode all day long."[1]

Vernon College cowgirl Jody Petersen Sarchett (front, 4th from left), the only cowgirl to qualify to compete in the team roping at the 1997 College National Finals Rodeo, won the reserve national champion team roper title with her partner Josh Crow from New Mexico Junior College, a first for a female. Petersen's 4.0 GPA also won her an academic scholarship. (Photo by Sylvia Gann Manoney)

The games that the ranch kids played were often played on horseback. When the ranch families gathered, the competition began. Tad Lucas also commented on those days. She said that when she was about thirteen, she and other children rode wild cows and other outlaw stock brought to town by local ranchers each Saturday. She became hooked on riding broncs in 1918 when she won twenty-five dollars in Cody, Wyoming, in a cowgirl steer riding contest.[2]

These young women were apparently no different than any other girls except that they just happened to be born in ranch country. Tad Lucas commented on this, stating that cowgirls are "rugged daughters of a rugged frontier. In fact, she thinks, any eastern 'perty' lass of the lipstick and fluffy female type might have taken to bronc busting if born in the leathery surroundings of a daddy-owned stock ranch, cradled in the saddle, teethed on a cinch buckle, and nourished on cooked cow."[3]

These early cowgirls were limited only by their daring. Some joined the early wild west shows, such as Buffalo Bill's Wild West Show and Pawnee Bill's Historical Wild West Show. In 1885, Annie Oakley signed on with Buffalo Bill as the first female Wild West star; however, she was a sharpshooter, not a cowgirl. Within two years from this beginning, several cowgirls had been hired for their beauty and riding skills. In 1896 in Fort Smith, Arkansas, the first mention of a lady riding a bronc was made. In 1897, at the first Cheyenne Frontier Days Celebration, Bertha Blancett was asked to give an exhibition ride in a water-soaked arena caused by a sudden downpour. None of the cowboys wanted to ride, so the chairman of the rodeo committee hoped Bertha's appearance would placate the audience and save reimbursing the gate money. Not only did she ride, but the cowboys decided if a woman could ride, they could, too. By 1901, lady bronc riding was a featured attraction at many rodeos.[4]

By the 1920s, three events for ladies had become regularly featured at rodeos: bronc riding, trick riding, and a relay race, if a track was available. However, some entered the steer roping and competed with the men. In the bronc riding, most ladies rode with their stirrups tied together.[5] These hobbled stirrups were supposed to be easier to ride; however, a lady bronc rider at Pendleton, Oregon, Bonnie McCarrol, was unable to free herself when she lost her hold. She died from her injuries eight days later.[6] In trick riding the cowgirls rode a horse at full-speed doing various tricks, which were judged on grace and difficulty of execution. The relay race required three horses and a race track, so this event was limited to places like Cheyenne and Pendleton. Steer roping was also a favorite for some early cowgirls. Once, Lucille Mulhall, on a bet to show her roping prowess for President Theodore Roosevelt, roped a coyote. Lucille was the lady for whom the word *cowgirl* was coined in 1899, when she was competing in her father's wild west show.[7]

However, by 1941 the Golden Age of the early cowgirl had passed. The bronc riding was dropped at most rodeos, as were most of the other events. One of the major reasons was the effects of the Depression. Rodeo cowgirls had always been few in number, and because of the expense of providing stock for both men and women, the women's events were eliminated. Some of the women found employment at the rodeos, especially the trick riders, who were hired for exhibition riding.

Meanwhile, cowgirls were blazing the trail to a new frontier: college rodeo. However, the barriers in this frontier were slow to erode. Women's first role at the college rodeo arena was to be displayed for their beauty. The first college to hold a rodeo on campus for students was Texas A&M University in 1920. Sixteen women were invited to participate. An article in *The Battalion*, The Texas A&M newspaper, stated, "A Duchess will be accompanied by sixteen of her most royal attendants. The Duchess and her attendants have been selected by a committee and will consist of the most popular and most beautiful debutantes of College Station and Bryan." Later, cowgirls rode in the grand entry at the Texas A&M rodeos, and some did trick riding. They always had a special section in which to sit. "The girls," according to one of the Aggie cowboys, "were a drawing card because of the all-male school."[8]

Barriers at the colleges and universities also had to be challenged by the cowgirls. The colleges, according to one early cowgirl, were not interested in having their coeds enter any kind of a rodeo. Fern Sawyer, a cowgirl who began rodeoing in the 1930s, commented on the problems she had when she enrolled at Texas Tech. Fern said, "I went to Texas Tech, and they were going to kick me out because I went to a rodeo."[9] She said that she had to sneak out to go to a rodeo, so she finally quit college. She said, "Since then, I have gone back to Texas Tech to judge their college rodeos."[10]

A cowgirl played a major role in starting intercollegiate rodeo. Advertised as the first intercollegiate rodeo, the event was held at a college cowgirl's ranch in Victorville, California, on April 8, 1939.

Jeanne Godshall, a cowgirl and trick rider who attended the University of Southern California, hosted the rodeo at her parents C Bar G Ranch. Eleven colleges and universities fielded forty-two men and eighteen women. Events for the women were the potato race, cow milking, and bareback and saddle riding. An editorial writer in the 1939 *Victor Press* commented on the cowgirls. He said, "If a cowboy gits bucked off, his gal friend most likely kin jump into the saddle an' show him how it really should have ben did."[11]

From that time college rodeos appeared like baby calves in the spring; however, women's events continued to vary, often changing with each rodeo. Various events appeared in the programs: the flag race, the cigar race, the stake race, and goat tying. In the flag race, a girl on horseback raced to a flag, retrieved it, and raced back across the finish line. In the cigar race, a girl was on horseback at a starting line; at the other end of the arena, a cowboy waited with a cigar and a match. The girl raced to the cowboy, dismounted, lit the cigar, remounted, then raced back across the finish line. The stake race was a barrel race run in a figure eight, instead of the clover-leaf pattern used today. In the goat tying, a girl on horseback raced to a goat staked in the arena, dismounted, and tied the goat.

In the early 1940s, as the Golden Era for the professional cowgirl was closing, World War II actually stimulated the evolution of the college cowgirl. On many of the ranches, the cowboys had been drafted, so their sisters had to fill their boots. They did, and they liked it. After the war, as the economy improved, many girls started to college along with the cowboy veterans, who made use of the G.I. Bill. Intercollegiate rodeo started again, strengthened by the maturity of the veteran cowboys and a larger number of cowgirls. Having a national college rodeo organization sanctioned by their schools and an organization to standardize rules and events became the topic of discussion at most of the rodeos. As one cowboy said, "The boy from the country coming to college needs an extracurricular activity to coincide with his classroom work the same as a city boy has his tennis, golf, or football."[12] Although no mention was made of the cowgirl, she was there competing in some event at every rodeo.

Women's events continued to be in a state of flux, as well as being viewed as something extra. In 1948, at the first Sul Ross State University rodeo in Alpine, Texas, twelve colleges entered a total of 134 contestants. The cowgirls wore a variety of outfits. One Sul Ross cowgirl, known as Beverly "Bonnet" Weyerts, wore a bonnet when she competed. Also, some cowgirls entered if they could find a horse to ride. Sul Ross' Mary Ellen Chandler borrowed a roping horse and won the barrel race and placed second in the other event, goat tying. As a point of comparison, during the 1994 college rodeo season, several college cowgirls bought new barrel horses for which they paid as much as fifty thousand dollars each.

Women played a major role in the launching of the National Intercollegiate Rodeo Association, known as the NIRA. During the Sul Ross rodeo, a group of contestants got together and elected a committee to start a student-led organization. Three students, one of which was a woman, emerged as the guiding force to launch the idea: Sul Ross' Hank Finger, Texas A&M's Charlie Rankin, and Sul Ross' rodeo club secretary Evelyn Bruce Kingsbery. With the able leadership and endless reams of correspondence from the three, the NIRA was chartered in 1949. By 2004, the NIRA's membership included approximately 135 colleges and universities and 3300 members.

Even with the women competing at every rodeo and helping to start the new organization, women still had some barriers to cross. The first College National Finals Rodeo (CNFR) in 1949 was an invitational rodeo. The secretary-manager of the Cow Palace in San Francisco heard about the new organization and invited college teams to have a rodeo restricted to full-time college cowboys at the Cow Palace during the Grand National Junior Livestock Exposition; no mention was made of inviting women. Possibly, they were unaware of the fact that women competed.

Vernon College cowgirls gathered from many states to rodeo. (l–r) Christi Sultemeier and Kelli Sultemeier, sisters from New Mexico, Molly Swanson and Jody Petersen from Montana, and Cheyenne Wimberly from Texas liked the rodeo program, the scholarships, and the coach at Vernon College, so they came to Texas to compete in the Southwest Region of the National Intercollegiate Rodeo Association. (Photo by Sylvia Gann Mahoney)

Also, the number of women contestants at that time was small. It was not until 1951, when the CNFR was officially moved to Fort Worth, that the first NIRA all-around champion cowgirl was named: Sul Ross' Jo Gregory Knox. At the 2004 CNFR, 379 men qualified and 142 women. The number of cowgirls continues to grow. For example, at one recent college rodeo, 57 calf ropers competed, 57 breakaway ropers, 60 bull riders, and 63 barrel racers.

Women now compete in four events: barrel racing, goat tying, breakaway roping, and team roping, a co-ed event. Some of the cowgirls are even complimented by cowboys with the statement, "She ropes like a man." Tie-down roping was once an event for the women. The 1961 national all-around champion Donna Saul won a national championship in tie-down roping. Today, at the men's professional rodeos, barrel racing is the only event for women, which illustrates the restricted access cowgirls still have in rodeo.

Cowgirls also challenged other barriers at the colleges and universities. Many administrators continued to view college rodeo for women as something other than desirable, even though their schools had college rodeos. The 1954 national all-around champion from Hardin-Simmons, Becky Jo Smith Doom, recounts how she was asked to leave through the back door of the dorm when she wore her jeans. Leaving without a chaperone was an even more difficult problem for her to surmount.

With women contestants being in the minority, the gender barrier on the national student governing board was typical of a board elected by a majority. The NIRA has always been governed by a national student board with faculty advisors. A student director and a faculty director from each of the regions (now eleven) are elected by the contestants from each region. They, in turn, serve on the national board. In the early years, few women were elected as regional directors, so the men tried to help out by giving women representation on the national board by electing national women event directors. This was eventually eliminated when more women were elected as regional directors. Finally, on the NIRA's fortieth anniversary, Molly McAuliffe of Montana State University was elected as the national student president, the first woman to serve as president. One cowboy board member, when asked about the election of the first female student president, said, "We elected Molly because we thought she would do a better job than anyone else on the board, not because she was a woman."[13] Molly's credentials supported this attitude. She had won the national all-around title in 1986 while studying to be an environmental attorney.

Finally, college cowgirls moved toward having equal status in the minds of the college cowboys. The 1991–1992 NIRA national board, which was elected by all the contestants with the cowboys still having the majority, had five female members and six males.

Not only did the cowgirls serve on the board, but as regional directors, they also handled all the problems in the regions for all of the events—men's and women's.

One national student director, Holly Foster, a senior business major with an emphasis in computers and public relations, was a primary example of the reason that cowgirls had gained the respect of cowboys. Holly proved herself in the arena by being a member of the Cal Poly-San Luis Obispo women's team that won the 1989 national championship. She also trained her own barrel horse and won the national barrel racing title in 1987 and 1989. She had experience working with the corporate world as a Wrangler poster personality, appearing with professional rodeo cowboys.

Women have also been challenged by being appointed to the position of rodeo coach. The college rodeo coach position is another area that has fought for recognition, since it requires as much experience as does coaching football or basketball. Women are now being hired who are cowgirls, but this has not always been true. For example, at New Mexico Junior College a woman was hired to teach English. The rodeo club sponsorship had been the responsibility of the previous college English instructor, so that came with the teaching job. Through a series of administrative decisions, the rodeo program was moved to the athletic department. She became a coach, and had to go to coaches' meetings and compete with the others for a percentage of the budget. So, her motto was "if you don't rodeo, recruit cowboys and cowgirls so good that you don't have to teach them." However, she did have to learn how to recruit, brand cattle, take care of stock, order stock for rodeos, put on a rodeo, work with a slim budget, have stalls built, solicit scholarships, and meet with the college board. However, she used local rodeo cowboys and ranchers as consultants and volunteer help.

Many of the coaches are now qualified former college contestants. For example, Betty Gayle Cooper, the 1972 national breakaway roping champion, helped her Eastern New Mexico University team win the 1972 national women's team title. After graduation she was hired to be the rodeo coach at Southeastern Oklahoma State University. Her teams won seven national titles, with both the men's and women's team titles going to her school in 1980. Winning both titles in the same year had only been achieved two other times prior to that in the forty-five year history of the NIRA. No other coach has as many titles to his or her credit.

The college rodeo queen's role has become more than a pretty face. She has to compete in horsemanship, be knowledgeable about rodeo, and be able to make public appearances. She visits apparel markets, and she appears at professional and youth rodeos. Many go into public relations and television broadcasting. Some, like Carolyn Seay Vietor of Philipsburg, Montana, and Joni James won the National Miss College Rodeo title (in 1965 and 1987, respectively) and went on to win the Miss Rodeo America title. However, due to lack of funding, the Miss College Rodeo Pageant has now been eliminated.

Along the way in college rodeo, the word *girl* gave way to the word woman. The borrowed horses gave way to her own trained horses and her own truck and trailer. The debutante became recognized as an athlete, respected for her roping skills and her horsemanship. She no longer had to have a position of leadership given to her; she was duly elected. She no longer had to leave by the back door if she wore jeans or did not have a chaperone. She is now raising her daughters and sons to follow in her boot tracks. Some of the all-around champions returned to the ranch, and some went to universities to teach and to coach, while others went into the business world. The barriers for women in college rodeo have come down, not by decree, but by cowgirls earning respect for their skills and leadership.

College cowgirls did not give up being recognized for their beauty; they just added being contestants, leaders, and coaches as choices. The college cowgirl blazed the trail in the collegiate world, bringing independence, freedom of expression, and competition that early professional cowgirls enjoyed at the turn of the twentieth century. The little cowgirl who rode her stickhorse to school was a harbinger of the college cowgirl who has her horse waiting for her when she gets out of the college classroom today.

ENDNOTES

1. Jordan, Teresa. *Cowgirls: Women of the American West*. Garden City, New York: Anchor Press, 1982. 201.
2. Roach, Joyce Gibson. *The Cowgirls*. Denton: University of North Texas Press, 1990. 104.
3. Ibid. 105.
4. Jordan.189.
5. Ibid. 191.
6. Roach. 112.
7. Porter, Willard H. *Who's Who in Rodeo*. Oklahoma City: Powder River, 1982. 90-91.
8. "A&M Rodeo to be a Novelty Livestock Show." *The Battalion*, Texas A&M Newspaper. Nov. 5, 1920.
9. Jordan. 232.
10. Ibid.
11. "Desert Sage Says." Editorial. *Victor Press* 7 April 1939: np.
12. Rankin, Charlie. "New Blood for the Rodeo Business: College Students are Getting Interested." *The Buckboard* January 1949: np.
13. Patterson, Rocky. Interview with Sylvia G. Mahoney. Bozeman, Montana. June 16, 1989.

BIBLIOGRAPHY

"A&M Rodeo to be a Novelty Livestock Show." *The Battalion*, Texas A&M Newspaper. Nov. 5, 1920.

"Desert Sage Says." Editorial. *Victor Press* 7 April 1939: np.

Jordan, Teresa. *Cowgirls: Women of the American West*. Garden City, New York: Anchor Press, 1982.

Patterson, Rocky. Interview with Sylvia G. Mahoney. Bozeman, Montana. June 16, 1989.

Porter, Willard H. *Who's Who in Rodeo*. Oklahoma City: Powder River, 1982.

Rankin, Charlie. "New Blood for the Rodeo Business: College Students are Getting Interested." *The Buckboard* January 1949: np.

Roach, Joyce Gibson. *The Cowgirls*. Denton: University of North Texas Press, 1990.

20

Ghosts, Goblins, Virgins, and Other Supernatural Creatures:

Ghost Stories at Texas Tech University and South Plains College

by Mike Felker

W e're all familiar with those things that go bump in the night. Even my own fairly intelligent, usually level-headed wife refuses to go to sleep unless the closet doors are firmly closed. It was, however, her curious insistence on carrying all her textbooks to each exam that originally prompted me in 1986 and 1987 to survey my undergraduates at Texas Tech University about their own good-luck rituals. Of the over two-hundred responses I collected in one semester, the largest single category, by far, was "Luck on Exams and other Schoolwork," a not-unexpected finding. The dozens of good luck rituals included everything from wearing lucky hats, dresses, sweatshirts, or shoes, to "my nicest underwear because old underwear makes me feel inferior."

Because the survey was open-ended and anonymous—"What superstitions have you heard about school?"[1]—I also got a number of responses which didn't fit into the categories about college life. Many of these responses dealt, instead, with stories of ghosts and the supernatural on the college campus. When I remembered the undergraduate in a Renaissance class who had written that Shakespeare's contemporaries believed in "ghosts, goblins, virgins, and other supernatural creatures," I had my new categories neatly laid out for me. In some cases, I was even able to trace the origin of the stories I had collected. After I moved to South Plains College in Levelland in 1988, I discovered that my students there also had ghost stories that they wanted to tell.[2] There, as at Tech, the students seemed strangely insistent upon explaining that they didn't believe such stories themselves. Most didn't even sign their names to the questionnaire, although those who did are given credit here.

While I was at Tech, I collected several good ghost stories, including multiple reports of the ghost of a lady's head, or "a headless girl" on the sixth floor of Coleman Hall, which is a men's dorm: "It was seen floating underneath a desk in the room. During the summer, cheerleaders staying in Coleman for camp reported it, and a guy living there last year took a picture of it." (unsigned)

For some reason, the dormitories seem especially susceptible to such ghosts; I received a report from Adrianna White of a girl raped and killed on the second floor of Knapp Hall, and another student reported a girl murdered in Gates Hall: "When I lived in Gates we used to never go to the bathroom alone at night due to a story of a girl murdered there two years earlier. Girls say they often heard her crying" (unsigned).

Another young woman wrote, "In my dormitory, the room three doors down, it is believed there is something uncomfortable about the room. A friend of mine lives there and says that she and her roommate, as well as the two girls who lived in the same room last year, have not been able to sleep easily in the room. My friend says that there is something uneasy about the room and it sometimes has strange noises" (Cathy Wald).

One student had heard a story about ghosts in West Hall, a former dormitory which now houses Admissions and other offices, and this writer even identified the source of the story he had heard, "The Secretary at the Ag Ed Building told me a story about West Hall. She said that way back when, the top floor was closed up. There was [*sic*] ghosts living up there. She said at all hours of the night lights would come on and go off. She said that she went up there and peeked through the crack of the boarded up door and saw footsteps [*sic*] in the dust." (unsigned)

Of course, the dormitories don't have a monopoly on ghosts; other campus buildings are haunted, also. In the Administration Building, "a ghost rings the victory bell after each ballgame" (Patty Owens). In the Biology Building, one student wrote, "I heard there was a teenager a few years back that was playing on the elevator and climbed out of the trap door and somehow lost his footing and fell and was killed. So the superstition that goes along with this incident is that this boy haunts the Biology Building" (unsigned). This story might actually be a modification of a real event. Shortly after the new Biology Building was opened, a student did fall to his death there, but he committed suicide by jumping from the roof of the building; he didn't fall from the elevator.

Perhaps the ghosts reported at the Texas Tech Museum should be the least surprising; after all, Tech did move old ranch houses from all over the state to its Ranching Heritage Center. One student had heard "Some of the former inhabitants of the Barton House at the Ranching Heritage Center come to visit on certain days of the year; these ghosts are apparently not hostile but rather curious" (unsigned).

Even the air-conditioning and maintenance tunnels underneath the campus have their share of ghosts: "Ghosts run around in the tunnels under the campus" (Patty Owens); and, "a girl was raped in the tunnels and her screams can still be heard" (Jenny Britton). In addition, the tunnels are said to be inhabited by one very specific ghost—the ghost of "a campus cleaning woman who

The Texas Tech Biology building.

was stabbed in the tunnels by a guy stealing a test" (Adrianna White). The actual murder upon which this is based took place many years ago when a student did murder a cleaning lady who caught him trying to steal a test in the old Biology Building, not in the tunnels. And, of course, the cleaning woman's ghost, or usually her ghostly head, has also been reported in the old Biology Building, usually floating in front of one of the windows.

South Plains College (S.P.C.) has fewer ghost stories, possibly because the school is younger than Texas Tech and possibly because, as a two-year institution, students don't stay long enough for the stories to become part of their heritage. I did find a couple of students who had heard of a ghost that is seen at Brashear Lake (a small playa lake right next to the track). One student wrote, "I heard that a girl drowned in that little lake over here by S.P.C. She comes out on Halloween. I heard at night the spirit walks around and scares kids." A second reported, "It comes out mostly when it rains real hard." A former S.P.C. English instructor remembers well the drowning upon which this story is apparently based; Scott Yarbrough reported that a teenager drowned in the lake when Yarbrough was about eight, which would have been in the early 1970s. Levelland had had about a week of heavy rain and the boy and his brother had gone swimming on the first sunny day; he apparently got his feet tangled in the underbrush and drowned. Yarbrough said he remembered the grappling hooks going in and out of the lake all day. It took hours, almost the rest of the day, to find the body and, by the time they dragged the boy from the lake, several hundred people had gathered around the edges. The body was very white, pallid, and cold-looking. The next day at school, the rumor was that because the boy had been trapped that long underwater, his soul had been forced out of his body, and that the ghost still roamed the lake at night looking for his body.

Two unnamed sisters taking my class reported independently of each other the same story about their haunted apartment. The first sister wrote, "We have a very busy ghost by the name of Poindexter in our apartment because he frequently opens the door." The second reported, "Sometimes our apartment door opens on its own. My roommates and I think it could be a ghost by the name of Poindexter." When I asked how they knew the ghost's name was Poindexter, both were overcome with such a fit of the giggles that they couldn't answer. I still don't know how they knew the ghost's name.

Although two faculty members told me that the South Plains Theatre Building has a ghost, as all good theatres should, the Drama teacher at that time denied she had ever heard anything about such a story.

Although I collected superstitions about monsters in almost every building on the Tech campus, the students were far more fascinated by the world beneath those buildings—those spooky air-conditioning tunnels. In addition to being told that the tunnels are used to store nuclear weapons and Star Wars weaponry, I learned that, "A student once entered the tunnels looking for a way either into the girls' dorm or into a locked building to try to steal a test,

One of the infamous tunnel vents on the Texas Tech campus.

Will Rogers, apparently still mounted on Soapsuds.

and was never seen again" (unsigned). The tunnels are also said to be inhabited by monsters (non-specific), by a rapist who uses the tunnels to get into the girls' dorms and then make his escape, by a "looney," and by an "insane murderer years ago who would kill only girls and who cut off their heads; he used the tunnels to get around at night. These murders went on for months and if you were out after curfew, a police officer would pick you up and escort you home. Supposedly, these murders are the reason they put up the emergency phones." The young man added, "this story never worried me too much because I haven't heard of any murders in the past few years" (Michael Koett).

These tunnels are also inhabited by one very specific monster which emerges from the tunnels to "steal our clothes from the washers and dryers in the basement of Wells Hall. There is always something missing" (unsigned).

And I hesitate to call him a goblin or monster, but I also received multiple unsigned reports of "the guy who lives in the stacks of the library." This, I suspect, is probably just based on sightings of a doctoral candidate trying to satisfy his dissertation committee, but one girl added, "Several years ago he raped girls" (Adrianna White).

The campus at South Plains is much quieter, I'm sorry to say; I received only one report of goblins or monsters there: "I've heard that there are closet monsters in the dorm closets, so when you go to bed at night or you are alone in your room, keep the closet doors closed" (unsigned). My wife reminds me that these monsters are not college-specific: everyone knows that bad things live in the closet and good things under the bed, unless, of course, whatever is under the bed is drooling.

At Tech, as at many other schools, virgins are often attributed supernatural powers of their own. The most common stories relate to Tech's statue of Will Rogers sitting on his favorite horse, Soapsuds. The story goes that if a virgin ever graduates, Will Rogers will do one of the following:

- get off his horse and walk around Memorial Circle
- ride his horse around Memorial Circle (Texas Tech Professor Emeritus Kenneth Davis told me that several years ago, the Tech paper had a picture of hoof prints in the snow making a circuit of Memorial Circle; this was, however, never verified)
- get off and walk around his horse
- fall off his horse
- stand up in the saddle

- come alive and ride off into the sunset
- get off his horse and walk across the street (Adrianna White)
- climb down off of his horse (Jeffrey Otey)
- step off the pedestal with his horse (Angie Conde)

There were several other responses in the same vein, but with a twist: "If Will Rogers escorts a girl off campus, she's a virgin" (Debbie Byrd); "The day a virgin graduates, Roy Rogers will get off his horse" (Robert E. Parker); "If a virgin comes to Tech [this one doesn't even have to graduate], Will Rogers will dismount from his horse" (Patty Owens); and, "Will Rogers gets off his horse once a year for a virgin sacrifice" (unsigned). Now we know why so few of them graduate! Another student had heard that the Tech mascot, the Masked Rider "can never ride at football games again if a virgin graduates" (Britton).

I have heard similar stories about several other college campuses, involving the statue of a buffalo at West Texas State, and the statue of a bear at a school in Colorado. Unfortunately, I found no such stories on the South Plains campus. Whether this means that virgins do sometimes manage to get an Associate's Degree or, perhaps more likely, simply reflects the fact that we don't have a statue on campus, yet remains to be determined.

Endnotes

1. In 1986, I asked my Texas Tech students to write a daily journal entry on any college superstitions about which they had heard or in which they participated. Because the results produced so much more than luck rituals, I refined the question for 1987: "As part of a survey of superstitions at Tech, please list any and all superstitions which you personally believe, or have heard about, which pertain to college life in general or Texas Tech in particular. You may include things people do for good luck or to avoid bad luck, things people do in hope of scoring better on exams (wear the same clothes, carry a 'lucky' ballpoint pen), or rumors you have heard about 'mysterious' occurrences, serious or not, on campus (the statue of Will Rogers, the tunnels beneath the campus, the behavior of certain professors).

Please restrict your list to superstitions that people really believe or to those which, even if not taken seriously, are particularly widespread."

2. In 1988, I used the following prompt at South Plains College: "We've all known or heard of students who wear the same lucky shirt to all tests, or the same lucky tennis shoes to all basketball games. Perhaps you've also heard other superstitions that relate to college life or to South Plains College (a haunted dorm room, etc.). Please take a few minutes to write down all the superstitions you've heard of about school in general or about South Plains College specifically."

Language
and Study

Popular English Usage in Texas, or How You're S'posed to Talk

by Robert Duncan

Texas has a lot of colorful expressions in its everyday language, and it had many more a generation or two ago. When the folk don't have the nuances of expression provided by a full, "proper" vocabulary, they make up words and expressions in an effort to convey precisely what they mean. The language of the common people is magnificent in its intricacies and texture. Its phrases and proverbs are often much more revealing, vivid, and colorful than so-called proper English usage.

Texans reputedly exaggerate. However, in truth, the soul of western humor is understatement. But, then, we're not apt to call a five-acre homesite a ranch, either.

In the late 1970s, Larry L. King made his fortune by writing a musical comedy about the best little "chicken ranch" in La Grange, Texas. At about the same time, country disco became a popular mania. Suddenly, the rest of the country reappraised the Lone Star State, and Texas became the gleam in the eye of the Big Apple. Almost overnight the Northeast decided that we were no longer "chicken——."

Texans. Lo and behold, suddenly we had become Texas Chic. We might still be provincial, but all of a sudden that was a *good* thing! It was a classic case of feathers today, chicken tomorrow.

Across the nation big money changed hands to outfit the rhinestone/midnight/urban cowboy. Some dudes spent more for their hats and boots—and belt buckles—than a lot of *real* good ole boys used to pay for their ranches.

Meanwhile, of course, Texas itself continued to be infiltrated—well, okay, overrun—by Yankees. In 1936, folklorist J. Frank Dobie lamented that Texas was importing Yankees for three reasons: "to fill up space, raise the price of real estate, and pad the census rolls." I guess deep down inside we know that not *all* Yankees are *all* bad.

One of the worst things about 'em is that they just don't know how to talk right. Apparently, nobody ever went to the trouble to teach 'em.

Most of the people who broadcast the TV news and weather in Texas cities seem to be transplants from Yankee land. Our state's television station managers must consider local color and regional accents taboo. Hence, we wind up with announcers who mispronounce place names like "Waxahachie," "Mexia," "Celina," and "Bexar," while they pronounce correctly other words that we Texans are used to hearing mispronounced in daily conversation. They don't comprehend that *potent* is apt to be pronounced "potenent" and *incentive*, "incentitive," or that *right-smart* is a compound quantitative adjective, not a reference to one's I.Q. My grandfather once told me that one of his neighbors had lied to him about his income. My grandfather named what to him was an ungodly salary (or hourly wage) that the neighbor had quoted him. "But I know *in reason* that can't be so," he told me. "There ain't nobody that makes that kind of money, for that's a *right-smart* little bit." It wasn't really very much. I was making more than that myself, but, thank goodness, I had the grace to bite my tongue.

I don't know how many times I've explained to visiting (or transferred) northern businessmen that chicken-fried steak is not fried chicken, or that a good mess of butterbeans does not consist of green beans cooked in a butter sauce.

A few years ago on a trip through East Texas, I stopped at a service station to ask directions. I made the mistake of parking in front of the gas pumps. A good ole boy who worked there asked me, with friendly tactfulness, to move my car out of the way. He explained, "My boss-man is li'ble to jump right astraddle of my back if he thanks I let you park here." Being an indigenous Texan myself, I understood perfectly and was happy to oblige him.

When I was a boy over half a century ago, the talk was more natural and expressive than it is "in this day and time." A serious fight was a "knock down, drag out." A tough guy might be referred to as "a tough titty," though probably not to his face. If

"As drunk as a boiled owl" is a Texas expression for someone who "dranks." (Illustration by Georgene Wood)

my father saw a "good" fight downtown, he would come home and remark, "A tussle; now, they had it." If someone tried to pick a fight with him, he would challenge the guy to "have at it!" If he thought someone was getting too high and mighty, Daddy would remark, "He thinks he's got the world by the ying-yang with a downhill pull."

An alcoholic was not known as such; folks just said so-and-so "dranks." His affliction was not thought of as an illness; it was considered a character defect, a weakness. When the person was drunk, he was said to be "about half tight" (another understatement), "drunk as a boiled owl" or, more poetically, "drunk as a skunk."

In the good old days when you really liked someone, you "thought the world an' all of him." And if you fell deeply in love, it was "head-over-heels." If a woman went out on the town, she was "having a high-heel time." If you were mad, you were said to be on your "high horse." When you were sad, you were "down in the dumps." If a friend was overawed by an obstacle and didn't think he could "make the riffle," you could offer encouragement by saying, "That's not much of a hill for a high stepper like you." If a friend exaggerated, it was your duty to call his hand by saying, "Now that's a lie, and you know it!" If somebody was disappointed, you might say, "Her feathers fell" or, "That liked to have killed his soul." A pretty girl might be described as "purty as a spotted pup under a red wagon." An individual brick was called a "brickbat." A person didn't have plain diabetes; it was always "*sugar* diabetes." Someone could "throw" or "pitch" three kinds of fit: *wall-eyed, conniption,* and *hissie.* If we were bound and determined to do something, we vowed to do it even "if it harelips the nation" or, alternately, "if it harelips the governor."

If you were shy and quiet, it was because "the cat got your tongue." If you laughed or giggled, it was because you "had your tickle box turned over." And if you laughed loudly or abruptly, you "just cackled out." When somebody "got your goat," you would "raise old Billy" or "rare and faunch." Usually, the strongest by-words one heard were son-of-a-gun, son-of-a-biscuit-eater, durn, boy howdy, gosh, and golly bum. "Cotton-pickin'" was a derogatory adjective of somewhat obvious origin.

Probability was expressed simply by the phrase "more than likely." If we did use the word *probably*, we omitted a syllable and just said "prob'ly." Inevitability was "in spite of the world." An expression of excess was "till the world looked level." The concept of high frequency was signified by the phrase "ever' little whip stitch." If something occurred infrequently, it was said to happen only "once in a great while" or "once in a blue moon."

When you fed company, you encouraged them to "make out their meal," meaning to eat all they wanted. If you went visiting, you told the hostess that she had "done wonders with this house." And when you left, you said, "Y'all come to see us," and *meant* it. (Incidentally, we never said "you all"; it was always "y'all.")

One time in a hotel in Ohio, I asked the bell captain where I could find a "washateria." He didn't understand what I meant. After I used the word several times trying to get through to him, it dawned on me that in Ohio the magic word was not *washateria*, but *laundromat*.

We had homegrown words that described lack of symmetry. "Hind-part-before," "bassackards" or "backards," of course, meant backwards. "Bottom-side-uppards" indicated that something was inverted, or upside-down. If something was inside out, we called that "*wrong*-side-out."

Sometimes for emphasis, we would interrupt ourselves in mid-word, making up homemade phrases such as the reassuring "I guaran-damn-tee you" and the adjective "a whole 'nuther." The latter, of course, was a colloquial expression for "another whole (something)."

We used similes, too. A few of them were "poor (pronounced *pore*) as Job's turkey," "honest as the day is long," "full as a tick," "toucheous as a sore thumb," "ugly as homemade sin," "bald as an eagle," "hotter than a two-dollar pistol," and the now-dated phrase "sound as a dollar."

For clarity, Mexico was referred to as "Old" Mexico to avoid any possible confusion with the state that lies between Texas and Arizona. Iowa was called "Ioway." *Business* was simply "b'ness." The phrase "as a matter of fact" was "fact-o-b'ness." We didn't say *nude*—it was "naked as a jaybird." And the manly equivalent of "thank you" was "much obliged."

When you did your very best at something, it was your "dead level best." And when you worked extremely hard, it was "like a Trojan." Occasionally, in those pre-Viagra times, you'd hear a middle-aged fellow brag about his sexual prowess by saying, "I'm not as good as I once was, but I'm as good *once* as I *ever* was."

The words *irrespective* and *regardless* merged to form "irregardless." When we wanted to delay something briefly, we said that we would do it "dreckly," the colloquial form of *directly*. You could tactfully contradict someone by flatly stating, "It ain't no such of a damn thang!"

When something that you were trying to do turned out wrong, some smart alec would usually be on hand to say, "Maybe you just didn't hold you mouth right." If somebody did something without your permission, you might complain, "He never said kiss my hine leg, nor nothin.'" Then again, sometimes what he never said was "kiss my foot." Higher anatomical parts were unmentionable in mixed company. If poetic justice was done and someone got what he deserved, folks said, "His chickens have finally come home to roost."

Several of the words can be best explained in context. For example:

"Quietus," meaning a sudden, abrupt stop. This is a good example of how cultured we were, and are, in Texas. *Quietus* is from the Latin, as in *Quietus est*, which translates, "He is quit." We might say, "Joe Bob's wife found lipstick on his underwear, and boy, she put the quietus on that."

"P-turkey," meaning "even the first thing." As in "He don't know P-turkey about women."

"Owin' to," meaning according to (some circumstance). For example, "That's just *owin' to* whether you would rather ride bareback or walk. We ain't got no saddle."

"Onliest" was a colloquial word for *only*. For example, "I wouldn't have minded livin' in that trailer house. The *onliest* thang is, Linda Sue is scared to death of tornadoes."

If you didn't "have much use" for something, you might say, "I wouldn't give you a dime for a carload of 'em." If it was a person that you were talking about, you might say, "I wish I could buy him for what he's worth and sell him for what he *thanks* he's worth."

A few years ago I flew back from New York to Dallas just before Christmas. The airports were full of people who seemed to be annoyed, or intoxicated, or both. As I waited for my luggage, I saw a badly warped and mangled suitcase come down the conveyor. A little boy standing near me told his father, "Lookie yonder, Daddy. They like to have knocked that'n kindly whomperjawed." Sure as the world, that kid had just come home. He wasn't no New Yorker. As I stood there, worn to frazzle by my weeklong trip, that little kid sounded right as rain.

[Parts of this article have appeared previously in *McKinney Living* Winter 1994 (as "Texas Lingo: A Colorful Variation to Proper English") and in the February 6, 1983 *Dallas Times Herald* (as "Texas Lingo Offers Colorful Variation to Proper English").]

22

Talking Fancy

by James Ward Lee

When I was in the seventh grade, 'Fessor Jones, who drove the school bus and taught general science, told me that only thirteen people in the world could understand Einstein's theory of relativity. And I was not one of them. Nor would I ever be. And then Miss Pate, the English teacher who was widely thought to be a devil worshiper, introduced us to the works of two drunkard dope-fiend poets and a consumptive—Samuel Taylor Coleridge, Edgar Alan Poe, and John Keats. After two days of "Annabel Lee," "Kubla Khan," and "Ode to a Nightingale," my classmate Ellie Pearl Wallace, who at thirteen weighed exactly the same as Gene Tunney did when he defeated Jack Dempsey, expressed herself on the subject of poetry. "I hate it," she averred. "All it is is a bunch of them old hidden meanings." Actually, Ellie Pearl didn't "aver." I put that fancy word in her mouth, but I quoted her correctly about all "them old hidden meanings." Ellie Pearl, you might say today, "had issues" with poetry. Think about the phrase "having issues" for a second. Nowadays, we don't reject ideas; we don't hate things; we don't necessarily disagree violently with someone. We just "have issues and concerns." We then like to "address" them. Today, nobody actually solves a problem or admits to its insolubility. The best we can do is "address our concerns" if we indeed have issues. Remember the old program *The Honeymooners?* Once, at a disastrous golf game, Ralph told Norton, "First, you address the ball." Norton leaned over and said, "Hello, ball."

So, issues and concerns are not all we address in this modern world of ours of today in which we now live. My freshmen used to use that lengthy locution to fill space and impress me with their grasp of the English language. Let me backtrack for a moment: we don't have freshmen anymore, at least not at the University of

North Texas where I once taught in that ancient world of yesterday in which I no longer live. We don't have freshmen because a female graduate of that institution wrote a vehement and violent and vituperative letter to the alumni magazine protesting the use of the term "freshmen." The very word is sexist and must be replaced by "first-year student." Now, I worry about that. I watch a lot of football on television, and what are the announcers going to do. They denominate some of the "scholar athletes" as "true freshmen." Now you might think this is opposed to your faux freshman, but actually it is as opposed to your "red-shirt freshman," that is to say, a first-year scholar athlete who has been "redshirted," a verb we can all conjugate if we put our minds to it. For instance, "He will have been redshirted" is the future perfect tense. But I guess I can't worry much about sportscasters. They are what we now call a "conflicted" lot. Half of them want the Cowboys or Aggies or Raiders to get "on track," while the other half want them to get "untracked." But I must move on to fancier talkers than ex-scholar athletes like Terry Bradshaw and Dione Sanders.

Modern fancy talk, hereinafter referred to as modernobabble, is like poetry with all them old hidden meanings. Keats says he longs to "cease upon the midnight with no pain." My Granny Lee used to say the same thing in Alabama plain talk, "I just hope I wake up dead someday."

Miss Pate pointed out that the whole idea of poetry was to mystify and puzzle and obscure any meaning that might lurk therein. All we were supposed to do was soak up the beauty of such fancy lines as those about the "winged seraphs" coming to try to "dissever my soul from the soul of the beautiful Annabel Lee." Or Coleridge's "charmed magic casements opening on the foam of perilous seas in faery lands forlorn." Or Keats's "A savage place as holy and enchanted as e'er beneath a waning moon was haunted by woman wailing for her demon lover." Miss Pate loved such mystery. Most stunning of all to me in Miss Pate's class was the statement by Poe that a tale of mystery and suspense should "heighten the grotesque into the arabesque." I have puzzled over that phrase for some sixty winters and am no closer to understanding it than when I first heard it. But I, myownpersonalself, will try to "heighten the grotesque into the arabesque" because if I learned nothing else from Miss Pate and 'Fessor Jones it was to see the beauty of fancy talk. (Digressive note: a systems engineer at H. Ross Perot's Electronic Data Systems once used the locution "myownpersonalself" in this sentence: "I, myownpersonalself wants to thank you." This same man wanted to arm the guards of the sacred computers with .357 magnums because they have more power in the arena of personnel stoppage.)

Lordy, lordy, I do love fancy talk. Nothing makes my soul soar as when a politician introduces another political hack with florid phraseology such as, "I give you a man who has been tempered in the cauldron of hard work, a man who has fought his party's and this nation's battles from the rock-ribbed coasts of Maine to the sun-kissed shores of California." Or as Arnold would say, Cal-e-for-nee-a.

I have traveled far from my Alabama home since the seventh grade, but the love of fancy talk or obscure befuddling phraseology have remained with me. I abhor the simple. I love the convoluted. And I am sure you do, too, or you would not be writers and teachers and editors and folklorists. Suppose, for instance, that two manuscripts cross your desk. One is titled *Groundwork of the Metaphysic of Morals*, and the other *Rush Limbaugh is a Big Fat Idiot*. Well, you know right off that only one of these books will take you into those "perilous seas in faery lands forlorn" that Keats talks about. You may have no more idea than a goose what you are being told in *Groundwork of the Metaphysic of Morals*, but you know it is of heft and solemnity. And that is all we require. If Miss Pate were alive today and not down in some netherworld with her satanic masters, she would—sight unseen—choose the book by Immanuel Kant over the one by Al Franken.

Now you may say there is a time for plain talk and a time for fancy talk. I have issues with that, and I am willing to address them. Or as Richard Nixon used to say, "Let me say this about that." If somebody had asked Abraham Lincoln how old his grandmother was, he might have said, "Oh, let's see, she is eighty-seven." But put him in front of an audience on the ringing plains of windy Gettysburg and his simple "eighty-seven" becomes "four score and seven years." Housman confounded hundreds, nay thousands, of my students with his lines, "Now of my threescore years and ten, twenty will not come again." When I asked my freshmen—redshirted or true—how old the speaker in the poem was, I got answers ranging from fifty to seventy to thirty-five. Only Walter Sutphen of Borger, Texas, got it right. Walter had failed freshperson composition five times but was hell on math. I passed him with a D for discerning one line of fancy talk and coming up the correct answer of "twenty." Later teachers of Walter's had both issues and concerns with me for passing him out of English 131 into what was for him an impossible 132.

But I was young at that point in time. Don't you love "at this point in time" as a substitute for "now" or as Walter used to say, "rat now?" You can with some ingenuity enlarge on "at this point in time." Three years ago, the chief of police of Fort Worth, "the Queen City of the Prairies," confronted the television cameras for a lengthy interview and had to go into a stall. He used the phrase "at this particular point in time" eleven times as he told why a miscreant had not been captured and incarcerated. See, I didn't say, "caught and jailed." Fancy talkers don't jail, they incarcerate. You may be familiar with a game that is going about the Internet now. It is called "Bullshit Bingo." In any meeting—at any point in time— you make a grid and you list a series of fancy words and phrases such as "empower," "24/7," "at the end of the day," "window of opportunity," "in a timely manner," "outsource," "connect the dots," "PowerPoint," "access," "feedback," "input," "thruput," "impact,"—you know the jargon. Well, when you hear enough words to go across your card, down it, or at the diagonal, you cry "Bullshit" and leave the room. You have won the bingo game.

Now as you know, the fanciest talkers of all are in the world of haute couture, of literary criticism, philosophy, and in all the "ologies." Oenology, sociology, psychology, cosmology, and possibly proctology, but as the modernobabblists says, "I am not going to go there." I hope.

Now your philosopher may be the worst. I can struggle along with Aristotle and Plato, who are in the grand-scheme-of-things plain talkers, but when you get to your Kants and Wittgensteins and Heideggers, you have got some serious fancy talk. Kant says in *The Critique of Pure Reason*, "The apprehension of the manifold of appearance is always successive. The representations of the parts follow upon one another. Whether they also follow one another in the object is a point which calls for further reflection, and which is not decided by the above statement." I say amen to that. And amen to Kant, but let me note for the record that Kant is not pronounced Kant by Germans. But let me pass that on by; maybe I will take it up "on down the road" or "at the end of the day" or "perhaps in the fullness of time," as you might say.

But Kant—if that really were the pronunciation—is easy pickings if you contrast him with Heidegger. I am sure all of you know the passage from *Being and Time* that goes, "We always conduct our activities in an understanding of being. Out of this understanding arise both the explicit question of the meaning of Being, and the tendency that leads us toward its conception." We do not *know* what being means. But even if we ask, "What is Being?" we keep within an understanding of the "is," though we are unable to fix conceptually what that "is" signifies. The forty-second president of this great land of ours in which we now live put it much more succinctly when he said, "It depends on what 'is' is." He was a plain talker and on another occasion should have resorted to euphemism instead of saying plainly, "I did not have sex with that woman."

Mr. Clinton might have learned a lesson from an experience I had about the same time he was talking plain. A woman I know, a woman of a certain age if I might euphemize, called me one night with a sensitive question. She and her eighty-seven-year-old mother had been watching too much of the Ken Starr follies on TV, and they heard a new word. She asked me, "Do you know what fellatio is?" I said, "Yes, yes I do. Fellatio is a town down in Lavaca County somewhere between Sublime and Climax on Alternate Route 269." See, I really didn't know what fellatio meant, but I have a degree in English and hate to ever admit ignorance. Clinton might also have learned from an anecdote that belongs to my old friend Al Lowman. Lowman tells of a lawyer pleading the case of a rustler hauled up to the county courthouse. The old presiding judge was pure hell on cattle theft, and when he asked the bright young attorney what his client had done, the lawyer said, "Well, your honor, this fine young man purloined a heifer." The old judge, neither a linguist nor a lexicographer, said, "Oh, hell, boys will be boys."

I fear I am digressing. There is no better place to start really exploring fancy talk than in my former profession—literary criticism. Most of you know that in the rhetoric of signifiers, "we are able to avoid arriving at a 'final' decoding or reading of the aesthetic message, because each ambiguity generates further 'rule breaking' at other levels, and invites us to reassemble what the work of art seems at any point to be saying. . . . Therefore critics are forced in consequence to rethink their whole arrangement and ultimately, that of the realities they encode for him." I wish I could take credit for that wonderful exegesis, but I can't. I copied it from Terence Hawkes's *Structuralism and Semiotics*, published by a famous western university press, which shall remain nameless. And here is a quotation from University of Chicago professor of English Homi Bhabba:

> If for a while, the ruse of desire is calculable for the uses of discipline soon the repetition of guilt, justification, pseudo-scientific theories, superstition, spurious authorities, and classifications can be seen as the desperate effort to "normalize" formally the disturbance of discourse of splitting that violates the rational, enlightened claims of its enunciatory modality.

Friends and neighbors, this wonderful and fancy talk was reprinted by the *Dallas News* in 1999. Is it any wonder that I retired fully from the profession in 1999? I simply didn't have the goods to compete. While I was trying to figure out what Poe meant about "the grotesque heightened into the arabesque," young scholars were "amping up" the tonality of the discourse. Or were they "ramping it up?" I am not sure because I have no idea where they get "ramping up." I know that Japan is ramping up its national computer grid. I read about it in *InfoWorld* just day before yesterday. Here is what I read about the ramping up: "This is a national project that provides a 10gbps photonic backbone network that branches from the nodes and bridges with optical cross-connects called MEMs which is optical circuitry without carrying the signal to an electronic signal by flipping very tiny mirrors at very high speeds." I could be wrong, but I bet even 'Fessor Jones would have trouble with that scientific concept.

But that is not all the ramping up we do. *The Dallas Business Journal* had this headline about a local searchlight company. It is "Ramping Up for War," and *Off-Road Expo* noted that it was "ramping up to make a media blitz for the 2003 show." And we are told in *Business Line* that even in far-off India the India Cement company's troubles are ramping up. And finally, the British Music Industry is "Ramping up to attack mode" to combat music piracy. I think "amping up" is a figure of speech that comes from the practice of turning up the amplifiers so that rock stars can deafen even more people. But when the news people are not "ramping up," or "amping up," they are "ratcheting up." I know what ratcheting up means since I own a perfectly good set of ratchets. You think I am "gaslighting" you don't you? Well, I am not. I never gaslight. In case you don't know, "gaslight" is one of the newest fancy verbs. I only learned it Friday when a friend told me the word. Then I saw this headline on Maureen Dowd's column in *The New York Times*. "Is Condi Gaslighting Rummy?" I accessed my computer (see I didn't just turn it on. I accessed it) and then I accessed "Ask Jeeves" and learned that the verb "to gaslight" means to drive crazy. It comes from an old play and movie called—you got it, *Gaslight*. In the movie, Charles Boyer tries to drive Ingrid Bergman

James Ward Lee, gaslighting an audience.

insane by turning the gaslight up and down and denying that there is any change of light. I think he also moves the furniture around and denies that it is not in its usual place and other brainwashing stuff. He is trying to find her cache of jewels or something. Anyway, old Ingrid won an Academy Award for this 1944 movie. Here is something I don't know about the verb "to gaslight": is the past perfect "I had gaslighted" or "I had gaslit?"

I do not have a protocol for gaslighting you. Have you noticed that nobody has a plan anymore? If it is serious it is a protocol. But, hey, I fear I may be getting "off message" here. I just need to prioritize and return to examples of fanciness. Here is one from *Variety*: Some famous director had "helmed a couple of movies." And another had "lensed" several. I stand in awe. I mean, you know, like awesome. Speaking of awe, the annoying Joe Theisman, a football announcer, says that Donovan McNabb's playing fifty-seven minutes on a broken leg was "the most awing thing" he had ever seen. Well, since old Donovan is black, this is probably some hype by the liberal media. I will call Rush Limbaugh when he gets out of rehab and see what he thinks. I can't seem to quit being amazed by fancy words. Robin Wright of the *Los Angeles Times* said on the *MacNeil/Lehrer NewsHour* that somebody came into information and "onpassed it to the FBI." Not long ago, somebody called in to C-Span about the energy crisis and said that if we drilled in Alaska we could be "independent energetically." And Bob Portman (R, Ohio) said the Bush tax cut would be "incentivizing" for business investment. And I am sure he is right, for as President Bush told Paula Zahn in 2000, "a tax cut is really one of the anecdotes to coming out of an economic illness." And I will never misunderestimate Mr. Bush.

Wait. I am getting off message here. I have more fancy talk to talk. Here is the kind of thing the fashion people say. This is from the latest issue of *Vogue* about designer Rick Owens. His new line is:

> through-and-through Rick. Right down to the unmistakable Owens tanks and frayed, pock-marked denims that underpin the tufty shrugs of mink, goat, fox, ostrich, and horsehair, and wispy vests of vulture feathers, this line is a very obvious continuum of his work. Look closer, though, and there's been a subtle amping up of the Owens aesthetic. . . . there are chicly delicate details like chiffon scarves knotted on the back of a coat or fluffs of goat hair sprouting from long leather gauntlets.

These clothes were worn by super models. Have you noticed that there is not a plain old model left in America? They are all super models dressed by uber designers.

Fashion folk are wonderful. Do you remember the late Stanley Marcus, the man who invented culture? Well, maybe he didn't invent it in Boston or New York, but he brought it back to Dallas many years ago. He introduced Texans to the word "fortnight" with his celebrated Neiman-Marcus Fortnights. As he grew old and satisfied that he had done all he could to civilize Dallas, he took to writing newspaper columns. In one he wanted to drop the name Ludwig Bemelmans, the man who wrote the "Madeline" stories. Stanley wrote, "In the course of my life, I have met a lot of well identified people. By that I mean people who have a sufficient number of accomplishments to qualify for a bit more attention than many of their contemporaries." What he meant was, "I know a lot of famous people." I can match him, for I once saw Chubby Checker in person. My late friend A. C. Greene left us with a posthumous book called *Chance Encounters*, in which he enumerated every famous person he had ever seen. And A. C. collected "well identified people" the way a blue serge suit attracts lint. On one occasion, he was taking to some other famous person, probably Lily Pons, in the Baker Hotel lobby and saw a man he thought was the great folklorist and reciter of "Lasca," Hermes Hye. He told Lily Pons or Princess Grace or Madame Maria Oudspensky or whoever he was with, "There is Hermes Nye." Well it turned out not to be Hermes, but A. C. put his picture in the book anyway.

Much of this stuff drives me crazy. I may need a self-help guru to address my concerns about modern fancy talk, someone like Stephen Covey, the *Seven Habits* guy who threatens to teach us "to create synergy with others through Quadrant II activities such as creating shared vision and empowering stewardship agreements. We will show you how to create a common compass that will empower you to form complementary teams that leverage your strengths." Or I could do as Don Henley advises in one of his Eagles songs and "get in touch with my inner child and kick its little ass." Or, as Doctor Phil says, "Open up a big old can of Whoop Ass." Well, maybe there is a time to talk plain.

One of the great things about the present Iraq war is that we have added some fancy talk to the language. Our forces have to be "robust," that is to say we simply have to put more "boots on the ground." Robust does not mean healthy as it used to in plain talk. It now means overwhelming in force, it means that we have to have a serious "footprint" in the Middle East. Now, footprints are also applicable to many other things. They are not simply prints of the feet. My computer has a footprint, as does my car. My vehicle needs a moderate, not robust, footprint or my garage will not hold it. The capacious Cadillac Brougham, the official dowager's (that means old lady's) car of Fort Worth has too robust a footprint for my garage. It has the same number of tires on the ground as my Toyota, but it is more generous as to size.

Some of the fanciest talkers in the world are the oenologists. Daniel Johannes, a wine critic for *Gourmet*, suggests "staying away from the powerhouse wines, which tend to dominate or even clash with a diverse assortment of canapés. Modest wines with a crisp acidity and fresh fruit flavors are more flexible." Here is what he says about a 1997 Sauvignon Blanc from the Russian River Valley: "It has citrus and melon aromas and is concentrated yet crisp, with a dry zesty finish." And a red from Santa Barbara: "a great all-purpose choice. It is light-bodied enough so as not to overwhelm the food, but it has plenty of juicy, red-berry flavor." It ain't none of what my old Navy pals used to call Dago Red. I can't read about vinobabble without remembering what John Steed says on an old *Avengers* TV show. Steed and Mrs. Peele break into a house, and Steed opens the fridge, pulls out a bottle of wine and says, "Plucky, but from the wrong side of the hill."

We all need a wine that is "user-friendly," that is "muscular," that has "a clean nose and a nice finish." I got that from the *Dallas Morning News* of 17 March 1999. But Fort Worth will not be outdone on fancy talk. Bud Kennedy in the *Star-Telegram* once wrote of a 1993 Reisling: "It is a classically racy, snappy reisling that starts off as very tight and austere, and takes years to unveil itself from behind its girdle of acidity." But what do I know, I was raised on Thunderbird and Richard's Irish Rose and Annie Greensprings.

I have to admit it: I am not edgy. Edgy does not mean nervous, which I am, but means out on the edge. With it. Unremittingly avant garde. I am not one of those people referred to in the *New York Times* as "people of money" who "have snapshot lifestyles." I am an old country boy from Alabama who is simply trying to learn to live in the world of the sophisticated. Back in Leeds, Alabama, T. B. Whitmire, the undertaker and furniture store owner, used to tell us that when we went to Birmingham, we had to say "those" and "came." My mother and her cousin Ruby Lathem, who had a child out of wedlock and passed him off as her cousin, once had a long discussion on whether the correct English was, "I took a dose of medicine" or "I takened a dose of medicine." They settled on "taken" as the most proper. I was all right to say "took" in Leeds, but if you went to Birmingham, you had better say "taken." Louie Dill, one of my father's World War I friends used to be called "Old I Were." Louie would make sentences like, "I were going down to Silura to buy me a mule." Or "I were here on time but where was you at?" I have tried to follow the advice of T. B. Whitmire and also learn from what I once saw in a *New Yorker* cartoon, where one woman says of another, "she is so refined that she never uses the objective case." So just between you and I, I am trying hard to come into this modern world of ours in which we now live today. At this point in time, as you might say.

Define the following terms (in native Texan)

fixin' to: to be about to commence an activity

carry me over to . . . : to give someone a ride in
an automobile

whole 'nuther:

frog strangler:

coke:

ABC's

Report Card

$2 + 5 = 7$

23

Folk Use of Mnemonics

by Jerry Crouser

There is little argument that everyone has a desire to have a much better memory. After all, we make comments to the effect of, "I sure do wish I could remember that person's name!" or, "I wish I could remember when that English paper is due." Yes, we all have times when our memory seems to go out the window, and most of us seem to spend a portion of our life explaining our dilemma by using the expression, "It's right on the tip of my tongue!" How many times have we been forced to say that—and then admit, "But I just can't remember it!"

Many people, however, have developed the ability to create meaningful memory skills. These skills are the subject of mnemonics—techniques which people deliberately use in order to help them recall information. Mnemonics comes from the Greek and literally means "of the mind." It is the science of organizing new information and filing it in the mind by connecting it to something that is already known. It is very different from repetition and rote memorization. Because mnemonics is the art of remembering, it is a person's intentional and thoughtful construction of a memory aide to recall information more efficiently.

Before giving a report about the methods people employ in order to help them remember things, a very vital question must first be answered. Why do we forget some things and remember others? The crux of an effective system lies in learning how we remember *anything* at all.

For example, my son, Ryan, knows the names, faces, and statistics of literally hundreds of baseball players, but he really struggles in his lessons at school. Being a concerned parent, I asked him how he managed to remember so much baseball information. "I'm interested in baseball, dad. Who cares about that other junk?" Yes, the biggest reason for remembering is interest. Interest begets attention, and when one pays attention he concentrates, and concentration sends a mental impulse though the "mental switchboard operator" who routes this impulse to the senses to file an impression that results in memory.

Since the biggest spark plug of memory recall is interest, it is always easier to remember things we are interested in rather than things we are not. The human mind has a tremendous ability to remember, and by doing the following exercise, you might well begin to appreciate how successful the memory can really be:

> Recall as many details as possible about your high school graduation.
> Recall as much as you can about a party or event you attended more than five years ago.
> Make a list of three schoolmates you haven't seen in five years, and describe some things you remember about them.
> Write the names of ten people you remember from your childhood.
> Make a list of ten important dates you remember.

After spending some time on these lists, try to analyze the reason why you succeeded in remembering some things better than others.[1] If you are like most people, your mind went through a process of mental images in which you were forced to picture in a literal way the times, places, and events involved in making the lists. Perhaps there were even things you wanted to recall, but simply could not come up with a mental picture, and therefore, could not remember.

In other words, when a person attempts to recall information, he is forced to create images in his mind. These images, in turn, act somewhat as a file retrieval system, and by a process of association a person suddenly remembers things that have long been hidden in the mind![2]

Efficient file retrieval systems, however, are created by direct effort, or by unusual and/or traumatic experiences. For example, if you walked out of your home and a few drops of rain splattered on you, you would quickly forget it ever happened. If, however, buckets of water were suddenly splashed upon your head, you would remember the event and probably recount it in detail for years. If you stopped to rest in a picnic area, and a cow or two wandered by, you might enjoy the pleasant moment. But if a crazed bull came into sight and you had to run for your life, you would never forget it. This is the reason why people remember exactly where they were and what they were doing when they first heard the news of President John Kennedy's assassination, an event that happened many years ago.[3]

When file retrieval systems are created by direct effort, we are entering the world of mnemonics. One popular mnemonic technique uses the association of rhyme and/or rhythm in order to retrieve information. Because it is used quite extensively, many fond memories may even begin to appear when you are reminded of these rhymes and rhythms. For example, I always remember, "I before e, except after c or when in the sound of a, as in *neighbor* or *weigh*" (remembering spelling rules). "Thirty days hath September, April, June, and November. All the rest have thirty-one, except February, which has twenty-eight in fine, 'til leap year gives it twenty-nine" (remembering how many days each month has). "M, I, crooked letter, crooked letter, I, crooked letter, crooked letter, I, hump back, hump back, I" (remembering how to spell Mississippi). "In fourteen hundred and ninety two, Columbus sailed the ocean blue" (remembering history facts).

One of my wife's friends told me that when she was in school, she had a hard time recalling adverbs. Because she wanted so badly to remember when a word was an adverb and what it actually did, she composed a song that used the same tune and rhythm as "When the Saints Go Marching In":

Who, what, where, to what extent and why,
Who, what, where, to what extent and why,

> Who, what, where, to what extent and why,
> Adverbs go marching on.[4]

Another mnemonic device used by some people involves "linking," the process of visual association and image forming. That is, it is the active process of taking a mental picture, and then associating the picture to something you wish to remember. Actually, visualization is so basic and obvious to our memory that we sometimes "Can't see the forest because of the trees." For example, think of a zebra. Don't you see a black and white striped horselike animal in your mind? Of course you do! In fact, if someone came up to you and said, "Don't you dare think about a large pink elephant," you could not help but picture the image in you mind! Therefore, if something can be visualized, it can be easily remembered.[5]

The process of linking is commonly taught by memory experts, but I found that very few folks actually employ such a mnemonic device. People frequently have a need to bring to mind lists of information, like notes for a test, a grocery shopping list, or a list of chores that need to be done. While most people make use of pen and paper for most of these types of records, it is not always convenient to write them down, nor is it advisable to depend upon such a written list for an exam. Therefore, the application of linking can solve this dilemma. For example, suppose someone gave you an inventory of fifteen items, and you were asked to repeat the inventory back in a few minutes without the use of notes. The list is as follows:

Car, spider, tree, cloud, goldfish, fireman, windmill, book, toothbrush, television, snow, rabbit, house, cigar, Frenchfries.

Most people would panic at the thought of having to repeat the items by memory only, but creating unusual pictures in the mind will provide instant and lasting recall. The process might go something like this: (Remember to make a deliberate effort to form vivid mental pictures as you read this story.)

The first word is car, so picture in your mind an old Model T car. A *spider* is driving the car, and the car runs into a *tree*, causing a cloud of smoke. Out of the cloud falls a *goldfish*, and out of the goldfish pops a fireman. The fireman spots a *windmill* on fire and runs to put it out. He can't get in because it is full of *books*. Suddenly, a *toothbrush* picks up all the books and walks off to his home. The toothbrush lives in a *television* set which is filled with *snow*. Out of the snow pops a *rabbit*, who builds a house made of *cigars*. The cigars smell just like *Frenchfries*.

The key to remembering lists is simply to create a bizarre and unusual mental picture, linking it to the item, and connecting the pictures in a story. Because the story is funny and silly, the items are easily recalled. In fact, the more bizarre the story, the easier it is to remember.[6]

Of all of the mnemonic devices that are available, perhaps "mental hooking" is the most commonly used by folk groups. Mental hooking establishes association by simply creating a clever sentence, saying, or trick in order to help recall. Knowing that there are so many exceptions to spelling rules in English, sometimes it's just good common sense to build mental hooks to abstract spellings. I was especially lucky to have a fourth grade elementary teacher who understood this mnemonic concept. Here are some examples of her wisdom:

At one time, I was experiencing great difficulty in spelling the word *motorcycle*. No matter how hard I tried, it always ended up *motercycle* on a test. My teacher asked me to picture two wheels with spokes, and these two wheels would represent the two "o's" in the word *motorcycle*.

The two words *capitol* and *capital* were often mixed up in my mind. My teacher suggested that the "o" in *capitol* would represent the big domed building in Austin. Then, she explained that since "a" is the first letter of the alphabet, I should remember capital when thinking of capital letters.

Since my elementary years, I have continued to use this method to help with spelling skills.

One of my own favorite mental hooks involves how to remember *asphalt*. In my mind I imagine a little worm, called an asp. The asp is crawling on the road and comes up to a stop sign. The stop sign is yelling out, "Halt!" Then, by putting *asp* and *halt* together, I remember how to spell *asphalt*. Other people make use of similar methods in spelling clues, but instead look for internal word clues that may trigger the memory: In trying to remember how to spell *separate*, it's a good thing to remember that there is "a rat" in *separate*.[7] When thinking of the word, *believe*, think of the sentence, "Never beLIEve a LIE."[8] When wanting to know how to spell *piece*, think of slicing a "PIEce of PIE."[9]

Never beLIEve a LIE

Slice a PIEce of PIE

When trying to remember how to spell *island*, just know that an island "is land" out in the middle of a body of water. In trying to remember the difference between *principal* and *principle*, just recall that the school princiPAL is your PAL, and that a principLE is a ruLE.

One of my neighbors just got back from Germany, and shared an interesting hook device used to remember how many days there are in each month:

Children are told to place their left hand in front of them, clench their fist, with the knuckles turned upward. In that way the knuckles of the little finger on the hand is January (raised and therefore a long month—thirty-one days), the valley beside it is February (lowered and therefore a short month). They continue across the knuckles in the same fashion, and then start over after the last knuckle is counted (July). July and August are the only months that have an equal number of days consecutively. The children are told that all the "hills" have thirty-one days, while all of the "valleys" have thirty days, except February.[10]

An interesting variation to this mnemonic device is found in Spain, where the children use both hands in the counting process instead of only one. The counting process starts either from the right or from the left fist.[11]

My wife's father recently visited Mammoth Cave in Kentucky, where the tour guide offered an interesting trick so that the tourists could remember the difference between stalagmites and stalactites: The middle letter in *stalagmite* is "g" which represents the ground. They are the ones that start on the ground and grow upward. The middle letter in *stalactite* is "c" which represents the ceiling. They are the ones that hang from the ceiling and grow downward. I remember a similar memory trick shared by a tour guide years ago while visiting Carlsbad Caverns in New Mexico: The middle letter in *stalagmite* is "g" which means they want to "grow up." The middle letter in *stalactite* is "c" which means they want to "come down."

Another traditional mnemonic device that is extremely widespread and popular is the application of acronyms, words that are made by taking the first letter from each word that a person wants to remember, and making a new word from all of those letters. The thing about acronyms is that some are so common that most folks do not think of them as mnemonic memory aides, and yet they offer tremendous recall efficiency. For example, what do you think of when you see IRS, MADD, SOP, NRA, or PMA? Most folks readily recognize these acronyms as representing the Internal Revenue Service, Mothers Against Drunk Driving, Standard Operating Procedure, National Rifle Association, and Positive Mental Attitude.

Since this method is usually a fairly simple process for mental file retrieval, it seems to have a special, enduring, and "high-brow" appeal for many folks. Students especially make use of acronyms prior to exams, because they seem to provide high success rates for memory recall. Infinite numbers of examples could be listed, but a few that have proven to be successful in folk cultures are as follows: HOMES is a good way to remember the five great lakes—Huron, Ontario, Michigan, Erie, Superior.

ROY G. BIV helps one to recall the colors of the rainbow (light spectrum). The colors are Red, Orange, Yellow, Green, Blue, Indigo, and Violet. ASK is used to help remember the order of sentences that compose a certain Bible verse. "Ask, and you shall receive; Speak, and you shall find; Knock, and the door shall be opened unto you."

ACTS is used by one pastor of a church in order to help him remember certain elements of a prayer—Adoration, Confession, Thanksgiving, and Supplication. STAB is a good memory aide used by music majors in order to remember the four voices in a choir—Soprano, Tenor, Alto, and Bass. SCALP helps one anatomy student to remember the actual layers of the scalp itself—Skin, Close connective tissue, Aponeurosis, Loose connective tissue, and Pericranium. O-RAGE is an acronym that I developed when wanting to remember the five major folk groups—Occupational, Regional, Age, Gender, and Ethnic.

		#1	#2
O	Oral	(the Old)	(Old)
T	Traditional	(Testament)	(Toys)
V	Variable	(Verifies)	(Vaporize)
A	Anonymous	(Adam's)	(After)
F	Formulaic	(Fall)	(February)

This is the mnemonic device the editor learned to remember the defining elements of folklore (column #1), and the updated version he uses when speaking to elementary age audiences (column #2).

With a little bit of imagination, one can really create some interesting acronyms that will serve as invaluable memory aides, but perhaps the most inventive of all mnemonic tricks rests within the world of "acrostics." Since an acrostic is a sentence that is made by taking the first letter from each word or symbol that you want to remember and inserting another word beginning with that same letter, people invent some very interesting and humorous sentences—as evidenced in the following examples: "King Phillip Came Over For Green Stamps" is used by many biology students in order to remember the classification system of living things—Kingdom, Phylum, Class, Order, Family, Genus, Species. Other variations include "King Philip Came Over For Good Spaghetti" and "Kick Prince Charles Out For molesting Girl Scouts."

"Every Good Boy Does Fine" is a common acrostic used to distinguish the musical notes that are on the lines of a musical staff—E, G, B, D, and F. I learned that, "All Cows Eat Grass" distinguishes the space notes on the Bass Clef—A, C, E, and G. "Mary's Violet Eyes Make John Sit Up Noticing Purple" is a good way to list the planets of the solar system, from the one nearest to the sun to the one farthest away—Mercury, Venus, Earth, Mars, Jupiter, Saturn, Uranus, Neptune, and Pluto. Another variation includes "My Very Educated Mother Just Served Us Nine Pizzas."

"Oh Be A Fine Girl, Kiss Me" (or "Old, Big, And Fat Girls Kiss Maggots," as I learned it) are acrostics invented by physics students to help them remember the spectral temperature classifications of stars, ranging from the hottest to the coolest—O, B, A, F, G, K, and M.

There is no doubt that all of the mnemonic devices discussed so far require a person to make a certain amount of deliberate invention—a certain level of creativity. Some memory clues and tricks are taught, but the vast majority are invented by common folk for common occasions. Perhaps the most demanding of all mnemonic invention centers around a person's need to remember names.

The reason why most names are hard to remember is because most modern names seldom lend themselves to obvious mental imaging. Originally, most names were descriptive—either of the person or of his occupation or particular skill. Names of American Indians were descriptive of the person or of the person's deeds. Names like Sitting Bull, Running Deer, and Growing Flower are easy to remember because of the associations that are naturally created in our minds. Even the names of Butler, Wolfe, Carpenter, Forrest, Brooks, Rivers, and so forth establish mental images for most people without even thinking about it.

When obvious mental associations are not available in a name we hear, a person must link some visual characteristic or something about the person's name to some mental picture. Sometimes, this is a very difficult task, but some association must be created. For example:

Name	Assimilation	Mental Picture
Bill Goff	Pay Bills, Play Golf	Picture Mr. Goff paying his bills at the golf course
Jerry Crouser	Bald Head, Bearded, Wearing Trousers	Picture Mr. Crouser as Jerry (rhymes with hairy) Crouser (rhymes with trouser)

By use of this method, remembering names can be as simple as 1, 2, 3. After hearing a name, simply form a substitute word, phrase, or thought that will remind you of the name. Then, find an outstanding feature about the person, whether it be a feature of his face or something he has said about himself. And finally, simply associate the two things into a visual image.[12]

In conclusion, memory is neither like a static storehouse where data is kept, nor is it like a library where knowledge is stored in random fashion. Rather, it is an organized system whereby accessible knowledge is consciously stored with a deliberate effort for future recall, using the basic skills of mental picture association. As Plato once said, "All knowledge is but remembrance."[13]

We have seen that there is already extensive use of mnemonic devices by many folk people from many backgrounds. We owe it to ourselves to become as familiar with memory development techniques as we can. As we build upon our own skills, we will be able to accomplish so much more. What good is an education if nothing is ever learned, and what good is learning if nothing is ever remembered?

ENDNOTES

1. Bryne, Brendan. *Three Weeks To A Better Memory*. Philadelphia: John C. Winston Co., 1951. 29.
2. Lorayne, Harry. *Page A Minute Memory Book*, New York: Holt, Rinehart, and Winston, 1985. 7.
3. Ibid.17.
4. Robinson, Beth. Student at Angelo State University.
5. Lorayne. 7.
6. *Memory Techniques*, Cassette College Audio Tapes, Nashville: 1987, Tape 1, Side A.
7. Wade, Wes. Manager of West Texas Bearing Co., raised in San Angelo, Texas.
8. Crouser, Jan. Housewife, born in Illinois, raised in west Texas.
9. Galloup, Juanita. Housewife in Odessa, Texas, raised in Duncanville, Illinois.
10. Baumgardner, Lynn. Housewife, raised in Kentucky.
11. Lorenzano, Jenny. Housewife, raised in New Mexico.
12. Lorayne. 47.
13. Weber, Linda. "You Can Improve Your Memory." *Good Housekeeping* Vol. 206, No. 3, March 1988. 195.

24

Some Aspects of Language in Selected Cowboy Poetry

by Mary Jane Hurst

The popularity of cowboy poetry increases every year. The Cowboy Poetry Gathering in Elko, Nevada, which debuted in 1985, has become an annual event, attracting world-wide media attention. Cowboy festivals have sprung up throughout the country, and recitations by cowboy poets have become a regular part of county fairs, folklore meetings, museum shows, and even business openings in the West and Southwest. Cowboy poets have achieved a kind of celebrity status, appearing, for example, on the Tonight Show and being written about in *People* magazine. Collections of cowboy poetry, cowboy stories, and cowboy songs have sold well for university presses and other publishing companies. For its intrinsic merits and because of its widespread popularity, cowboy poetry deserves serious academic attention.

In an earlier article in *Concho River Review*, I discussed ways in which cowboy poetry is related to other, more traditional forms of American literature, and I argued that a full appreciation of contemporary cowboy poetry requires a recognition of the genre's critical and thematic ties to history, particularly to a strong oral folk tradition in America and to the Old Southwest Humor of the nineteenth century. More recently, in "'The Rain is the Sweat of the Sky': Cowboy Poetry as American Ethnopoetics," Scott Preston also places cowboy poetry within its larger context of American literary history, noting that "cowboy poetry demands a reexamination of assumptions about the development of American literature and its role in the life of the country."[1] David Stanley's summative "Cowboy Poetry Then and Now: An Overview" not only references Alan Lomax's tracing of cowboy poetry's roots to the "verbal art of soldiers and sailors, largely English and Irish in origin, which combined with the songs and hollers of black cowboys and the *corrido* tradition of the vaqueros,"[2] but extends those roots to include first, the expressions of herding cultures throughout the centuries and second, many educated borrowings "from the forms, metrics, and images of folk song, the Bible, classic literature, and contemporary verse."[3]

Notwithstanding its clear ties to mainstream elements in history and literature, cowboy poetry utilizes a distinctive idiom. In the present essay, I would like to examine a few notable aspects of cowboy poetry's language, contrasting cowboy poets' use of certain features of language with that of other poets.[4] As David Stanley has said, "Far from being doggerel, cowboy poetry, both classic and contemporary, is more complex and subtle than it may seem on the surface."[5] The present discussion will draw primarily on eight poems chosen at random from Hal Cannon's 1985 collection entitled *Cowboy Poetry: A Gathering*. The selected group includes Omar Barker's "Jack Potter's Courtin'," Allen McCanless's "The Cowboy's Soliloquy," Gail Gardner's "The Dude Wrangler" and "The Sierry Petes," Bruce Kiskaddon's "That Little Blue Roan," Georgie Sicking's "Old Tuff" and "To Be a Top Hand," and Don Ian Smith's "Old Horse." All of these are now cowboy classics, though some have been composed more recently than others. About half of the poems are centered on descriptions of people or animals, and about half are narrative.

Verb usage is always an important indicator of style. These selected cowboy verses make use of relatively few linking verbs.[6] *Be* verbs are outnumbered by almost a five to one margin; only eighty-two linking verbs appear in the eight poems, compared with 357 action verbs. This figure even includes the fifteen *be* verbs in "Jack Potter's Courtin'," which appear in the poem specifically to illustrate the difficulty a shy cowboy has in keeping a conversation going with "a gal named Cordie Eddy, mighty purty, sweet and pure,"[7] whom he wishes to marry. The poem notes that Jack rides a hundred miles to see her:

> . . . a-sweatin' with the thought
> Of sweetsome words to ask her with, the way a feller ought:

"I'm just a humble cowhand, Miss Cordie, if you please,
That hereby asks your heart and hand upon my bended
knees!"

It sounded mighty simply, thus rehearsed upon the trail,
But when he comes to Cordie's house his words all
seemed to fail.

'Twas "Howdy, Ma'am, an' how's the crops?
An' how's your Pa and Ma?"
For when it come to askin' her, he couldn't come
to taw.[8]

Except for the portions of direct discourse between the cowboy
and Miss Cordie, which are intended to convey the cowboy's awk-
ward inarticulateness during a romantic situation, this poem, like
the others, contains few linking verbs.

The variety of action verbs in cowboy poetry is striking. Animals are said to *bush up, buck, fight, react, outfigure, moan* and
frisk, for example. Cowboys *understand, learn, forget, shoot, figger,
recall, savvy, suffer, kiss, smash, blink, build, spy,* and *die.* The range
of verbs describes typical actions of a cowboy, roping, branding,
and riding, but the verbs also ascribe specific qualities to cowboys.
For instance, the verbs *understand* and *learn*, or synonyms for
them, such as *figgered out* or *savvy*, appear in almost every poem.
The cowboy, then, is portrayed as thinking about his life and
adapting to his environment.

Verbs with particles are quite common in cowboy poetry, as in
sets up, look out, coiled up, branded up, and *lapped on.* Previously
used in informal or colloquial expressions, particles today are quite
common in writing as well as in speech. Normally, we do not even
notice particles in standard contemporary English except when
purists, mistaking them for prepositions, object to their position at
the end of a sentence, as in "She took the trash out" or "He tried
the sweater on." The appearance of particles in early cowboy

poetry would have been more of a distinctive feature, marking the language as casual and non-traditional.

A number of verbal idioms are also used in cowboy poems: cowboys "get to talkin'," "take a hint," "fall in love," "pop the question," and "keep under control." These idioms add to the informal, oral, and free-spirited tone of the poetry. Yet, many verbs are formed in ways more typical of older dialects of English. In Gail Gardner's "The Sierry Petes," for instance, the cowboy "sez" he "aint a-goin" but starts "a-packin," while the devil can be seen "a-prancin" and "a-bellerin." The orthographically-represented pronunciation of *sez* and the deletion of final -g, as in *packin* rather than *packing*, along with the nonstandard grammar shown by *aint*, mark regional and social dialect. Verb forms in cowboy poetry are also notable in the use of the prefix *a-*, as in *a-packin* or *a-bellerin*. Whereas particles represent a newer development in the English language, *a*-prefixing reflects a much older form. Long ago featured in standard English, *a*-prefixing now appears as a fossilized presence in older nursery rhymes, stories, and songs (as in "a-hunting we will go") and in certain socioeconomic dialects within certain geographical regions. Linguist Walt Wolfram describes the *a*- as "an older form which has now become socially stigmatized."[9]

Although commonly associated with Appalachian English or other rural southern dialects, the appearance of a-prefixing in cowboy poetry proves its wider usage. Of course, some of the cowboy poets or their ancestors originated in the Appalachian region or elsewhere in the South. Another literary example of a-prefixing occurs in Mark Twain's *Huckleberry Finn*; even when that novel was published in 1885, Huck's language was meant to depict him as a lower-class, backwoods boy.[10] It might be argued, of course, that *a*-prefixing is not a stigmatized feature to those individuals in whose dialect the form appears. Indeed, in some cowboy circles, *a*-prefixing might be said to mark in-group status.[11]

Although good poetry is not nearly as full of adjectives and adverbs as the popular stereotype would suggest, cowboy poetry contains noticeably fewer modifiers than do other types of poetry.

Built almost exclusively around strong, active verbs, cowboy poetry is far from being exclamatory or flowery. Adjectives in cowboy poetry are as scarce as trees on a West Texas ranch. There might be a few groves scattered around, but mostly there is only an isolated example here and there. The 1885 classic "The Cowboy's Soliloquy" by Allen McCanless, for example, includes thirty-four action verbs (such as *emigrated*, *started*, *stretches*, *hint*, *ride*, and *bake*), but only three adjectives (*all*, *luckier*, and *small*) in its ten stanzas about the cowboy's way of life.

In all, the eight cowboy poems selected for this discussion contain only seventy-nine adjectives and thirty-three adverbs.[12] The adjectives are thus outnumbered by the 357 action verbs almost five to one. Many of the adjectives are quite ordinary, such as *big*, *silver*, *good*, and *patient*. The adjectives *sad* and *gentle* appear numerous times. A few adjectives, such as *ancient* and *artistic*, are a bit more unusual for this ordinarily plain and unostentatious verse. Some adjectives, such as *sweetsome*, are formed through compounding, which is more typical of older forms of English. Hyphenated adjectives are common, as in *pump-tailed*, *long-yered*, and *Gawd-forsaken*. Dialectical pronunciations of these adjectives and adverbs are often rendered through variant spellings or distinctive orthography, as in *yeller* for *yellow*, *shorely* for *surely*, and *ol'* for *old*.

To see how these proportions and types of verbs and adjectives in cowboy poetry compare to other types of verse, we could examine the language in some familiar canonical poems. For purposes of the present discussion, the following seven poems have been selected at random from a classic anthology: Randall Jarrell's "The Death of the Ball Turret Gunner," Edgar Allan Poe's "To Helen," Theodore Roethke's "Dolor," two sonnets by William Shakespeare, Sonnet 18 ("Shall I compare thee to a summer's day?") and Sonnet 29 ("When in disgrace with fortune and men's eyes"), Karl Shapiro's "Auto Wreck," and Alfred, Lord Tennyson's "Break, Break, Break." These canonical poems are drawn from a range of time periods and reflect various styles and themes. Obviously, this is just a small sample, and there are, admittedly, limitations in comparing one small group of poems with another equally small group.

The seven traditional poems contain slightly fewer linking verbs than do the cowboy poems. The traditional poems contain 101 action verbs and fourteen linking verbs, at a seven to one margin, compared to the five to one margin of action verbs to linking verbs in the selected cowboy poems. The verbs in the mainstream verse, such as *dips, spatters, invites,* and *blooms,* are just as concrete as in the cowboy verse.

However, a great difference can be found in the use of adjectives between the two sets of poetry. The mainstream poems contain sixty-five adjectives and thirty-seven adverbs, thus using almost as many modifiers (102) as verbs (115). In the two Shakespearean sonnets, the number of modifiers is the same as the number of verbs (eighteen). This compares to the cowboy poetry in which the 112 modifiers are dwarfed by the 439 verbs. Moreover, the adjectives in the canonical poems are more learned, as in *inexorable, unalterable, occult, expedient, sullen, Nicean,* and *agate.* The adjectives in these poems are not necessarily more flowery, but they are multisyllabic and somewhat out of the ordinary.

Shakespeare's extensive vocabulary of some 30,000 different words is often contrasted with the King James Bible, which contains only about 8,000 different words.[13] No one would dispute the richness of expression in the King James Bible, despite its more limited vocabulary. Similarly, it would be nonsense to disparage cowboy poetry because it uses simple and unadorned words. Still, many people associate a varied and developed vocabulary with clarity and precision of thought. So, why would cowboy poets express themselves with few direct and ordinary adjectives, relying mainly on plain, active verbs to convey meaning?

There are at least three answers to this question. The most obvious answer is that cowboys are writing in their native idiom, expressing themselves honestly and truthfully in the same plain, direct, and action-oriented manner found in their everyday speech. A second and related explanation for the language patterns in cowboy poetry could be associated with the fact that in some ways, cowboy verse resembles prose more than poetry, a connection to be expected given cowboy poetry's ties to tales, stories, and the old southwest tradition of humorous legends. But, third, it seems that cowboy poets are also somewhat self-conscious in avoiding fancy or unusual language, as if in reaction against the popular stereotype that poetry should be exclamatory or flowery. In fact, however, David Stanley sees the imagery in "The Cowboy's Soliloquy" as being "taken directly from Shakespeare's *As You Like It*."[14] Just because a cowboy poet writes with simple and direct language, it does not necessarily follow that the author is uneducated.

Poetry can be written in diverse forms and can appeal to diverse types of people. Cowboy poetry expresses itself in its own fresh and authentic idiom, and we need not wish that it were anything other than its own natural self. The cowboy poets' efforts may sometimes be the object of bemusement or even satire, but their poems will also be the object of appreciation for their form as well as for their content because, in addition to the information cowboy poems provide about the cowboy's life, the poems also tell us about the cowboy's language. As shown in the present discussion, elements of conservatism (as in the preservation of older forms of language such as compounding and *a*-prefixing) and elements of innovation (as in the presence of particles and other free and informal manners of expression) coexist within the social and

Mary Jane Hurst, May 2005.

geographical dialects of cowboy poetry. This linguistic finding cor-
relates well with the philosophy of life typically attributed to the
cowboy: conservative and traditional in some regards, but fiercely
independent and free-thinking in others.[15]

ENDNOTES

1. Preston, Scott. "The Rain is the Sweat of the Sky': *Cowboy Poetry as
   American Ethnopoetics.*" Cowboy Poets & Cowboy Poetry. David
   Stanley and Elaine Thatcher, eds. Urbana: U of Illinois P, 2000. 50.
2. Stanley, David. "Cowboy Poetry Then and Now: An Overview."
   Cowboy Poets & Cowboy Poetry. David Stanley and Elaine Thatcher,
   eds. Urbana: Illinois P, 2000. 3.
3. Ibid. 6.
4. Those interested in the meter and rhyme of cowboy poetry should
   consult David Stanley's discussion of those subjects in "Orderly
   Disorder: Form and Tension in Cowboy Poetry." Stanley's core
   observations about the significance of language in cowboy poetry
   are similar to mine. He concludes that "cowboy poetry exemplifies
   this continued questioning of language and of the stability of the
   text" (123). Among others who have given specific attention to
   language issues in cowboy poetry are Scott Preston in "'The Rain is
   the Sweat of the Sky': Cowboy Poetry as American Ethnopoetics"
   (especially the section subtitled "Linguistic Parallels between Cowboy Poetry and Ethnopoetries") and Buck Ramsey in "Cowboy
   Libraries and Lingo."

   One other study of language in cowboy poetry that deserves particular notice is Barbara Barney Nelson's "Every Educated Feller
   Ain't a Plumb Greenhorn: Cowboy Poetry's Polyvocal Narrator."
   Nelson argues that public performances of cowboy poetry are creating changes in or even the loss of a "collective narrative voice" (49).
   She claims that, "In old cowboy poetry the dramatic . . . narrator
   usually speaks with a plural voice (we) representing the culture, usually as a minor character within the drama, watching from the fringe
   of the action" (49). Modern cowboy performances, she says, have
   changed the genre so that "new cowboy poetry seems to address a
   spectating audience rather than speak on behalf of and to a specific
   dramatic audience of working class cowboys. The narrative voice
   changes from polyvocal to first person singular and becomes more
   autobiographical, didactic, and omniscient" (55). Undoubtedly, Nelson is correct that media attention, popular performances, and new
   audiences are influencing developments in contemporary cowboy

poetry. However, all living entities, including languages, are constantly changing. Changes in language or in anything else can be, but are not necessarily, bad.

Nearly everyone who writes about cowboy poetry comments upon its distinctive language and upon its roots in the oral traditions, but the point still needs to be emphasized that part of what cowboy poetry is all about is language.

5. Stanley, David. "Orderly Disorder: Form and Tension in Cowboy Poetry." *Cowboy Poets & Cowboy Poetry.* David Stanley and Elaine Thatcher, eds. Urbana: Illinois P, 2000. 122.

6. For present purposes, forms of *be* were not included in tallies of linking verbs if they were used as auxiliaries, as in "He had been walking." Only *be* verbs used as the main verbs of a clause (as in, "He was cold and hungry") were counted as linking verbs.

7. Barker, S. Omar. "Jack Potter's Courtin'." *Cowboy Poetry: A Gathering.* Ed. Hal Cannon. Salt Lake City: Peregrine Smith Books, 1985. 15.

8. Ibid. 16.

9. Wolfram, Walt. "A-Prefixing in Appalachian English." *Locating Language in Time and Space.* Ed. William Labov. New York: Academic P, 1980. 108.

10. Lamont Antieu discusses a-prefixing in "'I'm a-going to see what's going on here': A-prefixing in *The Adventures of Huckleberry Finn.*" While Huck Finn's portrayal as an unsophisticated, backwoods boy is carefully represented by his speech, his language actually proves him to be an "active and discriminating" speaker and listener (Hurst, *Voice of the Child* 103). Throughout the novel, Huck Finn uses language for maximum effectiveness, whether he is implying a falsehood, pretending to be someone else, or engaging in some other complex linguistic maneuver.

11. *A*-prefixing can be better understood after a review of its historical origins. Wolfram ("*A*-Prefixing") attributes the form to prepositional phrases. Pyles and Algeo (264) specifically attribute the *a-* in *aside*, *alive*, *aboard*, and *a-hunting* to an earlier form of *on* plus the word. Oliver Farrar Emerson (151) attributes the prefix *a-* to various origins: from Old English *of-* in *adown*, *on-* in *away*, *and-* in *along*, and *ge-* in *aware* and *afford*; from Old French *en-* in *anoint*; and from other borrowed sources in other words. Such diversity in the origins of the *a-* prefix can also be traced through entries from the *Oxford English Dictionary* and from the *Middle English Dictionary*. The prefix *a-* has actually been lost from some verbs since the Middle English period; Emerson's *Middle English Reader* (321) reveals, for example, that Middle English *afinden*, derived from Old English

gefindan, has now lost the *a-* to become the streamlined *find*. All living languages change over time, and modern English is substantially different from Old or Middle English. Readers today even have difficulty with Early Modern English texts such as the King James Bible or Shakespeare's plays.

In Old English, of course, *ge-* was used to mark past participles, as in *fremman* "to do," *fremede* "did," and *gefremed* "done" (Pyles and Algeo 125). So, in addition to the phonological connection of *ge-* with *a-* (as indicated above in *find*, *afford*, and *aware*), could there be other connections between the two forms? For example, could remnants of *ge-* from the past participle have become erroneously associated at some point with the emerging present participle in some dialects? I know of no hard evidence for such a possibility, but it is unsatisfactory to try to explain *a*-prefixing solely by the prepositional phrase theory. Actually, Wolfram has also stated that "the form may function differently in different constructions, as suggested by the differences in serialization for progressive and adverbial *a*-prefixing" ("Reconsidering" 252). Frazer's subsequent essay "More on the Semantics of A-Prefixing" sheds further light on this complex and interesting form.

12. For purposes of this discussion, articles (*a*, *an*, and *the*), possessive pronouns (such as *my*), and demonstrative pronouns (such as *that*) were not counted as adjectives. Words such as *paper* clip and *Holy Land* were treated as double nouns rather than adjective plus noun formation. The word *not* was not counted as an adverb.

13. McCrum, Robert, William Cran, and Robert MacNeil. *The Story of English.* New York: Viking, 1986. 91–125.

14. Stanley. "Cowboy Poetry." 5.

15. Jim Hoy plots *the future* of cowboy poetry on the same axis the present essay finds reflected in *the language* of past and current cowboy poetry: conservatism and innovation. He predicts that "the best cowboy poets will take cowboy poetry down two paths in the future: the innovators will expand the possibilities for the genre, while the traditionalists will preserve the best of the past" (295). The present discussion revises and updates an earlier article of mine ("Linguistic Innovation and Conservatism: Dialect in Cowboy Poetry") which appeared in the *New Mexico Humanities Review*.

BIBLIOGRAPHY

Altenbernd, Lynn, and Leslie L. Lewis, eds. *Introduction to Literature: Poems.* New York: Macmillan, 1963.

Antieu, Lamont. "'I'm a-going to see what's going on here': *A*-prefixing in *The Adventures of Huckleberry Finn.*" *Language and Literature* 10.2 (2001): 145-57.

Barker, S. Omar. "Jack Potter's Courtin.'" *Cowboy Poetry: A Gathering.* Ed. Hal Cannon. Salt Lake City: Peregrine Smith Books, 1985. 15–17.

Cannon, Hal, ed. *Cowboy Poetry: A Gathering.* Salt Lake City: Peregrine Smith Books, 1985.

Emerson, Oliver Farrar. *A Brief History of the English Language.* New York: Macmillan, 1941.

————. *A Middle English Reader.* New York: Macmillan, 1908.

Frazer, T.C. "More on the Semantics of A-Prefixing." *American Speech* 65.1 (1990): 89–93.

Gardner, Gail. "The Dude Wrangler." *Cowboy Poetry: A Gathering.* Ed. Hal Cannon. Salt Lake City: Peregrine Smith Books, 1985. 5–7.

————. "The Sierry Petes." *Cowboy Poetry: A Gathering.* Ed. Hal Cannon. Salt Lake City: Peregrine Smith Books, 1985. 3–5.

Hoy, Jim. "Whither Cowboy Poetry?" *Great Plains Quarterly* 19.4 (1999): 291–97.

Hurst, Mary Jane. "The Historical Context of Contemporary Cowboy Poetry." *Concho River Review* 4 (1990): 59–66.

————. "Linguistic Innovation and Conservatism: Dialect in Cowboy Poetry." *New Mexico Humanities Review* 36 (1992): 103–12.

————. *The Voice of the Child in American Literature: Linguistic Approaches to Fictional Child Language.* Lexington: UP of Kentucky, 1990.

Jarrell, Randall. "The Death of the Ball Turret Gunner." *Introduction to Literature: Poems.* Lynn Altenbernd and Leslie L. Lewis, eds. New York: Macmillan, 1963. 488.

Kiskaddon, Bruce. "That Little Blue Roan." *Cowboy Poetry: A Gathering.* Ed. Hal Cannon. Salt Lake City: Peregrine Smith Books, 1985. 32–33.

Lomax, Alan. "Introduction." *Cowboy Songs and Other Frontier Ballads.* 1910. John A. Lomax and Alan Lomax, eds. New York: Macmillan, 1986. xviii–xxix.

McCanless, Allen. "The Cowboy's Soliloquy." *Cowboy Poetry: A Gathering.* Ed. Hal Cannon. Salt Lake City: Peregrine Smith Books, 1985. 1–2.

McCrum, Robert, William Cran, and Robert MacNeil. *The Story of English*. New York: Viking, 1986.

Nelson, Barbara Barney. "Every Educated Feller Ain't a Plumb Greenhorn: Cowboy Poetry's Polyvocal Narrator." *Heritage of the Great Plains* 33.2 (2000): 49–64.

Poe, Edgar Allan. "To Helen." *Introduction to Literature: Poems.* Lynn Altenbernd and Leslie L. Lewis, eds. New York: Macmillan, 1963. 316.

Preston, Scott. "'The Rain is the Sweat of the Sky': Cowboy Poetry as American Ethnopoetics." *Cowboy Poets & Cowboy Poetry.* David Stanley and Elaine Thatcher, eds. Urbana: U of Illinois P, 2000. 39–51.

Pyles, Thomas, and John Algeo. *The Origins and Development of the English Language.* Third Edition. New York: Harcourt, 1982.

Ramsey, Buck. "Cowboy Libraries and Lingo." *Cowboy Poets & Cowboy Poetry.* David Stanley and Elaine Thatcher, eds. Urbana: U of Illinois P, 2000. 88–106.

Roethke, Theodore. "Dolor." *Introduction to Literature: Poems.* Lynn Altenbernd and Leslie L. Lewis, eds. New York: Macmillan, 1963. 480.

Shakespeare, William. Sonnet 18 ("Shall I compare thee to a summer's day?"). *Introduction to Literature: Poems.* Lynn Altenbernd and Leslie L. Lewis, eds. New York: Macmillan, 1963. 92.

———. Sonnet 29 ("When in disgrace with fortune and men's eyes"). *Introduction to Literature: Poems.* Lynn Altenbernd and Leslie L. Lewis, eds. New York: Macmillan, 1963. 93.

Shapiro, Karl. "Auto Wreck." *Introduction to Literature: Poems.* Lynn Altenbernd and Leslie L. Lewis, eds. New York: Macmillan, 1963. 482.

Sicking, Georgie. "Old Tuff." Cowboy Poetry: *A Gathering.* Ed. Hal Cannon. Salt Lake City: Peregrine Smith Books, 1985. 77–79.

———. "To Be a Top Hand." *Cowboy Poetry: A Gathering.* Ed. Hal Cannon. Salt Lake City: Peregrine Smith Books, 1985. 76–77.

Smith, Don Ian. "Old Horse." *Cowboy Poetry: A Gathering.* Ed. Hal Cannon. Salt Lake City: Peregrine Smith Books, 1985. 126–27.

Stanley, David. "Cowboy Poetry Then and Now: An Overview." *Cowboy Poets & Cowboy Poetry.* David Stanley and Elaine Thatcher, eds. Urbana: U of Illinois P, 2000. 1–18.

———. "Orderly Disorder: Form and Tension in Cowboy Poetry." *Cowboy Poets & Cowboy Poetry.* David Stanley and Elaine Thatcher, eds. Urbana: U of Illinois P, 2000. 107–24.

Tennyson, Alfred, Lord. "Break, Break, Break." *Introduction to Literature: Poems.* Lynn Altenbernd and Leslie L. Lewis, eds. New York: Macmillan, 1963. 345.

Wolfram, Walt. "*A*-Prefixing in Appalachian English." *Locating Language in Time and Space.* Ed. William Labov. New York: Academic P, 1980. 107–43.

———. "Reconsidering the Semantics of A-Prefixing." *American Speech* 63 (1988): 247–53.

25

Some Past Directions of Narrative-Folklore Study

by James T. Bratcher

R egardless of how we choose to define it, presumably folklore has existed for as long as human culture has existed. But while the collecting of folklore must also have its roots in prehistory—in the first bard's notion of repertory—systematic collecting for the preservation of threatened species and for humanistic and scientific study belongs chiefly to the nineteenth century.

Two related political trends in eighteenth-century Europe, toward nationalism and toward democracy, awakened an interest in the folk-spirit as embodied in the common lore of the people. The word "common" has, of course, a double meaning; it implies the vulgar as well as the shared. Accordingly, educated Europeans schooled in the classics were slow to value the stories, jests, songs, and sayings of the unlettered masses. By and large, folklore was beneath notice except when taken over and transformed into literature by a Chaucer or Boccaccio. Near the end of the sixteenth century it had taken a courageous Sir Philip Sidney, a true knight and a gifted poet, to write uncondescendingly of a folk ballad, "I never heard that olde song of Percey and Douglas that I found not my heart moved more then with a trumpet."

By the mid-eighteenth century, intellectual attitudes began to change. The ideas of Jean Jaques Rousseau concerning popular sovereignty and artificial class distinctions swept Europe. "A man's a man for a' that," Robert Burns would write. One result among the many effects of the Romantic Movement and its democratic impulse was a new awareness of the lore of the folk. To three pioneers in the salvaging of texts—a Scots poet, an English churchman, and a Prussian philosopher and teacher—goes the credit for early spadework in folklore retrieval.

The Ossian poems of Scots poet James Macpherson contained genuine matter of Gaelic bards despite Macpherson's own imitations, which he falsely inserted. The fifty-year controversy raised by the 1760 publication of Macpherson's *Fragments . . . translated from the Gaelic or Erse language* called attention, throughout Europe, to the value of national literary remains, using the word "literary" broadly. Samuel Johnson became involved in the controversy. Considered as a catalyst to folklore collecting, the outcome of the Ossian debate had to be positive, whatever else is said of the Celtic survivals and Macpherson's lying about his sources.

The *Reliques of Ancient English Poetry* of Bishop Thomas Percy, published in 1765 from a rich manuscript store of ballads dated about 1650 and since known as the Percy Folio, shortly followed Macpherson's lead in the recovery of olden minstrelsy. Whereas Macpherson's motives were partly those of an unknown poet eager to see his creations in print, Percy's were those of the dedicated antiquary. He polished the ballads, notoriously so in the instance of "Sir Patrick Spens," in an attempt to stave off criticism of their imperfections; but it was his desire to see the old songs and romances valued for their own sake that inspired his work. The ballads remain a treasure, and anyone who does not respond to them must be lacking in human sensibility.

In Germany, schoolteacher Johann Gottfried Herder formulated theories of literary and linguistic nationalism starting with his first critical writing in 1764. Herder championed the cultural unity he saw in the scattered Germanic peoples, which included the Saxons and the Celts of Britain. Impressed by the Ossian poems, about which he wrote an essay in 1773, and by the favorable reception of Percy's *Reliques*, Herder urged that the remnants of popular poetry be collected for the formation of a national literature. In 1777, he wrote an essay on the similarities of Medieval English and German literature. His scope was international; the following year Herder published *Stimmen der Völker* (Folk Voices), an anthology of the native poetry of various peoples, which included Inca songs that had been translated by Garcilaso de la Vega, the learned son of an Inca princess, in his *Historia general del Perú*. A quarter of a century later, in 1805–1808, Achim von Arnim and his brother-in-law Clemens Brentano published *Des Knaben Wunderhorn* (The Lad's Miraculous Horn), exclusively a collection of German folksongs.

At the threshold of the nineteenth century, two brothers, Jacob and Wilhelm Grimm, who were college friends of von Arnim and Brentano, began what was to be their lasting achievement and, for folklore study, a crucial step forward. This was the famed Grimm collection of household tales, significant for the comparative study of folklore. Herder's writings, like some of the accomplishments of his promising student, Johann Wolfgang Goethe, himself a collector of Alsatian songs at his teacher's direction, had been both international in outlook and comparative to a degree. In England, John Aubrey's mid-seventeenth-century treatise on customs and beliefs, *Remaines of Gentilisme and Judaisme*, had been a comparative effort, seeking parallels in antiquity. But Aubrey was not very astute as a scholar; a contemporary described him as "magotieheaded." It is to the comparative methods of the Grimms, Jacob in particular, that folklorists owe the earliest progression of their subject to the level of a science.

A few more-or-less modern collections of folktales had appeared before the Grimms' *Kinder- und Hausmärchen* (Children's and Household Tales) came out in 1812–1814, collections based on oral tradition without undue literary tampering. These supplemented the familiar *buchmärchen* or doctored literary folktales bequeathed by Medieval and Renaissance Europe—of which those in Italian nobleman Giambattista Basile's *Pentamerone* perhaps ranked highest in total folklore value. In France as early as 1697 a courtier at the palace at Versailles, Charles Perrault, had written down the peasant stories with which he and his circle amused themselves. The result was *Contes de la Mére l'Oye*, the first in a long succession of publishers' wares presented under the auspices of Mother Goose. Perrault gave us well-known versions of the Cinderella and Puss-in-Boots stories, which the *Pentamerone*, too, had incorporated. In Germany, an anonymous *Kindermärchen aus mündlichen Erzählungen gesammelt* (Collected Children's Tales and Oral narratives) appeared in 1787; and in England, Benjamin Tabart's *Collection of Popular Stories for the Nursery* (in four volumes) starting in 1809.

But despite these and other forerunners, the premier work of the Grimms remains the single most important advance. Its sources were documented and its contents more sensitive to oral sources and style than were those of previous collections. It represented the work of serious scholars and was intended for intelligent adults, offering intellectual as well as entertainment appeal. Its reception and continued popularity encouraged the brothers to expand it and to widen their comparative investigations, taking in not only the fairy tales ("wonder tales" is the more accurate term) but also the German *sagen*, or migratory legends that had become localized. The brothers' *Deutsche Sagen* came out in 1816–1818, and later Jacob treated the residue of a Germanic mythology in his influential *Deutsche Mythologie* (1835). Finally, *Kinder- und Hausmärchen* inaugurated a state of affairs plainly vital to folklore research: international communication and cooperation.

Starting in 1814, Jacob corresponded with Sir Walter Scott, seeking books on peasant lore and information about British antiquaries such as Robert Jamieson, Joseph Ritson, and Francis Douche. Sir Walter cordially responded, dispatching books on antiquities.

In 1826, within a year of the publication of the first volume of T. Crofton Croker's *Fairy Legends and Traditions of the South of Ireland*, the Grimms translated it as *Irische Elfmärchen*, adding an introductory essay on the fairy mythology of Britain. For their introduction they combined Croker's findings with their own and consulted a collection Croker had missed, William Grant Stewart's *Popular Superstitions and Festive Amusements of the Highlanders* (1823). In 1828, Croker acknowledged their attentions by translating their essay for use in the third volume of *Fairy Legends*, an instance of one good turn being repaid by another.

Several years later Croker's associate, Thomas Wright, wrote "On Dr. Grimm's German Mythology" (1846), an article praising Jacob's *Deutsche Mythologie* as one of the best books out of Germany. Forty years after *Deutsche Mythologie* first saw print in German, James Stallybrass's English translation reached William Thoms and members of the recently formed (in 1878) Folk-Lore Society. Stallybrass's translation made available to all British antiquaries what Thoms, founder of the journal *Notes and Queries* in 1849, viewed as the Bible of Folklore. It was Thoms who, in a letter to *The Athenaeum* in 1846, coined the English term "folk-lore" to replace the cumbersome "popular antiquities" then used in Britain. Over the years, the Grimms corresponded with folklorists Peter Christen Asbjörnsen and J. Moe in Norway, Emmanuel Cosquin in France, Vuk Karadzic in Serbia, and Elias Lönnrot in Finland. All viewed folklore as a vehicle for promoting a national language, history, literature, and mythology.

In Germany and then elsewhere, one of the more scientific features of the Grimms' work underwent perversion and distortion. This was the historical-linguistics approach used by Jacob in his attempted recovery of Teutonic mythology. Along with philologists in England, German students of Sanskrit since the late eighteenth century had worked at reconstructing the parent language from which most of the languages from India to Ireland were descended. Himself a philologist and student of proto-Indo-European, in contrast to Wilhelm, who showed a literary inclination, Jacob saw in the narratives, superstitions, and ceremonies of the German peasant a kind of garbled code. Behind the code lay a toppled pantheon of gods and spirits (not necessarily harmful to man, as Christian devils and three-teated witches came to be) whose dim presences were detected partly in linguistic clues—key words having proto-Indo-European roots—embedded in German peasant lore. Jacob's conclusion that folktales with widely-shared actors and incidents were of Indo-European origin, opened up new vistas for philological speculation. Now the Sanskirt Vedas—the sacred writings of Hinduism—could be augmented by European peasant lore in unlocking Western man's cultural development at an extremely remote stage.

Unfortunately for folklore study in the decades following 1850, etymological sleuthing in the newly-opened territory was made to accommodate a theory of origins that too easily hardened into dogma. The emerging natural-phenomena school of mythologists saw in folklore not merely the debris of a fallen pantheon, as Jacob had suggested, but also (based on often ingenious linguistic equations) the hidden record of primitive man's earliest reactions to natural forces. The forces were celestial: the sun, moon, stars, clouds, rain, thunder, lightning, darkness, the dawn. Obviously, the Teutonic and Greek gods were but personifications of these phenomena. When rightly interpreted using proper linguistic techniques, however, the dramatis personae of fairy tales, legends, and rites disclosed an even deeper cultural layer: a primal nature worship that had never been reconstructed. Whereas Phaëthon of the Greek myth, who drove the sun chariot, was known to be the offspring of Helios, the sun, the golden-haired prince of the fairy tales had not been so identified.

The leading proponent of the solar mythology theory of origins, as it came to be called, was Max Müller, a German orientalist and Sanskrit scholar who in 1848 settled at Oxford to translate Sanskrit texts. Over the next four decades Müller published articles and books of articles on comparative mythology. Upwardly-mobile Victorian readers eagerly absorbed his fanciful reconstructions; this was, after all, the era of British ascendancy that gave us Darwin, archeological finds in Egypt, ouija boards, and the English fondness for peculiar causes. The Grimms' work had made the comparative study of folklore respectable and, in Jacob's researches, even erudite by wedding it to the methods of comparative philology. Now the sweeping revelations of Müller and his disciples—principally Sir George Cox, Angelo de Gubernatis in Italy, and the American mythologists Daniel Brinton and John Fiske—would carry one aspect of Jacob's scholarship to amazing heights. Thanks to historical linguistics, the unseemly Greek myth of Kronos devouring and then regurgitating his children could be seen for what it was: primitive man's way of expressing how the sun swallows the clouds on a cloudless day and later returns them to the sky.

Eventually, Müller's heady excesses were leveled by the anthropological school of British folklorists who looked to Andrew Lang, a canny Scot, as their main spokesman. In pungent article after article, Lang, a scholar-journalist skilled in controversy, lampooned and bombarded the solar-mythology reconstructions of Müller and his followers. So effective were his assaults, mixing common-sense with witticism and Lang's own formidable arsenal of knowledge, that by 1946 the American folklorist Stith Thompson could write with confidence: "Though some teachers of Greek and Latin mythology . . . still tell their students the 'interpretations' which their teachers had in turn learned from their teachers of the 1870s, the general absurdity of the whole doctrine [that folktales and myths are the fragmented remains of an early nature worship] has long been recognized."

Another offshoot of the Grimms' work was the single-source theory of folktale origins associated with Theodore Benfey, a Sanskrit scholar like Müller. Benfey addressed the question of exactly where, geographically, the familiar body of folktales spread over Europe came from. In 1859, Benfey published his German translation of the *Panchatantra*, an Indian collection of beast-fables made before A.D. 500. Many of the fables resembled European tales, and in an Introduction to his translation, and elsewhere, Benfey proposed India as the ultimate birthplace of folktales. Unlike Müller and his cohorts, he was generally cautious and level-headed in his arguments.

An anticipator of the Indianist theory, Louiseleur des Longechamps in his *Essai sur les fables indiennes* (1838), had suggested that certain of the Grimm tales might have their prototypes in India. Jacob Grimm's attributing some of the household tales to supposed Indo-European originals had been less specific in geographic placement. For their part, the natural-phenomena theorists were not so concerned with exact geographic placement as with linear descent from a parent culture and religion—speakers of proto-Indo-European who worshiped nature. But India was the prime begetter, Benfey argued, the tales having spread westward via three channels, undergoing changes along the way. Some tales had migrated westward before the tenth century in the normal course of individual and group wanderings. After the tenth century, movement was along the lines of expanding Islamic influence, especially through the Byzantine Empire, Italy, and Moslem Spain. Last, Buddhistic materials from India had entered the West via China or Tibet, or perhaps more directly with the Mongol invasions of Europe.

The Indianist theory mustered support, but critics soon disclosed, if not gaping fissures in it, troublesome cracks. Insistence on a one-way traffic and Eden-like propagation could not be maintained absolutely. The beast fables of the *Panchatantra*, as Benfey himself noted, involve animal actors whose basic traits are human. In this respect they differ from Western animal tales, in which a fox or a hare must emulate a real fox or hare, or the story loses point. Br'er Rabbit must be *at home* in the briar patch. Moreover, Joseph Bédier in France showed that European fabliaux, the risqué comic tales that satirists like Chaucer drew on, and which relied on quick wit and irony, had no true parallels in ancient India. Further, Lang in England echoed Cosquin in France by citing the discovery of Egyptian folktales put into writing in the thirteenth century B.C. What channel from India had affected Egypt before the thirteenth century B.C.?

For Lang, however, Benfey posed a lesser heresy. For him as for other British anthropologists—E. B. Tylor, G. L. Gomme, E. S. Hartland, and Edward Clodd—Müller and his disciples remained the targets of choice.

Though Edward B. Tylor, the "father of anthropology," made few attacks himself, Tylor's books *Researches into the Early History of Mankind* (1865) and *Primitive Culture* (1871) provided the basis for a rival hypothesis, the cultural-evolution theory. While a student at Oxford, Lang had been interested by Tylor's central premise that civilized societies evolve from lower states labeled "savagery" and "barbarism." The European peasant stood at the barbaric level. The human psyche reacts to its environment according to its evolutionary stage, the theory held, so that at the truly savage and naïve level the group and individual psyche will regard natural objects on a par with human life. The whole of creation, down to the smallest part, is thought of as being "alive" or possessing a spirit (animism). Müller relied on the same assumption about primitive psychology, almost a commonplace of the day, but for Lang and other cultural evolutionists the animistic belief that all things possess a virtue or power provided the main stimulus for folklore research. In general, Lang argued that arcane linguistic sleuthings were off track, in addition to being ridiculous when carried to extremes in elucidating folklore. Clearly, the primitive's belief in animism was the salient factor. Folklore everywhere demonstrated the belief in its constant recourse to magic: the fairy godmother's wand, the talking spittle, the musical instrument whose sound causes involuntary dancing, the hair of the dog that cures its bite.

Lang in particular reasoned further that, given the uniformity of the savage mindset wherever found, the idea of cultural exchanges—borrowings—was unnecessary to account for folklore similarities. A primitive society living in fear of a volcano is capable of inventing myths, tales, and rituals associated with the propitiation of a volcano god without input from outside sources. Polygenesis, or the assumption of multiple origins, Lang thought sufficient to explain similarities.

Finally, though Lang and his colleagues approached folklore as preserving survivals from the savage state, as the Grimms and natural-phenomena theorists had, their concern as folklorists pretty much ended there: at noting the persistence of savage psychology among civilized peoples. Folklore research would unclothe and lay bare, to an extent, the pretensions of civilized man. Instead of sun worship, more likely it was a recall of cannibalism that underlay the myth of Kronos devouring his children. Freud, of course, was to build on this line of thought.

Lang's tendency to discount borrowings proved to be an Achilles' heel. Joseph Jacobs, editor of the British journal *Folk-Lore* from 1889 to 1900, published an article in which he stressed two currents affecting folk tradition, the vertical and the lateral, or the diachronic (descending through time) and the synchronic (introduced in the course of time). The lateral current—borrowings— often accounts for observed resemblances. In many instances similarities were simply too close to be unrelated historically. If an English charm warns that the ladybug's house is on fire and her children will burn, and a German charm says that her homeland is devastated and her parents need her, there must be (in fact, obviously is) an historical connection. Jacobs, however, also felt that the evolutionists' search for survivals was often premature in that all the facts about a given piece of lore must be gathered before calling it a fly in amber. Frequently, the evolutionists' arguments were skimpy on data.

Starting in 1890, a grand synthesis of ethnological data was assembled by Sir James Frazer in his monumental *The Golden Bough*, first issued in two volumes and later expanded to twelve. Pseudo-history tells us that Aristotle prevailed on his former pupil Alexander the Great to enlist observers from all over the Hellenic world to send in botanical and zoological reports. Something like that applies to Frazer's classic work, substituting the British Empire for the Hellenic world and ethnological data for botanical and zoological reports. Worldwide instances of fertility-inducing rites, charms, legends, and the primitive ideas behind them crowd the pages of *The Golden Bough*. Naturally, it is a flawed work (crucially in Frazer's thesis that a region's fertility once depended on a tribal leader's virility), as Theodor H. Gaster has carefully shown in his one-volume abridgement, with critical notes, available since 1959. But today it comes as no surprise that William Faulkner along with T. S. Eliot drew on Frazer. For the modern student of literature, a basic familiarity with Frazer seems as obligatory as being able to recognize the Old Testament stories when they turn up in novels.

Early cultural anthropology left its imprint at another crossroads where literary scholarship and folklore overlap, the question of ballad origins. Though overshadowed by the researches of the Grimms, Benfey, Müller, and Lang and the evolutionists, ballad study saw advances. Following the interest stirred by Macpherson, Percy, and Herder in the previous century, in 1835 the Finnish scholar Elias Lönnrot published his homeland's national epic, the ballad-cycle known as the *Kalevala*. The reconstructed cycle drew on an exhaustive range of Norse heroic ballads retrieved by Lönnrot, who combined them and gave them canonical form. A disciple of his, Julius Krohn, studied individual ballads intensively and devised a method of comparing all versions to determine the life-history of each ballad, a procedure that was to have a profound bearing on later folklore study.

In Great Britain in 1872, Scottish ballads were gathered by J. F. Campbell in his *Leabhar na Feinne: Heroic Gaelic Ballads Collected in Scotland* from 1512–1871, and in the United States the full range of British ballads was brought under one heading by Harvard's Francis J. Child in *The English and Scottish Popular Ballads* (1892–1898). Child, incidentally, was the teacher of George Lyman Kittredge of Harvard, who in 1907 encouraged one of his students, John A. Lomax, from Texas, to continue collecting cowboy songs and to start a regional folklore society in Texas. Two other Kittredge protégés built reputations as folklorists, Archer Taylor and Stith Thompson.

A leading Scandinavian collector was Svend Grundtvig, a Danish scholar whose published texts date from 1853 and continued to appear until 1912. Like Child, Grundtvig investigated the ballad internationally, and while he and Child thought of themselves as collectors, along with Julius Krohn they contributed the first analytical studies.

It was hints coming from Grundtvig and Child, and from the Grimms' early conviction that "the songs of the people are made by the people as a whole," that led Child's student, Francis B. Gummere, to propose his communal theory of ballad origins. Especially in *The Popular Ballad* (1912), Gummere argued that the oldest part of the ballad is the burden or refrain. Originally, it accompanied the carole or ringdance of the Middle Ages. The narrative portion built on the original refrain and arose from group improvisations made while dancing or in the course of ritualized observances. To support his theory, Gummere cited the field work of anthropologists. The improvised songs and dances of South American Indians, the impromptu group productions of Danish Faroe Islanders, the spontaneous worksongs of peasant cigarette-makers in South Russia—all pointed to communal authorship.

In 1921 Louise Pound's *Poetic Origins of the Ballad* contested the theory, citing contradictory evidence. Primitive groups like the Akkas of West Africa, the Andaman Islanders in the Bay of Bengal, the Australian bushmen, the Semangs of Malaya, the Seris of Mexico, and the Eskimos and American plains Indians, these groups danced without singing and sang without dancing. Sometimes special bards created tribal poetry. Pound advocated individual authorship.

At the same time, she failed to explain away such indications of group input as existed especially in northern Europe, historically the focus of much ballad research. Certain refrains in certain ballads seem to correspond to a break or a shift in the dance movement, as in the euphonious *Eh vow bonnie* of a British ballad. These have an improvisational flavor, as do the nonsense phrases of folksongs not classed as ballads. Interestingly, the earliest preserved refrain (without any narrative) seems to reflect a rites-of-spring context. Written down in Latin from words sung by a group of dancers (not in Latin), it implies that a Jack and a Jill have just gone into the leafy woods for dalliance, and it asks rhetorically, "Why stand we here?" Considering that the European ringdance called for a song to be sung by the dancers, group shaping of a song might be expected, a concept that is hardly foreign to folklore.

The communal theory still has adherents, though the modern student, if pressed on the issue, is apt to accept single authorship and grant that communal changes took place over time after a ballad entered tradition. Today's students welcome the tunes of all folksongs where known, noting that collections before Cecil Sharp's *English Folksongs from the Southern Appalachians* (1917), which transcribed 323 tunes, typically slighted this essential "other half" of the subject. Sharp's exemplary work was assisted by his secretary, Maud Karpeles, a trained musicologist.

An air of mystery pervades some of the older ballads. Their spareness, incremental unfoldings, and antique glow may be the reason, but regarded as an instance of subliminal expression, few pieces could be more realistic while evoking a magical and primitive universe than "Lady Isabell and the Elfin Knight," for example. Whether the work of individual poets or the products of group authorship, undeniably the ballads offer an instinctual appeal not always matched by other genres of verbal folklore.

Since 1934, when Harvard professors Milman Parry and A. B. Lord first visited Yugoslavia to observe metrical composition on the lips of living storytellers, the "oral-formulaic" character of folk epics has interested folklorists and literary scholars. *Beowulf* and Homeric studies have been affected. Parry eventually published his widely-read *The Singer of Tales* in 1960, and Lord wrote follow-up articles. They discovered that among the semiprofessional singers of Yugoslavia, the longer folk epics (rehearsing the exploits of traditional heroes) consisted of hundreds of stock elements, time-honored verbal embroideries or "fill-ins" that the singer at all times controlled at his fingertips. In beginning a recitation, he remembered only a vague general plot, which he then filled out using various formulas rather than knowing an entire epic word for word. Much earlier, in 1909, the formulaic character of folk as distinguished from literary productions was discussed by Danish scholar Axel Olrick in an important article, "Epische Gesetze der Volksdichtung" (Epic Laws of Folk Narrative). Earlier than that, in an 1864 article, Johann Georg von Hahn had listed some of the formulas he had noticed in folk narratives. Studies done by Arnold van Gennep (*Les Rites du Passage*, 1909) and Lord Raglan (*The Hero*, 1936) confirmed folklore's reliance on ready-made patterns and stock elements. Joseph Campbell's imaginative *The Hero with a Thousand Faces* (1949) has added to the list of demonstrations. Folklore's dependence on repeated patterns and stock elements now seems self-evident, though the question of how far conventional formulas go toward illuminating *Beowulf* and the *Odyssey* remains unresolved.

If for a time ballad study was overshadowed by concerns in other areas, it nevertheless yielded a significant procedure for analyzing folktales. This was the historical-geographical approach developed by Finnish scholars, a method that later saw fruition in the tale-type classifications of Antti Aarne and Stith Thompson, and in Thompson's massive *Motif-Index of Folk-Literature*.

In 1866 an English clergyman and antiquary, S. Baring-Gould, in his *Curious Myths of the Middle Ages*, extracted "story radicals" for several traditional narratives. Baring-Gould's "radicals" (root elements) went unnoticed, but the somewhat similar life-histories of ballads constructed during Julius Krohn's *Kalevala* studies led Krohn's son, Kaarle, to apply the life-history approach to multiple versions of an animal tale. Kaarle's doctoral dissertation, *Bär (Wolf) und Fuchs* (Bear [Wolf] and Fox), was submitted in 1866. He later urged that folktale scholarship proceed along the lines of that study. First, it should seek to identify as "types" folktales that showed a marked resemblance to one another; and second, it should concentrate on determining the genealogical history, or family-tree, of each general type. For a number of tale-types spread internationally, an abundance of written versions were available. The questions became: Within a given type, which of the exemplars were the ancestors and which the progeny? And, what was the original form of a given type, its archetypal form? The date at which a particular version was recorded was no sure guide; for example, the classical story of Cupid and Psyches as told by Lucius Apuleius in *The Golden Ass* (second century) was actually younger than versions still being told orally in Europe in the nineteenth century, in which an animal or monster took a loving but heedless girl for his bride.

Kaarle Krohn thus saw in his father's method of tracing the histories of the Finnish ballads a means of treating folktales. Once the tales were grouped into general types, the fact that narratives consist of separable components ("motifs"—Baring-Gould's "radicals") came into play. A sorting-out of the components in a broad sampling of texts belonging to a given folktale type would clarify, when analyzed, where changes had occurred and possibly why. Also, "factoring" of this sort would provide clues as to earlier vs. later forms, and to the geographic spread of a story from its point of origin. It should be noted that the criteria for establishing a tale's life-history are fairly complex when put into practice; Thompson discusses them fully in his book *The Folktale* (1946), chapter 5 of part IV.

By 1910 Krohn's student, Antti Aarne, assisted by Krohn and other scholars—Oskar Hackman, Axel Olrik, Johannes Bolte, and C. W. von Sydow—had worked out the main type classifications into which collected tales could be fitted. That year saw the publication of Aarne's *Verzeichnis der Märchentypen* (Index of Folk-Tale Types). Aarne had combed Scandinavian and German archives for tale-types sufficiently fixed in oral tradition to enter the canon. While acceptance of his type index was slow at first, within a few years scholars discovered its worth and called for an enlarged edition to include many additional tale-types that accelerated collecting had brought to light. Aarne's death in 1923 prevented his own revision, but his chief sponsor, Kaarle Krohn, invited Stith Thompson, who had studied North American Indian tales, to expand the catalogue and translate it for easier international use. The Aarne-Thompson *Types of the Folk-Tale* came out in 1928, and another edition, again expanded, followed in 1961. Enlargement of Aarne's index was extensive. Whereas the original contained only 99 pages, Thompson's 1961 revision has 588.

Thompson built on Aarne's foundational work in another way. In his original index, Aarne commented that an index might be made of motifs, or the smaller units of narratives. Reception of *Types of the Folk-Tale* encouraged Thompson to undertake the gargantuan task, for which a stationer's store must have had to replenish its supply of 3x5 cards many times over. Publication of Thompson's *Motif-Index* began in 1932 and was completed in 1936. An amplified edition, reaching to six large volumes counting an alphabetical index, appeared in 1955-1958. Though the past few decades have witnessed a decline in their use, it is still safe to say that the type and motif indexes rank among the most valuable references a comparative folklorist (or literary student, for that matter, since folklore themes are rife in literature) has at his or her disposal. They offer a starting place for research, assembling folk-narrative "facts" as Frazer had assembled ethnological data.

Both the method of the Finnish school and, by implication, the indexes that grew out of the method generated criticism. Published life-histories of tales furnished by advocates of the historical-geographical method failed to satisfy the respected Swedish folklorist C. W. von Sydow, for one, who had helped Aarne plan his groundbreaking work. For many folklorists, mere textual comparisons were one-sided and mechanical in their preoccupation with texts alone; the life-histories revealed almost nothing about the style, social aspects, and overall cultural import of folktales and myths. In 1959 anthropologist Melville Jacobs, who had investigated the culture of an Indian group living in Washington State, the Clackamas Chinook, forcefully spoke of the need to "wriggle out of folklore's historico-geographical collecting and archiving straitjackets, and its handful of concepts such as motif, plot, and archetype."

The quest for archetypes, the principal goal of the Finnish method, attracted criticism that echoed charges leveled at the psychoanalytical schools founded by Freud and Carl Jung—too little certainty attaches to the conclusions. More severe in their censure, scholars making up the structuralist school of analysts regarded the Finnish school as mistaken in its most basic construct, the "motif" as employed in the Aarne-Thompson and Thompson indexes. Three structuralist critics deserve mention here: the Russian Vladimir Propp, the American Alan Dundes, and the French anthropologist Claude Lévi-Strauss.

In *Morphology of the Folktale*, first published in Russian in 1928, Propp insisted on a higher level of abstraction than was used in the Finnish method. Intellectual abstracting—or close insight into broad underlying structural ideas as opposed to motif analysis— goes far in describing the structuralists' approach. Propp questioned whether, instead of the unstable motifs that are often interchangeable from one tale to the next, the more meaningful segments might be the larger and relatively stable substructures that correspond to dramatic episodes or scenes in literary productions and to movements in musical compositions. He proposed his term *function* as the basic unit of folktale analysis, by which he meant the broader separable "actions" that make up tales. This shifted emphasis away from the clutter of actors and objects labeled "motifs," that can change within a given tale and sometimes appear to move in and out of tales at random. By identifying typical actions or plot movements—rescue, revenge-taking, etc.—Propp managed to reduce Russian fairy tales to a few "plot guides" or sequences of actions that define the fairy tale as told in Russia.

His treatise also attempted to provide a model for the study of folklore outside Russia and apart from the European fairy tale. In 1964, Alan Dundes' *The Morphology of North American Indian Tales* took its cue partly from Propp's method. Dundes attempted a breakthrough in "folkloristics" by assimilating folklore analysis to the techniques of structural linguistics, a cross-discipline approach faintly reminiscent of Jacob Grimm. He suggested as the basic unit of analysis the *motipheme*, a coinage that combined the word *motif* with the linguistic unit of meaningful change in speech sounds, the *morpheme*. Along with a Proppian analysis of American Indian tales, Dundes also undertook a structuralist approach to superstitions. With regard to the Amerind tales, he emphasized a characteristic broad movement away from an opening state of affairs toward its converse, or from a specific "lack" (a monster impounds a tribe's water) toward its opposite, or the "lack liquidated" (the water is released). Thus the abbreviations L and LL stood for *motiphemes* in Dundes' system, intended to supplant the "motifs" of the Finnish school. Like Propp's *functions*, Dundes' *motiphemes* sought a way around the unstable motifs central to the historical-geographical method.

Earlier than Dundes, Belgian-born Claude Lévi-Strauss, before returning to Europe, taught in Brazil where he studied Indian culture beginning in the first half of the twentieth century. Lévi-Strauss's subsequent reading and his reflection on the Amazon materials he collected and brought back, ripened into a number of articles and books that laymen could appreciate. Among these, to cite only two, were "The Structural Study of Myth" (1955) and *Le cru et le cuit* (The Raw and the Cooked, 1964). One idea he advanced appealed to literary scholars and mythologists alike, since it concerned the "reconciliation of opposites," a recurring theme in literary criticism that reaches back through Samuel Taylor Coleridge to the German philosopher Friedrich Schelling. Lévi-Strauss recognized the mediation of opposites as the most pervasive drive behind myth formation. Myths and folktales he saw as externalizing intellectual and emotional tensions in man's response to his particular physical and cultural setting. Disregarding "motifs" as the minimal units of analysis, Lévi-Strauss tried to discern, always in the light of ethnological data, underlying conceptual polarities or "bundles of features," as he called them. His treatment of the Oedipus myth in its Greek form best exemplifies his thinking.

The myth, according to Lévi-Strauss, externalized a cultural trauma present in the psychology of the ancient Greeks: their inability to make a satisfactory transition between their inherited mythic belief-tradition that mankind is autochthonous, "sprung from earth," and their experiential knowledge that human beings are born of women. In the Oedipus story, the slaying of the sphinx, who poses the riddle about man's life-stages, beginning with men crawling, then walking upright, then hobbling with a cane, signifies the Greeks' common-sense rejection of autochthonous origin. Yet "Swellfoot," the meaning of Oedipus's name, denotes diehard persistence of the belief, since everywhere in world mythology men who emerge from the earth, at the moment of emergence, either cannot walk or do so clumsily. Oedipus's marriage to his mother culminates a "bundle of features" that stand for an overevaluation of blood relations (denial of being earth-sprung) while murdering his father represents an underevaluation of the same (affirmation of being earth-sprung, or not having human parents). In the fatalistic context of the myth, Oedipus's story demonstrates the difficulty the Greeks had in completely liberating themselves from belief in autochthonous origin.

While the theory might seem clever but farfetched, Harvard anthropologist Clyde Kluckhohn thought it feasible. Probably most mythologists and literary theorists would agree. In a valuable article, "Recurrent Themes in Myths and Mythmaking" (1959), Kluckhohn wrote judiciously: "Lévi-Strauss . . . suggests that mythical thought always works from awareness of binary oppositions toward their progressive mediation. That is, the contribution of mythology is that of providing a logical model capable of overcoming contradictions in a people's view of the world and what they have deduced from their experience. This is an engaging idea, but much further empirical work is required to test it."

Lévi-Strauss's *The Cooked and the Raw* contains observations on the origin of "rough music" as used by primitives to express disapproval of social behavior that runs counter to the natural order. In 1964, Texas scholar E. Bagby Atwood contributed an article to one of the Texas Folklore Society annuals, *A Good Tale and a Bonnie Tune*, dealing with the French-Louisiana custom of the *charivari* or shivaree. Typically, North American versions of the shivaree used rough music—beating on pots and pans, also using a "bull-roarer" device—to "serenade" a newly-married couple whose disparate ages (one of them old, the other young) offended a community's sense of decency. The quest for primitive survivals continues.

Thus far this cursory review has said little about the psycho-analytical approach to folklore, though Lévi-Strauss plainly was indebted to the psychoanalysts. For almost a century, critics influenced by Freud and Jung have examined traditional myths and tales, rites, customs, superstitions, games, taunts, riddles, and dirty jokes. But when the conclusions put forward verge on the laughable, as when the stories of Jack and the Beanstalk and Aladdin and his Lamp are linked to prurient practices, and for no better reason than the one that prompted a well-known "analysis" of Jonathan Swift because he named Gulliver's sea captain "Master Bates," skepticism is warranted. At other times, the psychoanalysts have something to tell us.

Mythologists of the nineteenth century were the first to apply terms like "survival," "fantasy," and "psychic projection" to folklore. But with notable exceptions, Freudian and Jungian interpretations which employ a similar vocabulary have received short shrift from the more orthodox folklorists, including Thompson. "Fantasies applied to fantasies" has been a catch phrase. But while sometimes justified, rejection out of hand can be wrongheaded. The relevance of Jungian archetypes (different, of course, from folklore's historical-geographical archetypes) seems clear to anyone who has read much creative literature. Jung's mentor Freud may have overreached in his theory of a primal patricide that imprinted itself on the racial memory of following generations (*Totem and Taboo*, 1913), but Jung, for his part, shed genuine light on the External Soul theme in folklore (*The Phenomenology of the Spirit in Fairy Tales*, 1945) and no literary critic today would fault his earlier classic essay, "Psychology and Literature" (1933). Surely a reader of *Moby Dick* would be disposed to assent wholeheartedly to Jung's assertion that a creative writer's subconscious pokes through in what he writes; that, if he is good (inspired?), he is not in complete control of his material, some of it originating beneath the surface. On the other hand, to argue, as one commentator did in 1922, that Tale-type 425A, *The Monster Bridegroom* (to which the story *Cupid and Psyches* belongs), began life as a dream experience which the dreamer shared with listeners who then told the dream to others, leaves too much to speculation.

Anthropologists of the past several decades who have worked in primitive societies have been attentive to psychoanalytical theory despite the "fearful woolliness" that attaches. While disavowing any desire to "enroll in the ranks of psychiatrically oriented folklorism," William A. Lessa, in his *Tales from the Ulithi Atoll* (1961), nevertheless considered non-Western (Micronesian) versions of Oedipus-like myths from a psychoanalytical standpoint. He could not have done otherwise. Field-worker Geza Roheim, who observed Australian tribes before writing *The Gates of the Dream* (1952), urged the importance of sexual dreams in myth formation. Though not a field-worker (neither was Frazer), Joseph Campbell in his poetically-charged *The Masks of God* (1959–1961) mixed Jungian and Freudian readings in his essentially Jungian approach to world mythology. Earlier in the twentieth century, Bronislaw Malinowski's *Myth in Primitive Psychology* (1926) and *The Father in Primitive Psychology* (1927) assessed Freud's Oedipal theory in relation to the folktales of Trobriand Islanders. Thompson, in *The Folktale*, praised Malinowski for clarifying the mythmaking of the Melanesians, while adding polemically that his findings "give no comfort to those who look for hidden meanings and fantastic origins for folktales." Kluckhohn, on the other hand, opined otherwise about psychiatry's contribution, writing in the article mentioned above: "The psychoanalysts have maintained that mythmaking exemplifies a number of the mechanisms of ego defense. I agree . . ."

It should now be clear that folklore study, "folkloristics," is often abstruse and far removed from the chimney corner and the whittlers' bench. Perhaps one reason for increased theoretical emphasis is a somewhat jaded interest in the text for its own sake. The truth is, we are unable to place a high intrinsic value on much of what we encounter as folklore; a good deal of it is either unimpressive when taken alone, culturally obscure, or both. But like moon rocks or half-buried meteorites, a text may be significant. The search for that significance necessarily requires theoretical insight.

To state it another way, the tales in Paul Radin's 1956 book *The Trickster: A Study in American Indian Mythology,* which carries learned commentaries by Karl Kerényi and C. G. Jung, are less than spellbinding. For interest, we might as well watch a TV cartoon about the coyote and the roadrunner. The half-human culture hero of the Winnebago tribe of Wisconsin and Nebraska—Wakdjunkaga—carries his penis in a box on his back; in one tale he sends it across a lake to have intercourse with a chief's daughter, only to suffer injury. This sounds like titillating adolescent stuff. In Radin's book, however, the commentaries by Radin, Kerényi, and Jung redeem the puerilities and bad jokes of a creature who only half understands normal behavior. With reason, Radin calls the Winnebago Trickster a "mirror of the mind" of archaic man, showing "man's struggle with himself and with a world into which he [has] been thrust without his volition and consent." Classical scholar Kerényi, in turn, likens him to capricious Greek demigods. Jung resorts to a more exotic metaphor: the Winnebago Trickster represents the "shadow" archetype of the mind, the "saurian tail that man still drags behind." In short, it is the commentaries in Radin's book—not necessarily the Winnebago tales themselves—that fascinate us and sustain interest.

Psychoanalytical interpretations of folktales and myths continue to attract notice. For example, Little Red Riding Hood and the widely-distributed myth of a universal Flood have been treated as psychic projections of mother-daughter rivalry in the Riding Hood instance, and of the sudden release of amniotic fluid during the travails of childbirth in the case of the Flood story. These are extreme examples. But at a time when corporate industry, the military, and conservative lawcourts have accepted the validity of applied psychoanalytical theory, it is difficult to dismiss these interpretations as completely misguided despite their "fearful woolliness." Actually they are not too far removed in spirit from an intriguing folktale study published eighty-four years ago, Archer Taylor's impressive monograph extending to a hundred pages, "Northern Parallels to the Death of Pan" (1922). Taylor concluded that a broad range of European tales that announce the mysterious death of a so-called King of the Cats had their origin in auditory illusion, or the common psychic phenomenon of misjudging noises heard in the night (runaway imagination). A variant of the story, collected from an African-American informant, occurs in one of the TFS volumes, *Spur-of-the-Cock* (1933), pages 99–100.

James T. Bratcher, March 2005.

In another of the TFS books, the aforementioned *A Good Tale and a Bonnie Tune*, anthropologist John Greenway quoted blues-singer Big Bill Broonzy as responding as follows when asked what the blues were good for: "[They] were like a knife. You could keep it on a shelf and look at it, you could cut bread with it, you could clean your fingernails with it, you could shave with it, you could pare your toenails with it, you could even cut a man's throat with it." Excluding throat-cutting and like harmful purposes, such appears to be the state of folk-narrative analysis in the twenty-first century. That is, given enough documentation—and today you are apt to find it—virtually anything goes.

[Although the author did not want to include this bibliography because it is noticeably dated, I believe it can still be a valuable resource for scholars wanting an overview of fundamental folklore texts. A few of these works are referred to in the article, and they are listed here only as a resource for those wishing to do further study, even though the citations listed merely scratch the surface.—*Untiedt*]

BIBLIOGRAPHY

Bascom, William R. "Folklore and Anthropology." *Journal of American Folklore* LXVI (1953), 283–90. (Reprinted in Dundes, 1965.)

———. "Four Functions of Folklore." *Journal of American Folklore* LXVII (1954), 333–49. (Reprinted in Dundes, 1965.)

Clarke, Robert T., Jr. *Herder: His Life and Thought.* Berkeley and Los Angeles: University of California Press, 1955.

Dorson, Richard M. "Theories of Myth and the Folklorist." *Myth and Mythmaking,* ed. Henry A. Murray. New York: George Braziller, 1960.

———. "Current Folklore Theories," *Current Anthropology* IV (1963), 93–112.

———. "Foreword." *Folktakes of England,* ed. Katherine M. Briggs and Ruth L. Tongue. Chicago: University of Chicago Press, 1965.

———. "Foreword." *Folktales of Germany,* ed. Kurt Ranke. Chicago: University of Chicago Press, 1966.

———. ed. *Peasant Customs and Savage Myths.* 2 vols. Chicago: University of Chicago Press, 1968.

Dundes, Alan, ed. *The Study of Folklore.* Englewood Cliffs, N. J.: Prentice-Hall, 1965.

———. "Ways of Studying Folklore." *Our Living Traditions,* ed. Tristram P. Coffin. New York: Basic Books, Inc., 1968.

Fischer, J. L. "The Sociopsychological Analysis of Folktales." *Current Anthropology* IV (1963), 235-295.

Gummere, Francis B. "The Ballad and Communal Poetry." *Harvard Studies and Notes in Philology* V (1897), 40–56. (Reprinted in Leach and Coffin.)

Hautala, Jouko. *Finnish Folklore Research 1828–1918.* Helsinki: Finnish Society of Sciences, 1968.

Jacobs, Melville. *The Content and Style of an Oral Literature.* New York: Wenner-Gren Foundation, 1959.

———. "Foreword." *The Anthropologist Looks at Myth,* ed. John Greenway. Austin: The University of Texas Press, 1966.

Jones, Ernest. "Psychoanalysis and Folklore." *Jubilee Congress of the Folklore Society: Papers and Transactions.* London: The Folklore So., 1930. (Reprinted in Dundes, 1965.)

Keith, Alexander. "Scottish Ballads: Their Evidence of Authorship and Origin." *Essays and Studies by Members of the English Association* XII (1926), 100 119. (Reprinted in Leach and Coffin.)

Kluckhohn, Clyde. "Recurrent Themes in Myth and Mythmaking." *Myth and Mythmaking,* ed. Henry A. Murray. New York: George Braziller, 1960.

Krappe, Alexander H. *The Science of Folklore.* New York: W. W. Norton & Company, 1964. (Reprint of the 1930 book.)

Leach, MacEdward, and Tristram P. Coffin, eds. *The Critics and the Ballad.* Carbondale: Southern Illinois University Press, 1961.

Lessa, William A. *Tales From Ulithi Atoll.* Berkeley and Los Angeles: University of California Press, 1961. (Reprinted in part in Dundes, 1965.)

Lévi-Strauss, Claude. "The Structural Study of Myth." *Journal of American Folklore* LXVIII (1955), 428–45.

Levin, Isidor. "Vladimir Propp: An Evaluation on His Seventieth Birthday." *Journal of the Folklore Institute* IV (1967), 32–49.

McKnight, George. "Ballad and Dance." *Modern Language Notes* XXXV (1920), 464–73. (Reprinted in Leach and Coffin.)

Propp, Vladimir. *Morphology of the Folktale.* Bloomington: Indiana University Research Center in Anthropology, Folklore, and Linguistics, 1958. (Translation and reprint.)

Richmond, Edson W. "The Comparative Approach: Its Aim, Techniques, and Limitations." *A Good Tale and a Bonnie Tune*, ed. Mody C. Boatright, Wilson M. Hudson, and Allen Maxwell. Dallas: Southern Methodist University Press, 1964.

Taylor, Archer. "Folklore and the Student of Literature." *The Pacific Spectator* II (1948), 216–23. (Reprinted in Dundes, 1965.)

Thompson, Stith. *The Folktale.* New York: Holt, Rinehart, and Winston, 1946.

———. "Myths and Folktales." *Journal of American Folklore* LXVIII (1955), 482–488.

Utley, Francis Lee. "Folk Literature: An Operational Definition." *Journal of American Folklore* LXXIV (1961), 193–206. (Reprinted in Dundes, 1965.)

von Sydow, C. W. "Folktale Studies and Philology: Some Points of View." *Selected Papers on Folklore.* ed. Laurits Bodker. Copenhagen: Rosenkilde og Baggers Forlag, 1948. (Reprinted in Dundes, 1965.)

Biographical Information

Mody C. Boatright (1896–1970) served as Secretary-Editor of the Texas Folklore Society for twenty years. He obtained his M.A. and Ph.D. from the University of Texas, where he taught for four decades. His contributions to folklore study and to the Texas Folklore Society are innumerable, and we continue to benefit from his research.

James T. Bratcher attended TCU and UT Austin. When young, undecided, and subject to mononucleosis, he had a brief stay at Harvard. Much of his life was spent as a cow-trader and horse-trader, however. (If that's not "Texas," he doesn't know what is.) At UT Austin he studied under Mody Boatright and Wilson Hudson. We also have him to thank for the *Analytical Index to the Publications of the Texas Folklore Society: Volumes 1–36.*

Ty Cashion is associate professor of history at Sam Houston State University in Huntsville. He received his Ph.D. from Texas Christian University in 1993. Among his publications are *A Texas Frontier: The Clear Fork Country and Fort Griffin, 1849–1885* (Univ. of Oklahoma Press, 1996) and *Pigskin Pulpit: A Social History of Texas High School Coaches* (Texas State Historical Association, 1998). He is also a past president of the East Texas Historical Association.

Charles Chupp is a direct descendant of Adam and Eve of Eden. Five books of his manufacture have been foisted off on an unwary public, and the factory is still in operation. A weekly eruption of "I Got No Reason To Lie" is available for viewing at www.charleschupp.com, which originates in the poverty sink addition to the city of De Leon, Texas. The G.I. Bill bankrolled his education in the dark of the night back in the fabulous fifties.

Lawrence Clayton (1938–2000) received his B.S. and M.Ed. from Stephen F. Austin State University, and his Ph.D. from Texas Tech

University. At the time of his death, he was Dean of Liberal Arts at Hardin-Simmons University, where he had taught English for nearly thirty years. He published over 170 reviews, 130 articles, and numerous books and videos during his lifelong pursuit of chronicling cowboy heritage.

Jerry Crouser currently resides in San Angelo, Texas. All the children have left the nest, and he works as a real estate investor while his wife of 33 years manages a GNC store. Jerry acknowledges that his paper represents an effort some 15 years ago to investigate how normal, everyday people try to remember things, as we all suffer from some degree of "memory fatigue." Since that time, many commercial publications have surfaced that are targeted specifically to help people build better memories, but it will always be interesting how common folks have incorporated the "little tricks" to help us remember the "little things."

Ellisene Davis was raised on a ranch in the rural community of Jacksboro, Texas. She received a Bachelor of Science degree in home economics from Texas Technological College, where she became a member of Phi Upsilon Omicron, the home economics honor fraternity. Ellisene taught homemaking as a substitute while her husband was in the Navy in Newport, Rhode Island. When they moved to Keller, Texas, she began teaching and going to graduate school at North Texas State University, where she received a Master of Education with chemistry as the teaching field. She taught earth science, life science, chemistry, physical science, and health; she also sponsored the Future Homemakers of America, the annual, and the junior class. Due to an extended illness, Ellisene began reassessing her career, becoming a student again (in creative writing) under the direction Dr. Clifton Warren at Central State University in Edmond, Oklahoma. A short story of hers called "Hard Candy Christmas" appeared in *Texas and Christmas*, edited by Judy Alter and Joyce Gibson Roach (TCU Press, 1983). She also contributed "The Story of Marbles" to *Texas Toys and Games*. Ellisene currently lives in the beautiful mountain community of Angle Fire, New Mexico—again reassessing her life.

Robert J. (*Jack*) Duncan is a former TFS president. He is a writer/editor/researcher for Retractable Technologies, Inc. He has taught in, and worked for, several colleges and, in his sixth decade, continues to take graduate courses in a variety of disciplines. Jack has written for both scholarly and popular periodicals, including *Reader's Digest*. Author Bill Porterfield calls him "a root hog who digs up the damnedest truffles!" Jack lives in McKinney with his wife Elizabeth, his McKinney High School sweetheart. Their sons and grandsons all reside within Collin county.

Mike Felker received his Ph.D. with a specialization in Renaissance Drama from Texas Tech University in 1990. Having taught at Texas Tech for eight years, in 1988 he moved to South Plains College in Levelland, Texas, where he is currently Chair of the Department of English and Philosophy. He has presented papers and/or facilitated sessions at the International Conference for Community College Chairs, Deans, and Other Institutional Leaders, South Central Modern Language Association, American Culture Association, Southwest Popular Culture Association, West Texas Historical Association, and the Texas Folklore Society on topics varying from folklore to West Texas history to English Renaissance poetry. He is the author of several articles on Renaissance literature, West Texas folklore, and Joseph Conrad, and is co-author of three books on Turkish folklore.

Elizabeth Hume Galindo (1930–2001) was born on November 15, 1930 in Tampico, Mexico. She was raised in Mexico, Texas, and Florida, and she attended the University of Miami. In 1950, she married Carlos Galindo, and they resided in College Station, Texas, where he was a student at the A&M College of Texas (later renamed Texas A&M University). In 1954, they settled in Alice, Texas, where Elizabeth enjoyed a successful career as a homemaker and became very involved in the community. She was a member of the St. Elizabeth Church Altar Society, and served various leadership offices in such organizations as the Alicean Study Club, Retama Garden Club, Cotillion, Petroleum Wives Club, and the Alice Public Library Board. She was a charter board member of the Alice Counseling Center. Elizabeth served as chairperson for several large fundraisers benefiting such organizations as the Alice Counseling Center, and St. Elizabeth School.

Mary Jane Hurst was elected to Phi Beta Kappa and received her B.A. *summa cum laude* at Miami University in Ohio. She earned her M.A. and Ph.D. at the University of Maryland. She is currently Professor of English and Associate Dean of Arts and Sciences at Texas Tech University, where, since 1986, she has taught graduate and undergraduate courses in linguistics and literature and has been the recipient of the President's Excellence in Teaching Award and other honors. Most of Dr. Hurst's research centers on language in literature. She is the former President and former Executive Director of the Linguistic Association of the Southwest and currently serves as an Executive Board member for the South Central Modern Language Association. For many years, she had been a member of the Editorial Board for the Texas Tech University Press and for the *Southwest Journal of Linguistics.*

Elmer Kelton is author of forty novels, including *The Time It Never Rained* and *The Good Old Boys,* as well as about a dozen non-fiction books. He worked as an agricultural journalist for forty-two years. Among his awards are seven Spur Awards from Western Writers of

America, four Western Heritage Awards from the National Cowboy Hall of Fame, and a number of career awards from such organizations as the Western Literature Association and Texas Institute of Letters. He holds honorary doctorates from Texas Tech University and Hardin-Simmons University.

James Ward Lee is a native Texan who was born in the Woodlawn Hospital in Birmingham, Alabama, when Herbert Hoover was president. (Lee declared himself a native Texan in 1986 during the Sesquicentennial when he discovered he was the only person who could pronounce the word on the first try.) Lee is one of the longest serving members of the Texas Folklore Society, though not nearly the oldest! He paid his first dues in 1958 and read his first paper in 1959. He taught at the University of North Texas for forty-two years until he was worn to a nub. He now lives happily ever after in Fort Worth. His latest book is *Adventures with a Texas Humanist*, a title he stole form the late Roy Bedichek, also a member of TFS when Lee joined.

Sylvia Gann Mahoney wrote the first history book about college rodeo, was a college rodeo coach, founded a cowboy hall of fame and western heritage museum, founded a national college rodeo alumni organization, was a rodeo photographer, a free-lance writer of western articles, and taught English at a community college. She has also been involved in helping to mark and preserve and promote the Great Western Cattle Trail that crossed Texas from the Rio Grande to the Red River headed for Kansas and Nebraska. She has served as the president of the Texas Folklore Society and presented numerous papers on rodeo cowboys and cowgirls and the Western way of life, all illustrated by slides that she has taken.

Rebecca Matthews became a volunteer Scouter when her oldest son joined Cub Scouts over twenty years ago. She has since been honored with the District Award of Merit and the Silver Beaver, given by the Boy Scouts of America for service to Scouting and to youth in the community. "You Can Tell a Scout from Texas," first presented in 1989, was the first paper she read at a TFS meeting. She now lives in San Antonio, where she teaches college-level English part-time, homeschools her daughters full-time, and remains an active Scouter even though her sons are grown.

Barbara Morgan-Fleming is an associate professor in the Department of Curriculum and Instruction at Texas Tech University. Her research interests include classroom performance of curriculum and informal aspects of teachers' knowledge. She has recent publications in *Teaching and Teacher Education, Curriculum Inquiry*, the *International Journal of Social Education, Social Studies, Educational Forum*, and the *Journal of Curriculum & Supervision*.

Palmer H. "Pat" Olsen (1894–1994), a naturalist and engineer, was born October 22, 1894 in Clifton, Texas to Norwegian immigrants. He lived most of his life in Clifton except for periods in Dallas and Gatesville during 1920-1940. Palmer was the first of three brothers to attend Texas A&M, where he was one of A&M's great baseball pitchers. He was president of his class and graduated with a degree in 1916 in civil engineering. Palmer joined the U. S. Army as a lieutenant in 1917 and served on the battlefields of France and Germany during World War I. He married Esther Swenson, his childhood sweetheart, in 1919 after returning from Europe and had two daughters, Virginia and Annis. At his request, Palmer was re-commissioned into the U. S. Army in the early days of World War II. He received a personal citation for service to Norway from Crown Prince Olav and later served as a military governor in Germany. Palmer was a model of physical fitness into his middle nineties. A great believer in walking and jogging, he ran in the Galveston marathon when he was in his 80s. He kept a lively interest in baseball and other sports, history, politics, and the natural sciences. He wrote many humorous articles about his life experiences, a number of which he read before the Texas Folklore Society's annual meetings. In later years, he was an avid participant in the Bosque County Historical Commission, where his remarkable memory of early days and people of Clifton made valuable contributions to the Commission's records. Palmer died on July 12, 1994 at the age of 99.

J. G. "Paw-Paw" Pinkerton was born and raised in Texas where he counts Junction as his hometown. He served in the U. S. Navy in World War II and graduated from The University of Texas at Austin with a Bachelor of Business Administration degree in 1952. He worked for Texasgulf, Inc. (a natural resource mining company) in Newgulf, Texas, Moab, Utah, Perth, Western Australia, Panama, and Stamford, Connecticut where he and his wife still reside. In 1982, six years prior to retirement, he started a second career in storytelling. By 1997, he was a Featured Teller at the National Storytelling Festival, "the granddaddy of them all!" in Jonesborough, TN. He has told stories at Festivals and Tellabrations! across the USA and as far afield as Australia, Ireland, Israel, and Japan. Also, he has told stories on radio and television, done voiceovers and appeared in commercials. He and his wife have three children and seven grandchildren.

Lou Halsell Rodenberger has published essays on Texas rural schoolteachers, as well as on Texas and western writers, and she is the editor of four books and a biographical study of West Texas writer Jane Gilmore Rushing. Lou is emeritus professor of English at McMurry University, Abilene, past president of the Texas Folklore Society, a member of the

Texas Institute of Letters, Fellow of the Texas State Historical Association, and a Distinguished Alumna of Texas Women's University. Her most recent books are *Quotable Texas Women* (State House Press) and *Writing on the Wind: A West Texas Anthology of Women Writers* (Texas Tech University Press).

Cynthia Savage was born in folklore-rich Southeastern New Mexico. She moved to the oil fields of West Texas from Roswell while in high school, and later attended the University of Texas at Austin, studying folklore under Américo Paredes. Cynthia credits Dr. Joseph Jones with encouraging her to major in English. After completing her degree at UT, she moved back to West Texas to teach and earned an M.A. in education. When attending an English teachers' meeting in El Paso, she decided to drop in on John O. West to discuss pursuing another degree in English. He decided she needed to speak with Lawrence Clayton, picked up the phone, and a great conversation about folklore began. Cynthia taught at Lee High School with Faye Leeper, who eventually insisted that she attend the Texas Folklore Society meeting in 1988 in Lubbock, which was hosted by Kenneth Davis. Since then, she has not missed a gathering of the TFS. She has served on the Board, hosted a meeting in Midland, and presented papers at annual meetings. She currently teaches at Lee High School in Midland.

Jean Granberry Schnitz was born in Spur, Texas. She graduated from Raymondville High School in 1948 and from Texas A&I College in Kingsville in 1952. She and Lew Schnitz were married in 1953. They have three sons and four grandchildren. A retired legal secretary, she now lives near Boerne. As of 2005, Jean has presented seven papers to the Texas Folklore Society, and she has been a Director on the Board since 2002.

Ernestine P. Sewell (1918–2001) began teaching in 1939 in high schools throughout East Texas and Arkansas. She later taught English at the University of Texas at Arlington after receiving her Ph.D. from East Texas State University in 1968. She and Charles Linck co-owned Cow Hill Press, and her book *Eats: A Folk History of Texas Foods* won the Best Non-Fiction award from the Texas Institute of Letters. In addition to her other books, she wrote many articles and contributed chapters to several publications.

Ernest B. Speck (1916–1995) served as TFS President 1974-1975. His publications include *Mody Boatright, Folklorist* (1973) and *Benjamin Capps* (1981), but he is also fondly remembered for bringing in young members to the Texas Folklore Society, namely Lee and Karen Haile.

Evelyn Stroder was born in 1930 and graduated from Corpus Christi High School in 1947. She received her B.A. in journalism/English from Baylor University, and finished her M.A. in American literature/mass communication at UTPB in 1977. She taught English/journalism/history for four years at old Sundeen High School (now in Corpus Christi ISD), as well as 28 years in Crane schools. Evelyn is now retired and still living in Crane, the place where she went for a last-minute opening in 1955 "just to get out where the salaries were better" because she was pregnant and her husband (a former geologist turned science/math teacher) would be the only breadwinner for a while. After shopping around for a few years, they decided they couldn't find a better place. She and her husband both do a little substitute teaching, historical research/writing, and church work, and as much traveling as they can get in—often to visit children/grandchildren in Burleson and Lubbock, Texas, and Trinidad, Colorado. Evelyn also judges journalism and ready writing in UIL meets and newspapers/yearbooks/literary magazines for scholastic press associations, and she writes an occasional history column in the local weekly paper and features for area newspapers.

Tierney Untiedt was born and raised in Iowa, but moved to Texas in 1986 because it doesn't snow as much here. She was a licensed day care director for seven years, and now she works as a Records Verification Coordinator in the Registrar's Office at Stephen F. Austin State University. She and her husband have four children.

Index

Note: Page numbers in *italics* indicate photographs and illustrations.